Key Stage 3
Classbook

History

NEW for September 2000

Fiona Reynoldson

First published 2000

Letts Educational
9–15 Aldine Street
London W12 8AW
Tel 020 8740 2266
Fax 020 8743 8451

Design and page layout: Ken Vail Graphic Design, Cambridge

Illustrations: Mark Bergin, Joan Corlass, Nick Hawken, Linda Rogers Associates (Trevor Parkin).

Colour reproduction by PDQ Repro, Bungay, Suffolk

Picture research by Brooks Krikler Research

British Library Cataloguing-in-Publication Data

A CIP record for this book is available from the British Library

ISBN 1 84085 419 7

Printed and Bound in Spain

Letts Educational Limited, a division of Granada Learning Limited. Part of the Granada Media Group

Acknowledgements

The authors and publishers are grateful to the following for permission to reproduce photographs:

Fig 41.2 reproduced by kind permission of the National Trust Photographic Library/Geoff Morgan.

Figs 41.2 and 41.3 reproduced by kind permission of the Weald and Downland Open Air Museum, Singleton, Chichester, Sussex; tel. 01243 811363; website www.wealddown.co.uk

AKG: unit 2.5, 11.3, 12.1, 13.2, 15.2, 15.3, 24.2, 25.4, 27.3, 29.2, 31.1, 32.1, 34.2, 35.1, 37.1, 38.1, 39.1, 43.1, 44.1, 46.1, 46.3, 48.2, 48.3, 54.2, 56.3, 57.4, 59.1, 71.1, 96.1, 97.2, 108.3; Tom Donovan Military Books: 89.4; e.t Archive: 19.3, 20.4, 31.3, 90.2, 99.3; Eye Ubiquitous: 2.5, 3.1, 17.3, 22.2, 66.3; Mary Evans Picture Library: 1.1, 1.2, 6.1, 7.1, 9.2, 11.1, 16.3, 22.3, 28.2, 30.1, 32.2, 33.1, 33.2, 36.1, 36.2, 36.3, 39.2, 42.3. 43.3, 47.1, 49.1, 50.2, 52.1, 53.1, 53.2, 55.4. 56.1, 57.3, 59.4, 60.1, 61.2, 62.4, 64.3, 65.1, 65.3, 67.2, 68.2, 69.2, 69.5, 70.3, 70.4, 71.2, 71.4, 72.3, 73.1, 73.2, 74.2, 75.3, 75.4, 77.3, 77.4, 78.3, 79.1, 79.2, 80.2, 80.4, 81.2, 81.3, 82.1, 86.1, 95.3, 96.4; Hulton Getty Collection: 5.2, 19.2, 20.2, 27.4, 40.2, 51.2, 55.2, 63.1, 81.4, 82.3, 83.2, 83.4, 84.1, 84.3, 85.2, 86.2, 86.5, 87.1, 88.2, 89.3, 92.3, 93.2, 94.1, 95.1, 97.3, 98.2, 98.3, 101.3, 102. 2, 102.3, 103.1, 103.5, 104.3, 105.4, 106.1, 106.3, 107.3, 109.1, 110.1 right, 110.1 left, 110.2, 111.1, 112.2, 113.1, 113.3; Paul Nightingale: 8.4; Frank Spooner Pictures: 10.1, 104.4, 113.4, 114.3, 114.4

Contents

Making of the United Kingdom 1500–1750 62

Expansion, trade and industry 1750–1900 123

Introduction

This Letts History classbook has been designed and written to help you learn and understand the topics you will cover during your Key Stage 3 History course. It covers the content of the National Curriculum and will guide you through the last 1000 years of history.

The book is divided into four sections:

1. Medieval realms;
2. Making of the United Kingdom;
3. Expansion, trade and industry;
4. The Twentieth century world.

Together, these sections contain 115 units, each beginning with a list of topics that you will cover. The information that follows is written clearly so that you can read the unit yourself. There are also many photographs, pictures, diagrams and graphs. These are as important as the writing, so study them carefully and always look at them before you answer a question.

Answer the questions as you go along; these will help you to focus on what you are reading. Any new or technical words are explained in the Key words section of each unit and in the Glossary at the back of the book. There is a Summary activity at the end of every unit, which will help you to develop some ideas further.

History is a broad and fascinating subject. This book gives an outline of events in English and British history from 1066 and, in the final section, looks at some of the world events in the twentieth century. There is a great deal more to find out. We hope this makes an interesting start.

1 England before 1066

In this section of the book you will learn the following things:

- **Edward the Confessor was King of England from 1042 to 1066;**
- **three men wanted to be King of England after Edward died.**

Edward, England and Normandy

Edward the **Confessor** was born in England between 1002 and 1005. However, soon after he was born, the Danish King, Cnut, seized the English throne. The young Edward was sent to relatives in Normandy for safety. He was brought up by monks and lived in Normandy for nearly 30 years. Cnut's family died out in 1042 and Edward came back to England to be King.

Edward as King of England

By this time Edward was a white-haired man of about 40 years old. He had lived in Normandy nearly all his life and much preferred the Normans to the English. The mainstay of his Government was Earl Godwin, the most powerful of the English **earls**. However, Godwin hated the way Edward gave land and the best jobs to the Normans. In 1051 the English rioted against the Normans at Dover. Godwin was sent to put down the riot but he refused to punish the rioters. For this the King banished him from England.

▲ ***Fig 1** Edward the Confessor in a scene from the **Bayeaux Tapestry**.*

Q1 Why do you think Edward preferred the Normans to the English?

Q2 Why did Edward banish Godwin?

Duke William of Normandy

While Godwin was away, Edward invited his cousin, William, **Duke** of Normandy, to visit England. This was the only time that William came to England before 1066. Ever afterwards, William claimed that Edward had promised to make him his heir to the throne of England. He also claimed that Harold Godwinson (Earl Godwin's son) had sworn to support his claim to the throne.

Harold Godwin

In 1052, Earl Godwin returned to England and many of Edward's Norman friends fled back to Normandy. Edward gave up even trying to be King. He had always wanted to be a monk and he spent the rest of his life devoting himself to religion. Among other things, he built Westminster Abbey. Meanwhile, Godwin's son, Harold Godwinson, rose to power and was the real ruler of England from 1053 to 1066.

▲ ***Fig 2*** *Harold Godwinson swearing to support William. From the Bayeux tapestry.*

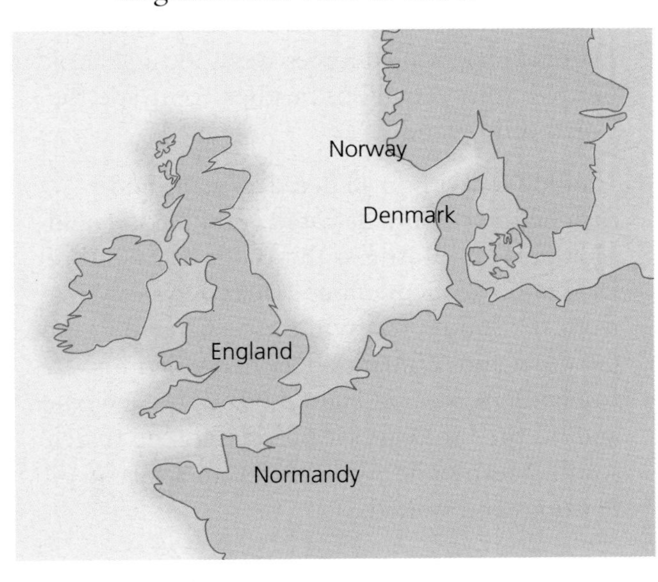

Harald Hardrada

Harald Hardrada was a warlike King of Norway. The Norwegians had strong connections with England. Harald saw that Edward was a weak king and, more importantly, he had no children. So who would be King of England when Edward died?

◀ ***Fig 3*** *Part of Europe in 1066.*

Key words

Bayeux Tapestry – an embroidered cloth about 70 metres long, showing events leading up to the Norman Conquest. It was made for the Bishop of Bayeux in Normandy between 1066 and 1077.
Confessor – a religious person
duke – a nobleman of higher status than an earl
earl – a nobleman

SUMMARY

- Edward the Confessor (1042–1066) had no children.
- Duke William of Normandy was Edward's cousin.
- William said that Edward promised to make him his heir.
- Earl Godwin and his son, Harold Godwinson, were the most powerful English earls at this time.
- The King of Norway, Harald Hardrada, wanted to be King of England.

SUMMARY *activity*

What were the two claims William made about being the heir to the throne of England? Do you believe him? Give reasons for your answer.

2 The Battle of Hastings 1066

In this section of the book you will learn the following things:

- **Harold Godwin became King in 1066;**
- **William of Normandy and Harald Hardrada prepared to attack England.**

Death of Edward the Confessor: Harold Godwinson becomes King

Edward the Confessor died on 5 January 1066. The day after his funeral, Harold Godwinson was declared King at Westminster, but both Harald Hardrada and William of Normandy prepared for war for the throne of England.

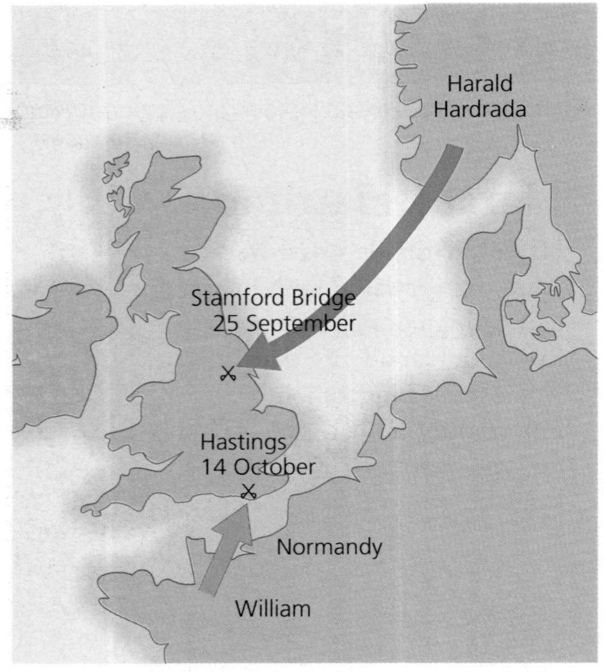

▲ ***Fig 1*** *Battle of Hastings: William and Harald Hardrada invaded England in 1066, before the battle.*

Invasions

During the summer, William prepared a fleet of ships in Normandy and waited for a southerly wind to sail to England. Meanwhile, Harald Hardrada had joined forces with Tostig, Harold Godwinson's rebellious brother, to invade the north of England.

Harold Godwinson gathered an army and marched north. He defeated and killed Harald Hardrada and Tostig at the Battle of Stamford Bridge on 25 September. Then news came from the south. The wind had changed in the Channel and William's fleet had sailed for England. As soon as Harold heard the news, he and his tired soldiers set off on a forced march south. Meanwhile, William set up a fort at Hastings and waited.

Harold and William's armies

On Friday 13 October William's scouts sighted Harold's army a few miles north of Hastings. There were probably about 7,000 soldiers, ranging from the fierce, well-armed **housecarls** of Harold's own bodyguard to half-armed peasants who had been recruited along the way. William's army may have been smaller but it was very well disciplined, up to date and had plenty of experience from fighting in northern France.

Q1 What advantages did Harold's army have?

Q2 What advantages did William's army have?

The Battle of Hastings: 14 October 1066

As day dawned on 14 October, William moved his army into battle order on the ground below Senlac Hill. Harold's army was crowded on top of the hill.

William's archers started the battle. The **knights** then attacked, but the two-handed battle axes of the English housecarls easily hacked through the knights' flimsy chain mail. The **Breton** knights turned their horses and fled, but William rode in front and not only stopped them, but rallied them to fight. This was a stroke of genius because some of the English, seeing the Bretons running away, rushed down the hill to 'finish them off'. William and the Bretons were able to encircle and kill them.

Having seen how well it worked, twice in the next few hours, groups of Norman knights pretended to run away. Then they turned and massacred the English who had chased them. By late afternoon the English were still holding Senlac Hill, grouped around Harold. However, Harold's two brothers had already died and when Harold was killed, some people think with an arrow in his eye, the English army was broken. William had won.

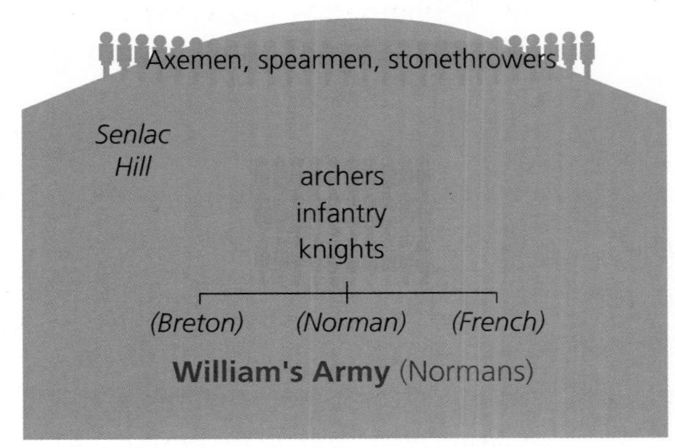

▲ ***Fig 2*** *Battle of Hastings: battle positions on 14 October 1066. William had knights from Brittany and France in his army.*

▲ ***Fig 3*** *Normans on horseback fighting the English, in a scene from the Bayeux Tapestry.*

Key words

Bretons – people from Brittany, near Normandy
housecarls – Harold's special soldiers
knights – soldiers on horseback

SUMMARY

- Harold Godwinson defeated Harald Hardrada at the Battle of Stamford Bridge on 25 September 1066.
- William of Normandy defeated Harold Godwinson at the Battle of Hastings on 14 October 1066.

SUMMARY *activity*

Why do you think William won the Battle of Hastings?

3 The settlement of England

In this section of the book you will learn the following things:

- **William was crowned King of England;**
- **William set up the feudal system.**

William the Conqueror

William of Normandy became known as William the Conqueror of England. He had won the Battle of Hastings, but could he win the peace? After the battle William took Dover Castle, the cities of Canterbury and Winchester, and marched north. When William finally met the English **barons** at Berkhamsted, they offered him the throne of England.

William had to make it clear that he was King in two ways:

- he was related to Edward the Confessor;
- he had won England by right of conquest.

▲ ***Fig 1*** *Westminster Abbey today is built on the same site as Edward the Confessor's original. Edward had built the Abbey, and it was important to William to be crowned there to show he was the* ***legitimate*** *heir to the throne.*

Q1 What did William do after the Battle of Hastings?

Q2 Who offered him the English throne?

'I will be faithful and loyal to you through life and in death; so God help me.'

◀ ***Fig 2*** *These words are from the oath of homage the barons had to swear to William.*

The coronation

The coronation was held in Westminster Abbey in front of the most important men in England. Not only did William swear to rule England justly, he added something new. He insisted that everyone there acknowledged him as King. The question was put in English and in French so there would be no mistake. The shouted replies filled the **Abbey** and could be heard outside. So much so that William's soldiers outside thought he was being attacked.

The feudal system

After the coronation, William kept many Englishmen in important jobs as long as they were loyal to him. He also introduced some new ideas. One of these was the **feudal system**. It was not a completely new idea in England, but William set it up as thoroughly as he did everything else. All the great men (often called barons) who were going to hold land had to kneel before the King and, placing their hands between his, swear an oath of **homage**. The lesser men (often knights) swore to the barons in the same way and held land from the barons above them (see also Unit 6). The peasants and farmworkers swore an oath of homage to the knights in return for their land.

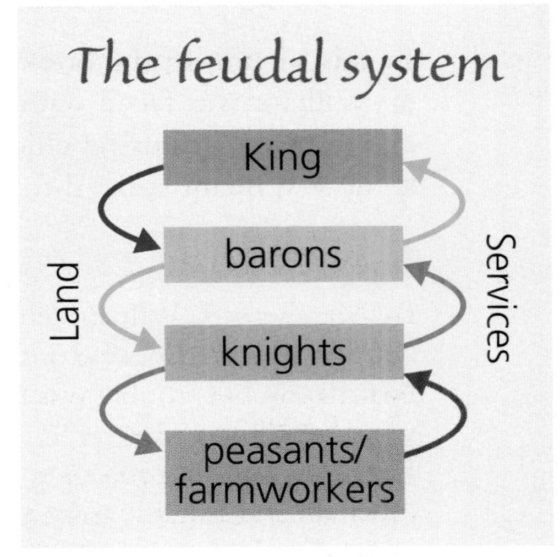

▲ ***Fig 3*** *The feudal system was based on land and services. Services included providing soldiers when the King needed them.*

Although William took land from the English who had fought against him and gave it to his Norman supporters, at first many Englishmen held land as well – until the rebellions started.

How William made sure the barons did not get too powerful:

- he gave them small amounts of land in different parts of the country;
- he made the knights swear an oath of homage directly to him as well as to their barons.

▲ ***Fig 4***

Q3 What was the oath of homage?

Q4 Why did giving the barons small amounts of land in different parts of the country stop them getting too powerful?

Q5 Why did making the knights swear an oath of homage direct to William stop the barons getting too powerful?

Key words

abbey – a church connected with a monastery
baron – a nobleman, often an earl
feudal system – a way of holding land for services instead of money
homage – loyalty and devotion
legitimate – legal

SUMMARY

- The great men of England offered the crown of England to William.
- William was crowned on Christmas Day 1066 in Westminster Abbey.
- William insisted everyone in the Abbey acknowledged him as King.
- William set up the feudal system so he could keep control.

SUMMARY *activity*

How did William make himself secure in England?

4 Rebellion

In this section of the book you will learn the following things:

- **William was faced with rebellions from 1068;**
- **the most serious rebellion was in the north of England;**
- **how William reacted to the rebellions.**

Rebellions crushed

By March 1067, William felt secure enough to leave England and visit Normandy, but trouble was brewing. There was a rebellion in Exeter. Returning to England, William rode there with a mixed Norman and English army and the city surrendered. More serious was rebellion in the north of England. This simmered on until 1070, when William finally crushed it ruthlessly.

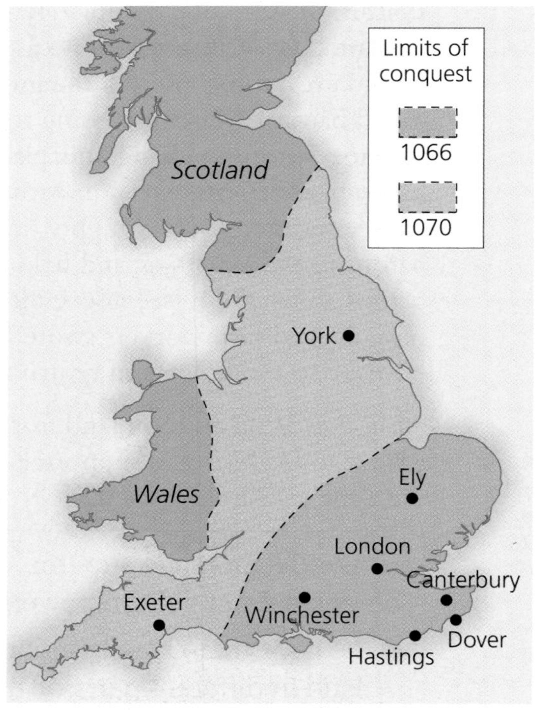

▲ ***Fig 1*** *How much of England William conquered.*

Q1 What was meant by 'the harrying of the north'?

'Harrying of the north'

Outbreak after outbreak of trouble in Yorkshire had caused William to ride north to deal with the rebel English, who were often helped by the Danes, Norwegians and Scots. William had had enough of the English. He devastated the land around York, destroying everything for miles so that no one could live there and rebel again and everyone would know what would happen to their land if they did. This was called 'the harrying of the north'.

Hereward the Wake

The last rebellion was led by Hereward the Wake, further south. A number of important Englishmen joined him and he held the island of Ely for some months against William's forces, but at last they were overwhelmed. Hereward himself escaped and was never found.

Replacing the English with Normans

One result of these rebellions was that William stopped trusting the English. He gave more and more land to his Norman followers. By 1086, there were only two English nobles who held large amounts of land. William also began to replace the leading members of the Church with Normans.

William and the Church

William was a religious man. He had ordered the building of Battle Abbey and the high altar was placed where Harold is supposed to have fallen. However, he also needed the support of the Church, which was a powerful organisation by this time. The Archbishop of Canterbury was the head of the Church in England and William gave this job to Lanfranc, a Norman. One way in which William gained the support of the Church was by agreeing that it could have its own law courts. This was going to cause trouble for later Kings of England.

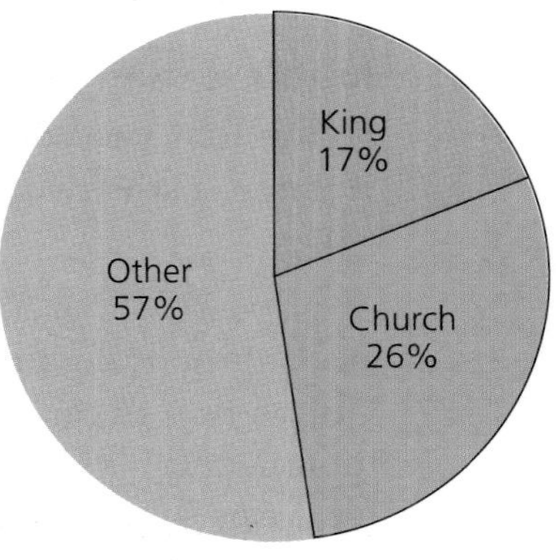

▲ ***Fig 2*** *Who controlled land in England by 1086? Although William owned all the land, he had to put it in the hands of the barons and the Church to run it from day to day. He only kept some as his own.*

Q2 How did William gain the support of the Church?

Castles

Another way in which William kept control of England was by building castles. At first these were simple castles. A huge mound of earth was built up and a wooden tower built on it. Wooden fences surrounded the base of the mound. This was called a **motte** and **bailey** castle.

▼ ***Fig 3*** *Motte and bailey castle.*

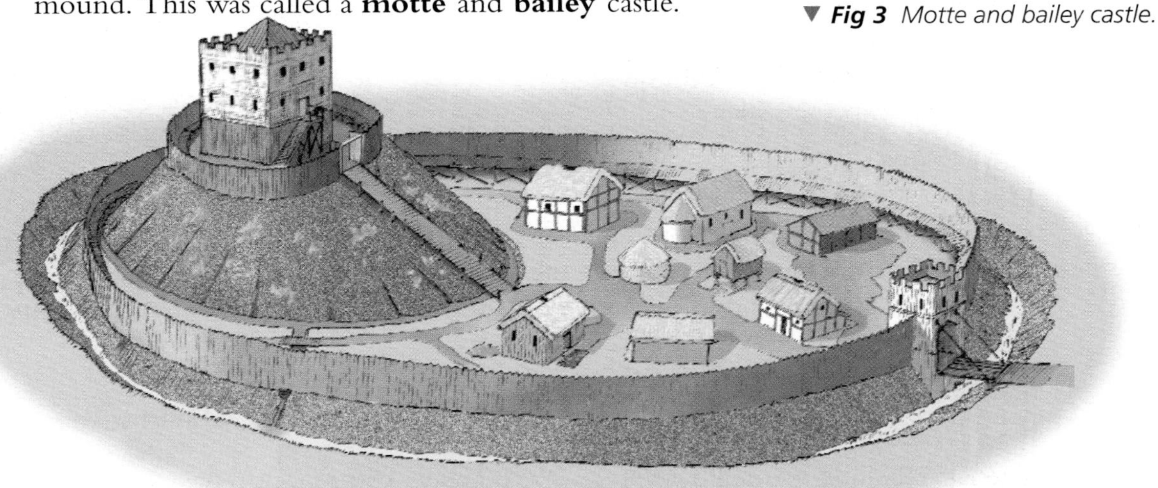

Key words

bailey – a large, level area below the motte, protected by a fence and ditch, used for keeping animals, stores, and as extra living space

motte – mound

SUMMARY

- William put down the northern revolts and destroyed much of the land in Yorkshire to prevent further revolts.
- William took land and power from the English and gave it to the Normans.
- William gained the support of the Church.
- William built castles to keep control of England.

SUMMARY *activity*

How did William keep control of England?

5 Castles

In this section of the book you will learn the following things:

- **the first castles were made of wood;**
- **later castles were made of stone.**

The first castle at Hastings

William built the first castle at Hastings while he was waiting for Harold Godwinson to join battle (fight). It took only 17 days to make the mound and build the wooden castle on the top (see page 9). Within a few years of the Battle of Hastings, there were castles all over England.

Why castles?

Not only did castles keep the people inside them safe, they also made it easier to keep the land around them under control. From their safe base in the castle, Norman soldiers could control all the countryside around within about half a day's ride on horseback. This was about 20 miles.

Q1 Why did the Normans build castles?

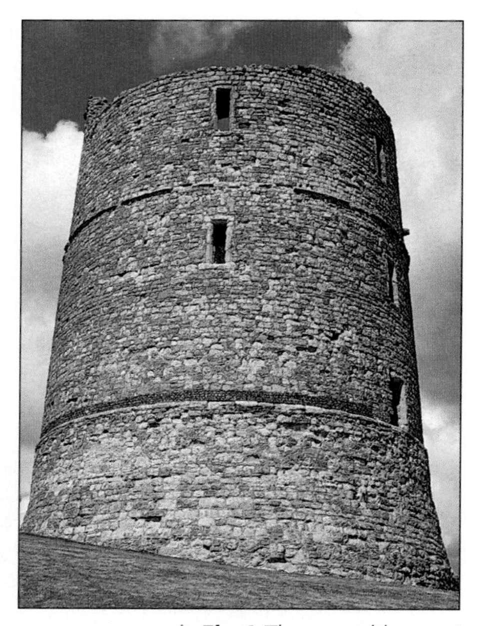

▲ ***Fig 1*** *The round keep at Hadleigh Castle, Essex.*

Stone square-keep castles

It was easy to set fire to a wooden castle, so the Normans soon began making them of stone. However, stone castles with walls up to five metres thick were too heavy to build on top of a mound of earth. They were built on the flat, but the narrow slits for windows and the doors on the first floor meant they were very difficult to attack.

Q2 What were the advantages and disadvantages of wooden castles?

◄ ***Fig 2*** *Dover Castle, showing the concentric walls.*

Round keeps, curtain walls and concentric castles

A weakness of square **keeps** were the corners. Soldier engineers could dig or mine under the corners so the building would fall down. Round keeps are stronger. Builders also added thick stone **curtain walls** around the keep so that the enemy found it more difficult to attack. The next step was **concentric castles**. Two walls were built around the keep for extra safety.

Q3 What was the disadvantage of square-keep castles?

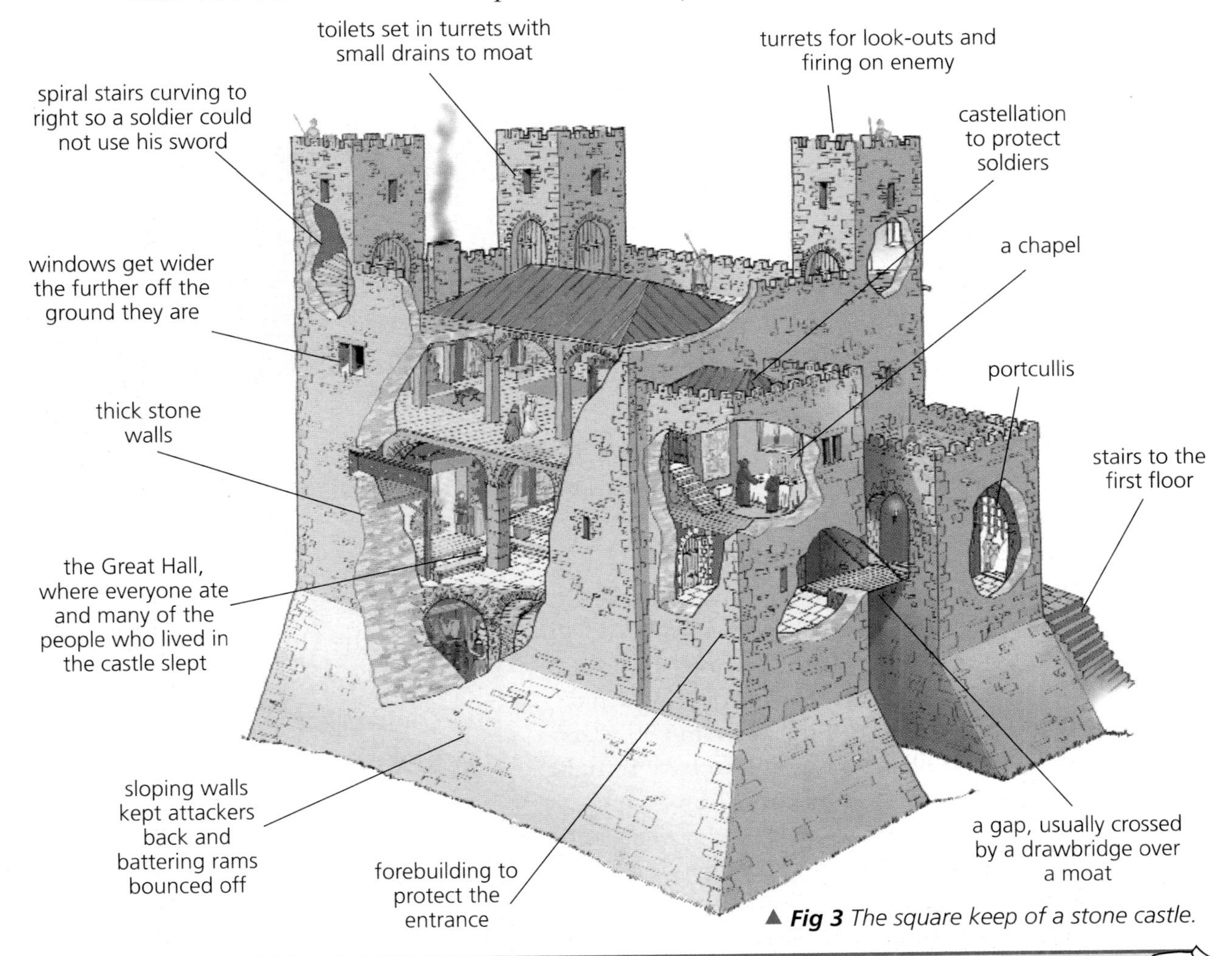

▲ ***Fig 3*** *The square keep of a stone castle.*

Key words

concentric castle – a castle ringed with two walls

curtain wall – wall surrounding a keep

keep – strongest, centre part of a castle

SUMMARY

- The first castles were motte and bailey castles.
- Castles were built to keep control of the country.
- Later castles were built of stone.
- There were square-keep and round-keep castles.
- Walls were built around the keeps for extra protection.

SUMMARY *activity*

Look at the diagram of a square keep and write about all the ways in which it was protected from attack.

6 The Domesday Book

In this section of the book you will learn the following things:

- why William wanted a survey of all England;
- the survey was called the Domesday Book;
- what the Domesday Book says.

England settled

By the 1080s, William felt secure within England. He had reliable men to run the government of England for him, to collect taxes and to keep the law. All over England he had castles of his own and castles built and run by loyal barons, to keep the peace. Three times a year he held a Great Council where he consulted the leading barons. At Christmas time this was usually at Gloucester.

► *Fig 1* *A modern artist's picture of a knight swearing fealty (loyalty).*

The threat of invasion 1085

At Christmas 1085, William was worried. The King of Denmark was preparing to invade England to claim the English throne because he was a descendant of King Cnut who had reigned in England some 50 years earlier. If William was going to have to fight another war, he had to know how much money he needed to spend on soldiers, and if he had to bring in foreign soldiers, how many he could expect his barons to feed. He realised that he did not know anything in detail about the land and people he ruled. He talked with the barons in his Great Council and decided to do a survey. As it turned out, William need not have worried. The King of Denmark argued so much with his followers that in the summer of 1086 one of them murdered him. However, by this time the survey was under way.

Uses of the Domesday Book:

- to know how much the King could ask in taxes;
- to know how many soldiers the King could expect a baron to support if he needed to billet foreign soldiers in England;
- to make sure everyone in England knew who was King, and had met his officials;
- to allow people to put their arguments over land to the King's officials.

▲ ***Fig 2***

Morin and Hugh hold Fletching from the Count. Cana held it from King Edward. Then and now it answered for 2 hides. Land for 5 ploughs. In lordship 1 plough; 11 villeins and 5 bordars with 4 ploughs. Meadow, 6 acres; from woodland 30 pigs. Value before 1066 £4; now 50s (£2.50).

▲ ***Fig 3*** *From the Domesday Book for Sussex. Knights Morin and Hugh held land from the baron, the Count of Mortain.*

The survey: the Domesday Book

William sent officials all over England to ask questions about the land. They wrote down the answers. Then William, being a very careful man, sent a second set of officials to check up on the answers of the first set. Eventually, everything was copied into two volumes, known today as the Domesday Book. The officials asked a number of questions, such as who held the land, how many people it supported and what it was worth in 1066 and at present (1086). The results give us some interesting information about how people lived at the time (see figs 2 and 3). It gives a rough idea of the numbers and types of people living in England in 1086 (see fig 4).

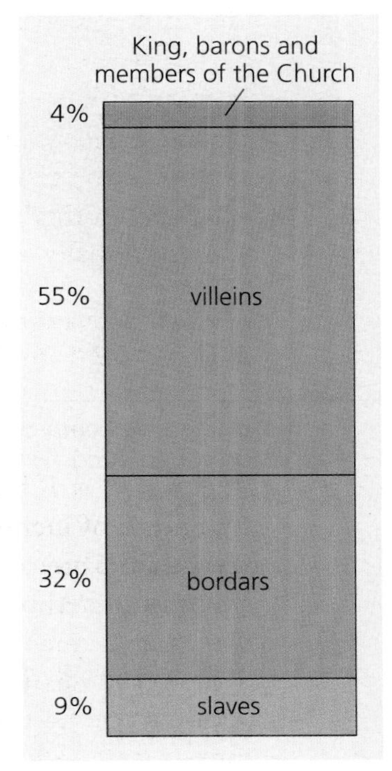

▲ ***Fig 4*** *Types of people living in England in 1086.*

Q1 What was the survey called?

Q2 What sort of people controlled the land in 1086?

Q3 What percentage of the total population did they make up?

Domesday and the feudal system

The survey shows the working of the feudal system. The King held all the land in England. Look at fig 3. The Count of Mortain held his land from the King. Morin and Hugh were knights who held land at Fletching from the Count. The **villeins** held land from Morin and Hugh. The **bordars** only held a cottage and garden.

Key words

bordar or **cottar** – just owned a cottage and garden, then worked for the knight

hide – a measurement of land, enough to support a family, usually about 120 acres

villager or **villein** – held some land from the knight

SUMMARY

- William wanted a survey so he knew all about England and the people in it.
- The Domesday Book listed the villages, who held the land, how many were supported by the land and how much it was worth.

SUMMARY *activity*

What use was the Domesday Book to William?

7 William II, Henry I and Stephen

In this section of the book you will learn the following things:

- William the Conqueror died in 1087;
- the Kings after William were William Rufus, Henry I and Stephen.

William II or William Rufus 1087–1100

▲ *Fig 1 A nineteenth-century engraving of King William II.*

William the Conqueror died in 1087 after a fall from his horse. His second son, William II, became King. He was a short, thickset man with a red face, which earned him the name William Rufus. He was a very harsh man and was hated by many people. On 2 August 1100, he was hunting in the New Forest when he was shot with an arrow and killed. It could have been an accident, but there was one man in the hunting party who would gain by his death. This was his brother Henry who, leaving his dead brother, rode straight to Winchester and took control of the **treasury**. Three days later, Henry was crowned King in Westminster Abbey.

The King and the Church

- William I allowed the Church to have its own Church Law Courts.
- William Rufus got Church lands back when he could.
- Henry I and the Pope rowed about who should choose the bishops.
- Stephen allowed the Church to do what it liked.

▲ ***Fig 2***

Henry I 1100–1135

Henry I was also a harsh king, but he kept law and order in England. At a time when there was no police force, most people preferred a king who made even his powerful barons keep the law, to a king who let people do what they wanted.

Henry was a good organiser. He set up:

- the Court of Exchequer to manage the King's money;
- the Court of Justice to make sure powerful criminals were punished by the law;
- the King's council to advise the King.

◄ ***Fig 3***

Q1 Why did most people tolerate Henry I as King?

The *White Ship* and the drowning at sea

Unfortunately, Henry's only son, William, was drowned at sea. He was sailing from Normandy in one of the most up-to-date ships of the day, the *White Ship*. With him were many other members of the royal family and important barons. However, it seems that everyone on board had been celebrating and the entire crew and passengers were drunk. In this state they raced to catch up some of the other English ships they were sailing with. The *White Ship* hit a rock and sank. Only one man escaped to tell the tale. Henry was heartbroken as well as concerned about who would rule after his death.

▲ **Fig 4** *Henry I used the same coat of arms as his father, William I, and his brother, William II.*

Henry made his barons swear to support his daughter, Matilda, as Queen after his death. When Henry died, however, his nephew, Stephen, seized the throne of England. It was about the only firm action Stephen ever took.

Q2 How did Henry I try to make sure that his daughter, Matilda, would be Queen after his death?

> Every baron built castles and held them against the King. Then they took all those they thought had any goods – men and women – put them in prison and tortured them

▲ **Fig 5** *What happened when Stephen was King (written by a chronicler).*

Stephen 1135–1154

Stephen was lovable and generous. In the 19 years he was King, he allowed the barons to do what they liked. They built castles where they pleased and paid no attention to him. Worse, Matilda did not give up her claim to the throne. Some of the barons became tired of Stephen's weak rule and supported Matilda. England was plunged into **civil war** which lasted for years. In the end Stephen, worn out, agreed that Matilda's son should be King after him.

Key words

civil war – fighting within a country

treasury – the King's money for running the country

SUMMARY

- William Rufus was a harsh king and may have been murdered on his brother's orders.
- Henry I was a harsh king but kept law and order well.
- Stephen was a generous king but could not keep law and order.

SUMMARY *activity*

Which king do you think was the best sort of king for England at this time? Choose between William Rufus, Henry I or Stephen. Give reasons for your answer.

8 The Church

In this section of the book you will learn the following things:

- **the Pope was the head of the Catholic Church;**
- **the Church was the whole organisation of churchmen;**
- **kings and the Church often argued.**

The Catholic Church

In the Middle Ages, almost everyone in England was Christian. They belonged to the **Catholic** Church, which was the only **Christian** Church. The head of the Catholic Church was the Pope, who lived in Rome. **Popes** had been elected to head the Catholic Church ever since Jesus Christ died over 1 000 years before. By now the Church was very powerful all over Europe.

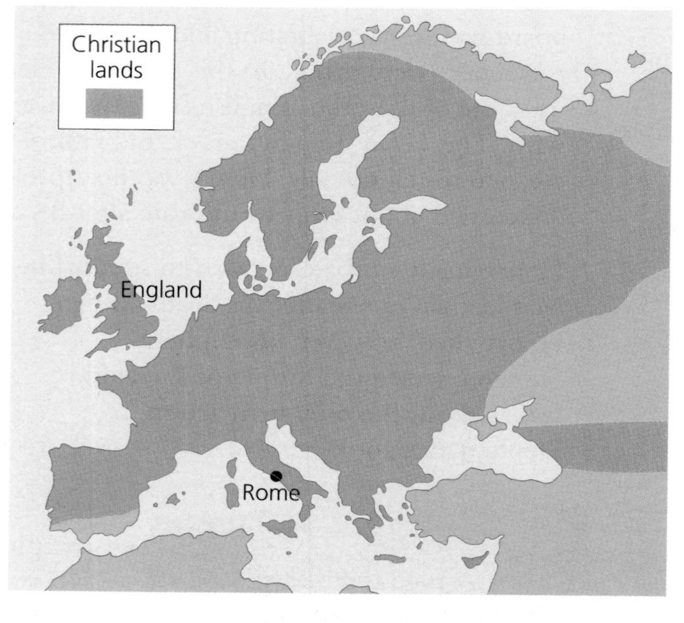

▶ ***Fig 1*** *Christianity in Europe in 1450.*

The Catholic Church in England

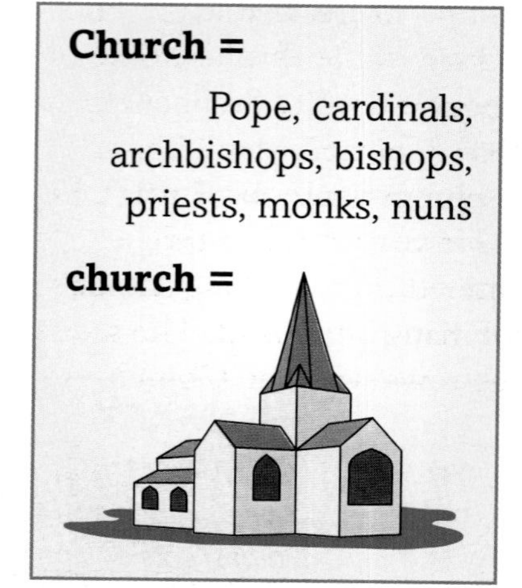

In England, the Catholic Church was run by two archbishops – the Archbishop of Canterbury and the Archbishop of York. Under them were many bishops. When William the Conqueror came to England he owned all the land, but gave out sections of it to his barons. In return, they had to fight for him and provide knights to fight for him. William gave land to the archbishops and bishops too.

◀ ***Fig 2*** *Church and church.*

Q1 Who were the other people in the Church besides archbishops?

Q2 What is the difference between the Church and a church?

How the Church was so powerful

The Church

rich in land and money ⇄ served God

owned land in England ⇄ head of the Church was in Rome

▲ ***Fig 3*** *Divided loyalty.*

Q3 Explain how the Church had divided loyalties.

William the Conqueror was a religious man so he wanted to help the Church, but he also needed the help of the Church himself for a number of reasons:

- churchmen were well educated. William needed men to help him run the country, to do everything from writing letters to acting as judges;
- the Church in Europe was very powerful and William could not afford to anger the Pope;
- William gave land to his bishops and archbishops so, like the barons, they would help him keep control of England.

► ***Fig 4*** *Ely Cathedral. The Church built magnificent cathedrals and churches for people to worship God.*

Weak and strong kings

▲ ***Fig 5*** *King Henry II's coat of arms.*

As the years went by after William I's death, the Church became more powerful. This was particularly so if there was a weak king. When Stephen died in 1154, Henry II became King. He was 21 years old, of medium height, with red hair. He would have run to fat if he had not exercised a lot. In fact, he never sat down unless to eat a meal or ride a horse. He was determined that the King should be the most powerful man in England. The scene was set for some huge rows with the Church.

Key words

Catholic – universal, as in the Catholic Church

Christian – follower of Jesus Christ

Pope – head or father of the Catholic Church

SUMMARY

- William the Conqueror allowed the Church to have its own law courts.
- Strong kings did not want the Church to be powerful.

SUMMARY *activity*

How did the Church become so powerful under William I and afterwards?

9 Henry II and Thomas Becket

In this section of the book you will learn the following things:

- **Henry II made his friend, Thomas Becket, Archbishop of Canterbury;**
- **Henry and Becket quarrelled and Becket was murdered.**

Thomas Becket as Henry II's Chancellor

Thomas Becket first became Henry's **Chancellor** or right-hand man. They were also friends. They both enjoyed hunting and worked together running the country. In 1162 it seemed to Henry a very good idea to make Becket Archbishop of Canterbury. This would mean that his friend held the top Church position in England and could help Henry gain control of the Church.

Q1 Why did Henry think making Becket Archbishop of Canterbury was a good idea?

Church law and Church courts

Anyone in the Church from the highest archbishop to the lowest priest could be tried for crimes in the Church courts, not in the King's courts. The Church did not have the death penalty or put people in prison. It usually disgraced them. This was all very well for sincere priests, but there were some very unsavoury characters in the Church, particularly after the chaos of Stephen's reign. Decent people were appalled at what these so-called priests got away with. It was said that in the first ten years of Henry's reign, there were over 100 murders committed by clerks (the lowest grade of priests). They all had the right to be tried by the Church courts.

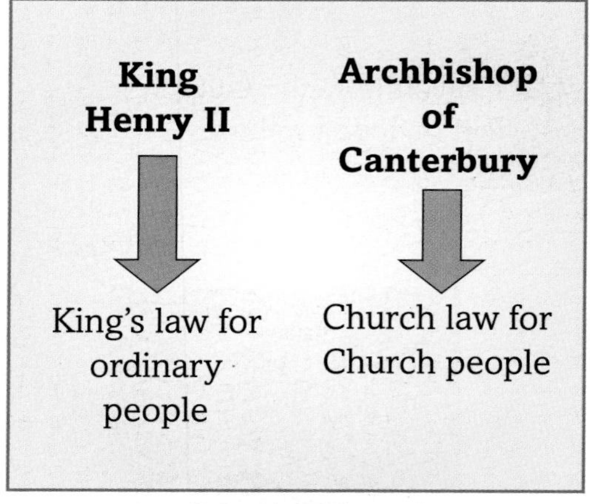

▲ ***Fig 1*** *Two laws in England.*

Thomas Becket as Archbishop of Canterbury

To Henry's horror, as soon as Becket became Archbishop of Canterbury, he changed sides. Far from getting rid of the Church courts, Becket now stood up for them. The rows between the two men got worse and worse. Becket fled abroad and stayed in France for six years. Neither he nor Henry would give in. Eventually, Becket came back to England, but no sooner did he arrive than he and Henry argued again. Becket sacked all the bishops who had supported Henry while he was away.

Q2 What happened as soon as Becket became Archbishop of Canterbury?

The murder of Thomas Becket

◀ ***Fig 2*** *An illustration of Becket's murder, drawn in about 1200.*

Henry was in Normandy at Christmas 1170; the bishops arrived to tell him what had happened. Henry flew into a rage and shouted out, 'Will no one rid me of this **turbulent** priest?' Four knights heard his words. They slipped away, sailed to England, rode to Canterbury and murdered Becket in Canterbury Cathedral.

> They wanted to get him outside the cathedral to kill him but he clung to a pillar. He was struck on the head and the fourth blow spilt his brains and blood on the floor.

▲ ***Fig 3*** *Death of Thomas Becket (described by his assistant, who was with him).*

After the murder

People were horrified, not just in England but all over Europe. Within two years, Thomas Becket **was made a saint** and Canterbury became a famous **shrine** for **pilgrims** to visit. Sick people prayed to Becket and many claimed to be cured. For Henry the murder was not only a shock, it was a huge setback. He had to leave the Church courts alone and ask to be forgiven for his rash words. He said he had not meant that anyone should murder Becket, but he agreed his words might have led to the murder.

Key words

Chancellor – the King's most important assistant
pilgrim – someone who journeys to a holy place
shrine – a holy place
to be made a saint – declared a holy person by the Pope
turbulent – troublesome, fiery

SUMMARY

- Henry made his Chancellor and friend, Becket, Archbishop of Canterbury in 1162.
- Becket refused to help Henry get control of the Church courts.
- Years of rows between the two men led to the murder of Becket in 1170.
- Thomas Becket was made a saint and people prayed to him.

SUMMARY *activity*

Write a paragraph about the murder of Thomas Becket. Include the reasons for the murder, where it took place and what happened afterwards.

10 Cathedrals and pilgrims

In this section of the book you will learn the following things:

- **cathedrals were the seats of archbishops and bishops;**
- **pilgrims travelled to cathedrals to pray to saints;**
- **styles of cathedral building changed.**

Archbishops, bishops and their cathedrals

There were 19 cathedrals in England in the Middle Ages and Thomas Becket died in the grandest one, Canterbury Cathedral. This was the seat of the Archbishop of Canterbury. The cathedral at York was the seat of the Archbishop of York. Between them, they ruled over the Church in England. Below them were the bishops, each with a cathedral. The word cathedral comes from *cathedra*, which means 'a seat' in Latin. Each bishop kept a seat or throne in his cathedral.

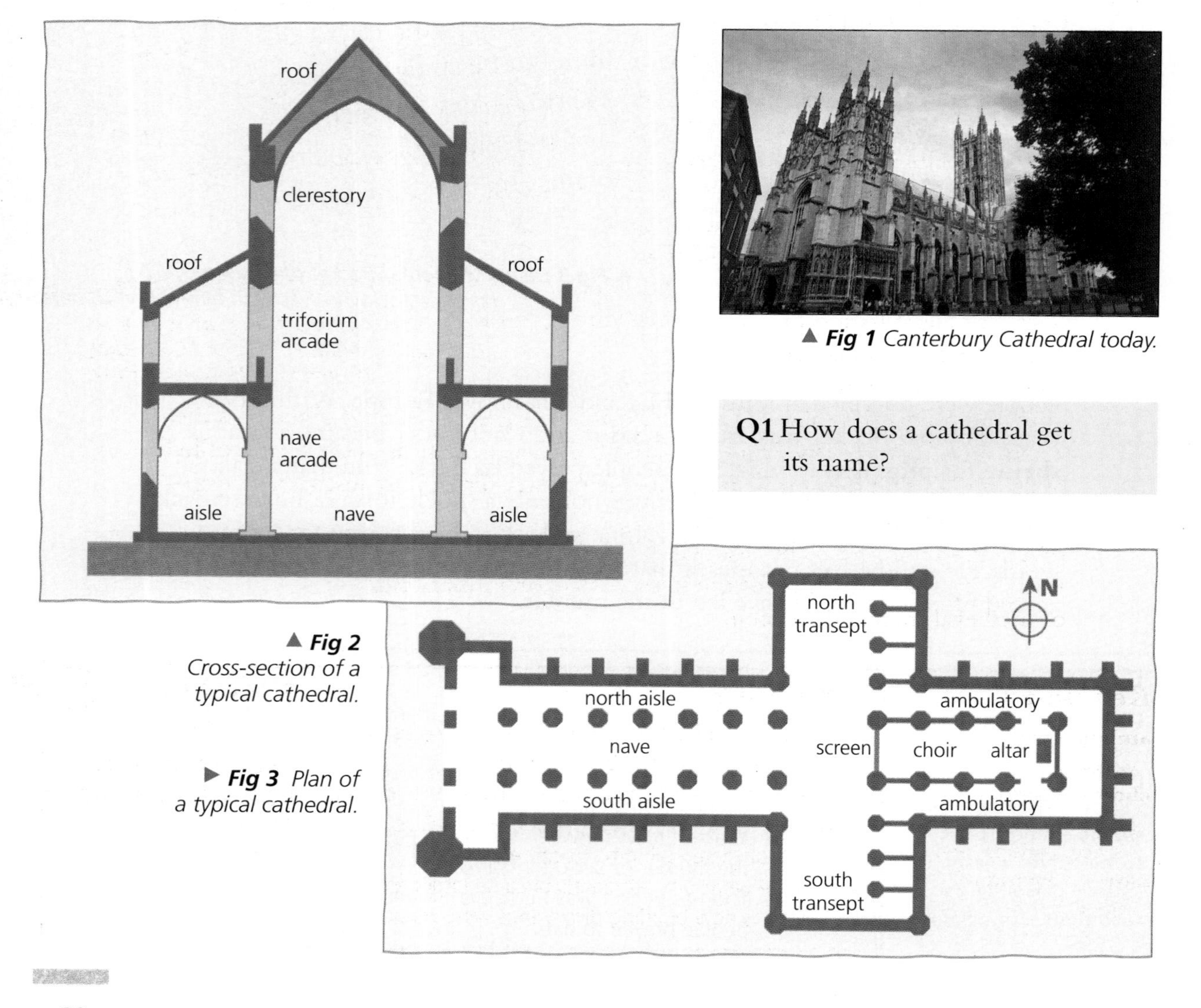

▲ ***Fig 1*** *Canterbury Cathedral today.*

Q1 How does a cathedral get its name?

▲ ***Fig 2*** *Cross-section of a typical cathedral.*

▶ ***Fig 3*** *Plan of a typical cathedral.*

Services and saints

These cathedrals were huge churches, built to praise God. Services were held in them all day, every day, and saints were buried in them, so many became centres of pilgrimage. People came from all over the country to pray to the saint to help them. Needless to say, Canterbury became the biggest pilgrimage centre in England. Not only did the cathedral have the body of St Thomas Becket, but he had actually been murdered there. Other famous saints at cathedrals were St Swithin at Winchester, St Etheldreda at Ely and St Cuthbert at Durham.

170	silver ships
129	silver models of bodies or parts of bodies
95	silk or linen children's clothes
108	walking sticks
515	gold rings and brooches
109	silver rings and brooches
	many jewels
	wax models of bodies, body parts (ears, etc)
	wax models of ships
1	prisoner's iron chains
	ship's anchors
	swords, knives, daggers
plus	money offerings not counted

▲ ***Fig 4*** *Some of the offerings at St Thomas Cantilupe's shrine at Hereford Cathedral, counted on 29 August 1307.*

Style of cathedrals

Styles of building changed. The Normans built solid cathedrals with rounded arches and small windows. Then builders made some interesting discoveries. If they made arches pointed they could make bigger spaces and bigger windows. Suddenly light and airy space flooded into the new cathedrals. Bishops with old cathedrals wanted modern ones, or at least to add on a new part. This is one reason why old cathedrals and churches are a mixture of styles. Other building discoveries followed and the cathedrals grew taller and grander as they reached towards the sky. Sometimes the builders, or masons as they were called, built so high that the spires and towers fell down. Then they just started again. People raised money to build and rebuild their cathedrals because God was a very important part of the lives of medieval men and women.

Q2 Why was the discovery of the pointed arch important?

Key words

ambulatory – a walkway
choir – where the priests or monks held services praising God
nave – main part of cathedral

SUMMARY

- There were 19 cathedrals in the Middle Ages that were the seats of archbishops and bishops.
- Cathedrals were huge churches built to praise God.
- Many cathedrals housed the bodies of saints, which attracted pilgrims to come and pray.
- As time went on, cathedrals became larger and lighter as new building discoveries were made.

SUMMARY *activity*

Why were cathedrals important in the Middle Ages?

11 Henry II and the law

In this section of the book you will learn the following things:

- Henry II restored order after Stephen's reign;
- Henry set up trial by jury and travelling courts.

Restoring order

▲ ***Fig 1*** *An illustration from an early fourteenth-century English manuscript, showing a monk and a nun in the stocks.*

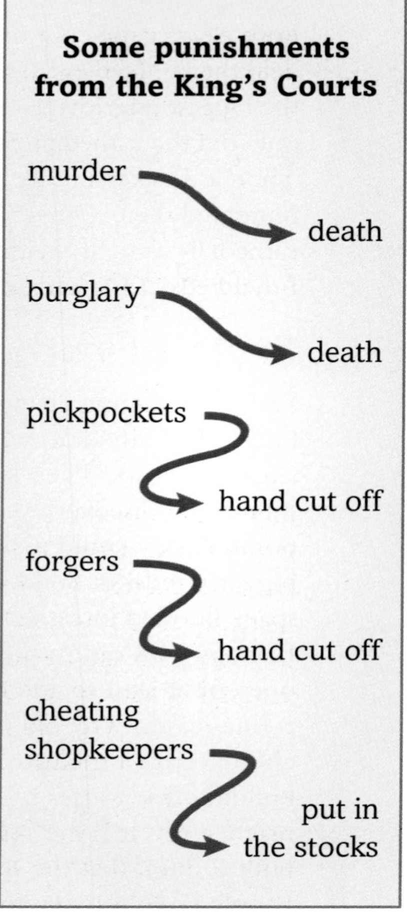

▲ ***Fig 2*** *Some punishments from the King's courts.*

The Church and Thomas Becket were not Henry's only worries. He came to the throne in 1154 and his first job was to restore order and make everyone in England obey his laws. Stephen had allowed the barons to do as they pleased. They had built castles without the King's permission and had terrorised farmers and merchants so that farming and trade were at a standstill.

Q1 What had the barons done in Stephen's reign?

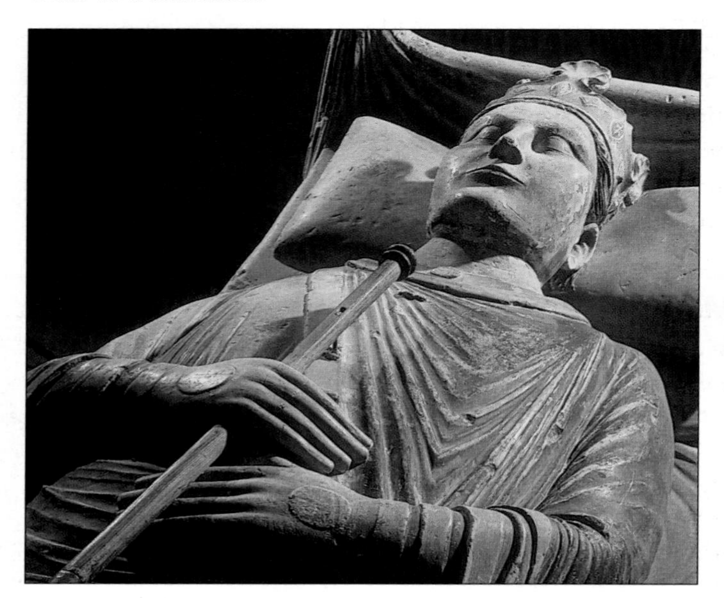

◄ ***Fig 3*** *Henry II's effigy (sculpture) on his tomb in France.*

Henry and trial by jury

For a long time **trial by battle** or **trial by ordeal** had been used to decide whether someone was guilty of a crime. There were three main trials by ordeal and one by battle:

- **ordeal by fire** – the accused person had to carry a red-hot iron bar and walk three steps. Then the wound was bandaged. If it healed in three days, they were innocent.
- **ordeal by boiling water** – the accused person had to pick a stone out of boiling water. If the wound healed in three days, they were innocent.
- **ordeal by water** – the accused person was thrown in the water. If they sank, they were innocent. (The water had accepted them.)
- **ordeal by battle** – barons could choose trial by battle. They or their champions fought. If they won, they were innocent.

Henry did not think these methods were either fair or sensible. Instead he encouraged trial by jury. The jury was made up of 12 men. They listened to all the evidence and decided if the person accused of the crime was guilty or not.

▶ *Fig 4*

What Henry II did to restore order:

- destroyed 365 illegal castles;
- had new coins made;
- restored Henry I's laws.

Travelling courts

Q2 What three things did Henry do to restore order?

Henry wanted everyone to respect the law. He therefore had to make sure that everyone saw that the law was carried out and wrongdoers were punished. So he sent judges all over England to hold courts of law. Often Henry went as judge himself. He had a very good reputation and people felt they would get a fair trial if he was the judge.

Key words

ordeal – suffering
trial – test

SUMMARY

- Henry restored order by pulling down illegal castles and bringing back the laws of Henry I.
- Henry brought in trial by jury and did away with trial by ordeal and battle.
- Henry sent his judges to different towns to try cases so everyone saw the law working.

SUMMARY *activity*

Why did many people think that Henry was a fair king?

12 Henry II: a great European king

In this section of the book you will learn the following things:

- **Henry II had a large empire;**
- **he married Eleanor of Aquitaine.**

English and French lands

Henry inherited English and French lands. He married Eleanor of Aquitaine so he gained all of Aquitaine as well. He ruled far more land in France than the King of France himself and, during his reign, gained part of Ireland too. Only a man of tremendous energy could hold all these different lands together. It was said of Henry II that he never stayed still. Even on his way to great meetings with his barons, he would pass the journey by hunting deer or **hawking**.

▲ ***Fig 1*** *The tomb effigy of Eleanor in France.*

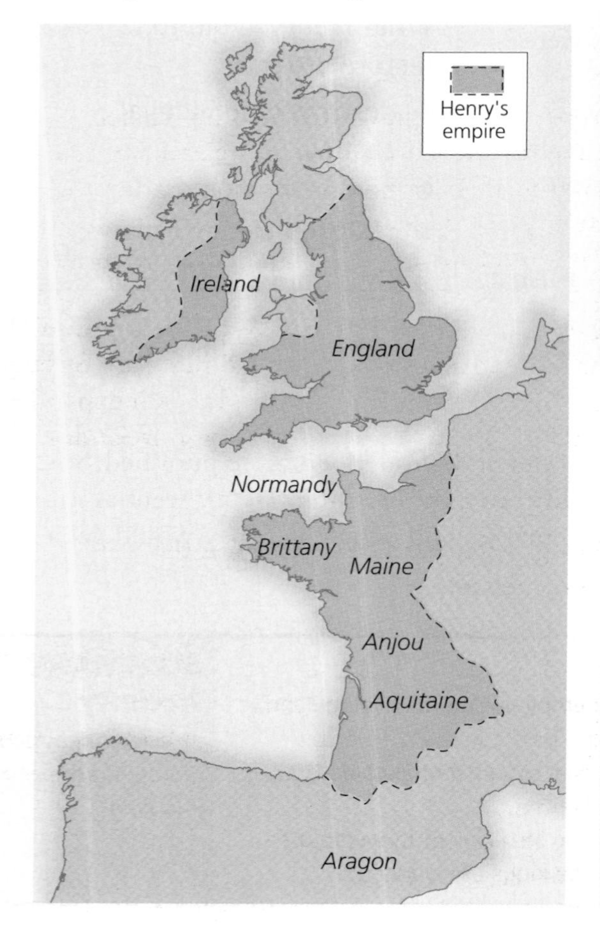

◀ ***Fig 2*** *Henry's European empire.*

Q1 In what two countries did Henry inherit land?

Q2 Where did he gain land during his reign?

Q3 Who did he marry?

Eleanor of Aquitaine

Eleanor was as strong a character as Henry and much of their marriage was spent rowing. They had many sons and daughters and Henry wanted to make sure all the lands stayed in the family. This led to more rows as the sons grew up and wanted to have land straight away. In the end all his sons rebelled against him, often aided by his wife.

Henry II's sons and what he said they could have when he died:

William – died very young

Henry – England, Normandy, Maine, Anjou (died young)

Richard – Aquitaine

John – Ireland

Geoffrey – Brittany

▲ *Fig 3*

Ireland

Ireland had many kings who frequently fought among themselves. This was no concern of the Norman kings in England until the reign of Henry II. Then two things happened. The Church was getting stronger and the Pope wanted more control over the Church in Ireland. He asked Henry II to invade Ireland on his behalf. However, even Henry II was too occupied. Then, a little later, one of the Irish kings, Dermot MacMurrough, asked for Henry's help.

Dermot MacMurrough: England gets involved in Ireland

Dermot stole another king's wife in 1152. Although he returned her to her husband, it led to such fighting that Dermot was driven out of Ireland. He went to England, where he asked for Henry's help. Henry was still too occupied, but gave his permission for any of his barons to help Dermot. A group of knights went out to Ireland, led by a baron nicknamed 'Strongbow'. Strongbow was so successful that he stayed there, married Dermot's daughter and became an Irish king. Henry was opposed to that. He said Strongbow must pay him homage and the King of England must rank higher than all the kings of Ireland.

Q4 Why do you think Henry did not want Strongbow to be an independent king in Ireland?

Ireland and John

Henry sent his son, John, to Ireland to **govern** parts of it. This was the beginning of the English occupation of Ireland.

Key words

govern – rule

hawking – hunting small animals using tame hawks

SUMMARY

- Henry had a great empire, with lands in England, France and Ireland.
- By marrying Eleanor of Aquitaine he gained Aquitaine (also in France).
- By helping one of the Irish kings, Henry declared himself King over the kings of Ireland.

SUMMARY *activity*

In what way was Henry II a great European king?

13 The forest

In this section of the book you will learn the following things:

- the Normans set up hunting forests;
- no one else was allowed to hunt in the forests.

Population and land

The Normans loved hunting and even Henry II was not too busy to go hunting. At this time huge forests and wild lands covered much of England. The population was still small – probably about 1½–2 million people – though no one knows for sure. Small farms were dotted here and there, but there was much spare land.

Hunting forests

As soon as William the Conqueror was settled in England he set up royal forests. These lands had enough trees to give cover to animals such as deer and **wild boar**, but were often open enough for men to ride horses through and hunt. Since the Norman kings and their friends loved hunting, they added more and more land to the royal forests. By the time of Henry II, about one-third of all the land in England was forest.

Q1 How much of England was covered in forest in Henry II's reign?

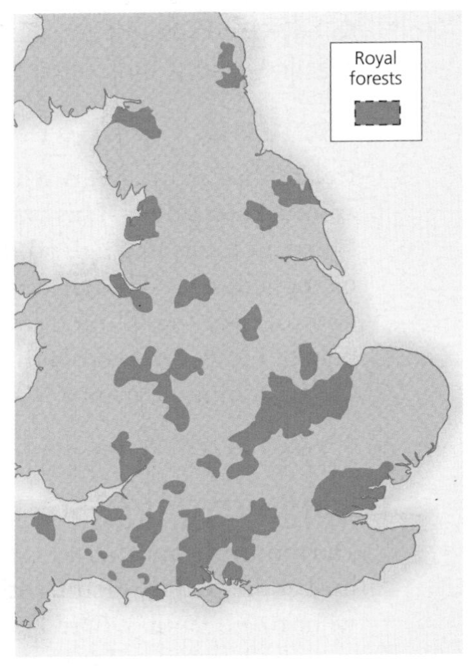

▲ ***Fig 1*** *Royal forests in about 1250.*

▼ ***Fig 2*** *A medieval deer hunt.*

Importance of the forests

Hunting in the forests provided food for the King's court – the men who travelled around with him, including his advisers and servants. The King used timber from the forests for making ships and royal buildings. The forests were also important for ordinary villagers, who were often hungry and would have liked to have been able to hunt as well. However, this was forbidden by the harsh forest laws.

Q2 What were the people living in the forest areas allowed to do?

Q3 What were they not allowed to do?

Animals of the forest

It was not only in the royal forests that no one but the King was allowed to hunt. All the animals he liked to hunt were protected in any wooded land. The King was particularly keen to preserve red deer, fallow deer and wild boar for his own hunting. Often he would grant rights of hunting smaller animals such as hares, foxes and cats to favoured men and women. For instance, he allowed the nuns of Wix to keep a small pack of hounds to hunt hares in the Essex forest to feed to sick people.

Q4 What animals were hunted?

People living in forest areas

Could:

- pay rent to graze pigs and cows all year except when deer had young;
- collect dead branches for fuel and repairing their cottages.

Could not:

- carry a bow and arrow;
- cut off a live branch or chop down a tree;
- Their dogs had to have three claws cut off their front paws so they could not hunt.

▲ ***Fig 3***

Penalties for breaking the forest laws

Men who were caught **poaching** in the forests were thrown into prison. Punishments ranged from death to **mutilation**, a prison sentence or a fine. There were times, no doubt, when one of the King's officials let a man go who had killed a hare to feed his starving family. However, the only cases that are written down for historians to read are the ones that came to court. There may also have been people who lived in the vast forests without ever being found, such as the legendary Robin Hood.

Key words

mutilation – cutting off a hand, etc

poaching – stealing animals from the forests

wild boar – wild pig

SUMMARY

- The population was small and there was a lot of open land in England.
- The Norman kings set up royal forests covering up to a third of England.
- The King liked to hunt red deer, fallow deer and wild boar.
- No one else could hunt without his permission.
- The penalties for poaching were very harsh.

SUMMARY *activity*

Who used the forests at this time?

14 The village

In this section of the book you will learn the following things:

- **how a medieval village was organised.**

A small population

The population of England was still very small in the Middle Ages. In the middle of the vast forests and stretches of open land sat tiny villages, surrounded by fields. Most people lived in such villages at this time and farmed the land around as their ancestors had done for hundreds of years. Their cattle and pigs grazed in the forests and they were allowed to collect dead wood from there; otherwise they relied for food on the crops they could grow in the fields and the animals they raised.

The three-field system

Most villages had three enormous fields. These were divided into strips. People in the village owned some strips in each field. Every year one whole field was left **fallow** so it could regain its goodness. Wheat or rye were grown in one other field and barley or oats in the other. Everyone ploughed together and harvested together. The wheat and barley were **threshed** and the grain sent to the mill to be ground into flour.

Q1 What was grown in each field?

The Lord of the Manor

Villages were based around the manor where the Lord lived. He might be a knight and hold land from the King under the feudal system. The Lord of the Manor had his own land (demesne) as well as strips of land in each field.

The villager

Most villagers were villeins. They had to work on the Lord's land. Some worked as much as two days a week and more at harvest time. They were tied to the Lord and the village. They worked from morning to night, ploughing, sowing, weeding, harvesting, repairing hedges and ditches and looking after animals. They often went hungry in winter if food was short. They lived in small, windowless cottages which they shared with their pigs and chickens. They had a fire on a stone slab in the middle of the mud floor, a few wooden stools and a table. There was a vegetable garden round the cottage.

Q2 Describe a villein's house.

A villein's duties

- work on the Lord's land for a fixed number of days per year;
- never leave the village without the Lord's permission;
- never let his children marry without the Lord's permission;
- pay the Lord; for instance when a villein died and his son inherited.

► *Fig 1*

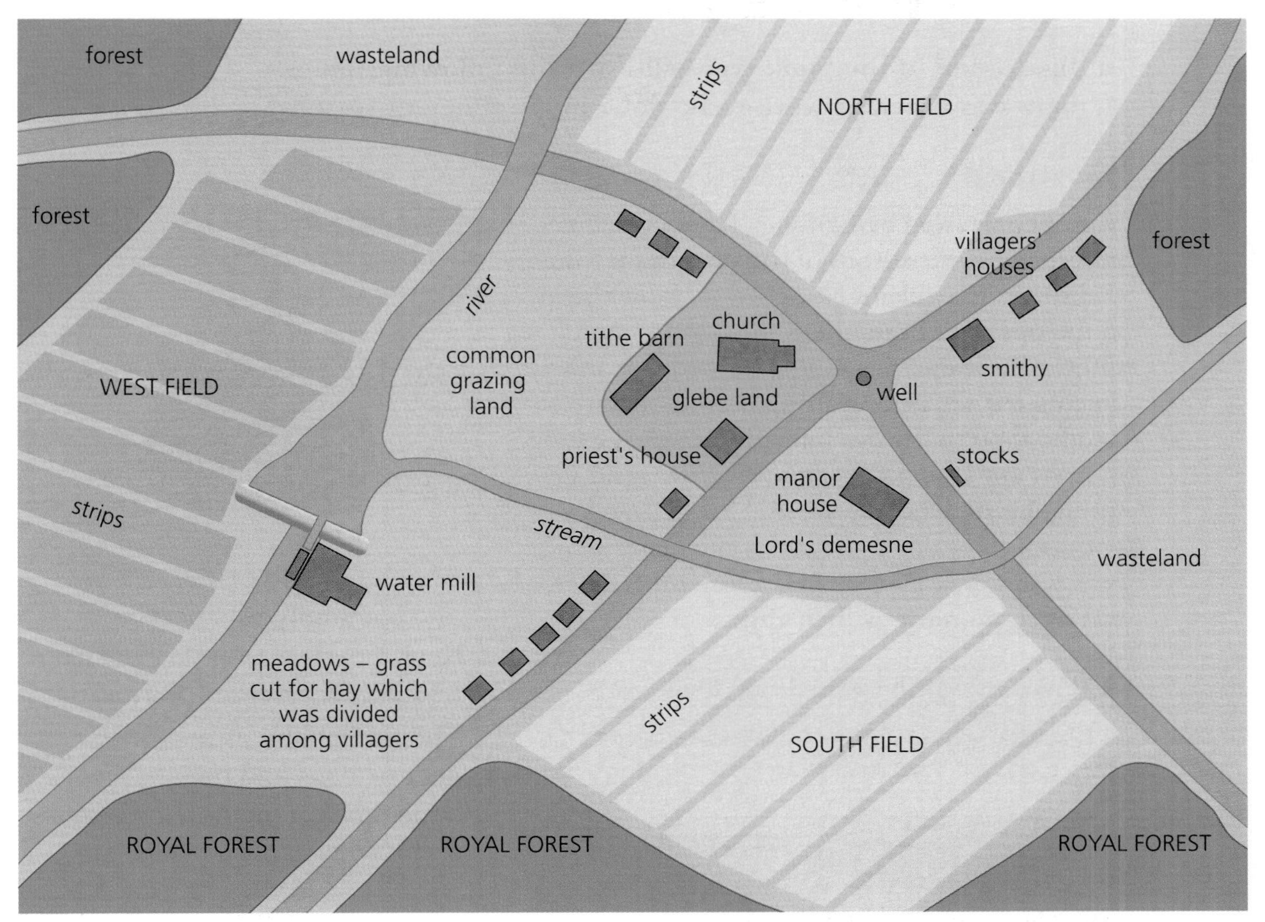

▲ ***Fig 2*** *The layout of a medieval village.*

Church, priest and tithe

The church was a large building. It was used for church services and for storing village possessions such as weapons, valuables and firehooks to pull down the thatch of burning cottages. The Manor Court (local law court) might be held in the church; it was also a good place to hold miracle plays (religious plays), local meetings and church ales (feasts). The priest lived in a house near the church and farmed his own land (glebe). He also had a right to **tithes** to keep him and the church. A tithe was one-tenth of each man's produce in the village. This was stored in the tithe barn.

Key words

fallow – resting
threshing – beating the wheat or barley so that the seed heads (grain) come off
tithe – one-tenth

SUMMARY

- The village had three large fields and was based around the Lord's manor.
- The church was the building used for services and meetings.

SUMMARY *activity*

Explain what each of the following was: the Lord's demesne, glebe land, tithe barn, meadows, fields.

15 The villagers' year

In this section of the book you will learn the following things:

- **there was different work to be done in the different seasons.**

Winter

Most people lived by farming. Their lives were governed by the seasons of the year. In the winter (February) the villeins ploughed their own strips in the open fields and their Lord's strips too. Otherwise winter was a time for hedging and digging out ditches, repairing farm tools and finding food to get the animals through the long months until the grass started to grow again in spring. **Lent**, which began on Shrove Tuesday with pancakes, when the last of the preserved eggs were often used up, was a lean time. There was often no meat by then either.

Q1 When was the ploughing done?

Q2 What other winter jobs were there?

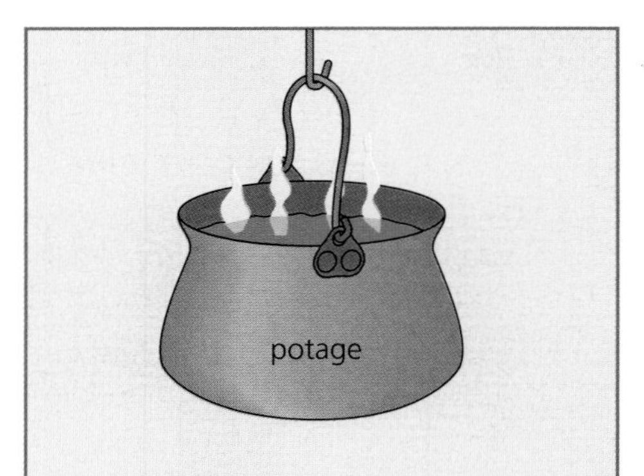

The main food of the villein and his family was potage, a thick vegetable soup. They also had bread, and ale to drink.

The availability of meat, cheese, eggs and milk depended on the time of year and how well off a villein was.

▲ ***Fig 1***

▲ ***Fig 2*** *Sowing seed in springtime by the* ***broadcast method****.*

Spring

When spring came it was time to sow seed. This was done by 'broadcast sowing'. A man walked along his strip in the field with a basket full of seed and scattered handfuls to right and left. At the same time of year he took his cows out to start grazing the new grass. Sometimes the animals were so weak after the winter they had to be carried. Chickens started to lay eggs again and pigs began to put on weight. It was a joyful time celebrated by the festival of Easter.

Q3 What were the main jobs in springtime?

Summer

Through the summer crops had to be weeded and animals looked after. In June the **hay** meadows were ready for cutting. The hay could be dried and stored to provide some winter feed. By August the wheat, barley, rye and oats were ready for harvesting. This was the busiest time of the year. Men, women and children worked from dawn to dusk to get the crops cut while the weather was good. Huge cartloads were taken to the barns for storing and threshing.

Q4 Why was it important to work from dawn to dusk at harvest time?

Autumn

As summer moved towards autumn there was more harvesting. Fruit such as apples and pears were picked, vegetables were gathered, the pigs foraged in the woods for acorns and beech nuts and cows grazed on the **stubble** after the crops were cut at harvest time. As winter came nearer, it was obvious that there was not enough food for most cows, pigs and sheep to be kept during the winter. Many were slaughtered and what was not eaten then was salted to last as long as possible through the winter. Only the best breeding animals were kept for the next spring and even they often ended the winter fed on holly and half starved.

▲ ***Fig 3*** *Harvesting in summer in a medieval village.*

Q5 Why did many animals have to be killed before winter?

Key words

broadcast method – scattering seed
hay – dried grass
Lent – from about mid-February to Easter
stubble – the cut-off stalks of crops sticking out of the ground after harvesting

SUMMARY

- Winter was the time for hedging, ditching, repairing tools and looking after animals.
- Spring was the time for sowing crops.
- In summer the crops were weeded and in late summer they were harvested.
- In autumn many animals were slaughtered and the meat preserved.

SUMMARY *activity*

Why was the weather very important to villeins?

16 Monasteries and nunneries

In this section of the book you will learn the following things:

- monks and nuns lived in religious houses;
- as time went by monasteries and nunneries became rich.

Lives devoted to God

Monks lived in monasteries, nuns in nunneries, and devoted their lives to God. They lived according to strict rules which had been laid down by St Benedict. They spent the day praying, studying and working hard. When they entered the monastery or nunnery, they gave up all their possessions and agreed to eat simple food and wear simple clothes. They even gave up their names and social status.

A monk's day

Midnight	go to church service
2 a.m.	back to bed
7 a.m.	rise for prayers and meeting in Chapter House
11.30 a.m.	dinner
12.30 p.m.	work
6 p.m.	church service followed by meal and church service
8.30 p.m.	to bed

▲ ***Fig 1***

Why did monks join monasteries?

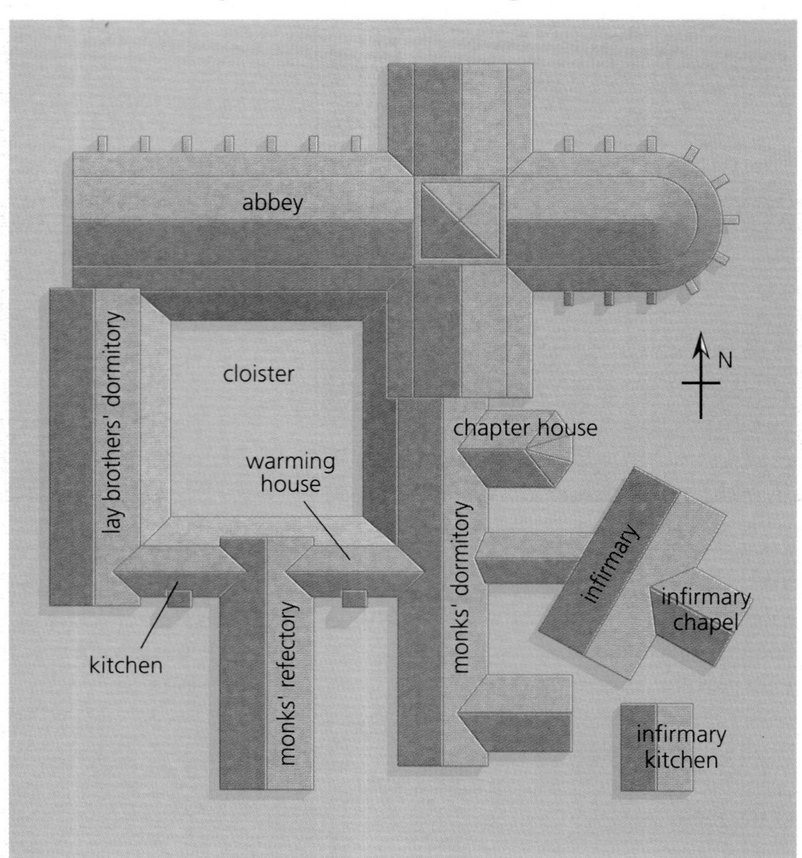

Many men joined monasteries in the Middle Ages. They felt they would be sure to get to heaven if they lived for God on earth. Some men retired to a monastery towards the end of their lives, others entered when they were very young because their families put them there. Some men felt secure in monasteries because, however simple and strict the way of life, they belonged to a group and were cared for. Women joined nunneries for similar reasons.

Q1 Why did men and women join monasteries and nunneries?

◀ ***Fig 2*** *The layout of a medieval monastery.*

Monasteries grew rich

Although monasteries started very simply, rich people often gave them money and land. Rich men and women felt that gifts to monasteries might help them get to heaven, and that was a good thing to do. Over hundreds of years, some monasteries became large landowners. As they got richer, they became less strict and spent more time managing their money than they did at prayer. On the whole nunneries were smaller and were given less money.

Q2 Why did monasteries become rich?

What did monasteries do?

By the time of the **Black Death** in 1348–49, there were 600 monasteries in England. Some of the large ones housed 700 monks. The monks grew their own food and did all the cooking. They grew herbs and, because there were no hospitals then, they might be both hospital and doctor. The monks learnt to read and write and often ran schools. There was no printing in those days, so some of the monks copied out and illustrated beautiful books by hand. As time went by and the monasteries owned more land, the monks became land managers, traders in wool and, in general, makers of more money!

▶ ***Fig 3*** *A fifteenth-century illustration showing nuns treating patients in a hospital.*

Key words

Black Death – the bubonic plague which killed many people in 1348–49

SUMMARY

- Monks joined monasteries and nuns joined nunneries to devote their lives to God.
- Over the centuries the monasteries grew richer because of gifts from rich people.
- By 1381 there were 600 monasteries in England and nearly as many nunneries.
- The monasteries were self-sufficient, looked after the sick, ran schools and copied out books.

SUMMARY *activity*

Why did men join monasteries and women join nunneries?

17 Crusades

In this section of the book you will learn the following things:

- **what a crusade was;**
- **about Muhammad and the Muslims;**
- **about the First Crusade.**

What was a crusade?

Crusade comes from the Latin word *crux*, meaning 'a cross'. It referred to the cross on which Jesus Christ was crucified and to go on a crusade meant going to fight for Christ. In 1100, it meant going to fight the **Muslims** in the **Holy Land**, around Jerusalem, where Christ had lived.

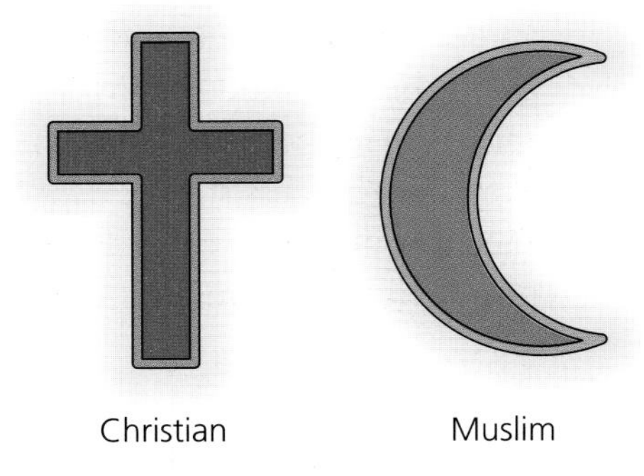

▲ ***Fig 1*** *Symbols of the crusades: the Christian cross and the Muslim crescent.*

Muhammad and Muslims

Muhammad was born in the city of Mecca in AD 570. He founded a great religion and his followers were called Muslims. Some of his followers were warlike and over the next few hundred years they captured land around the Mediterranean Sea.

In AD 637, the Muslims captured the city of Jerusalem, which was a holy city to **Christians** because Christ had lived and died in that area.

Q1 How does the word crusade get its name?

Q2 What was a crusade?

Q3 What were Muhammad's followers called?

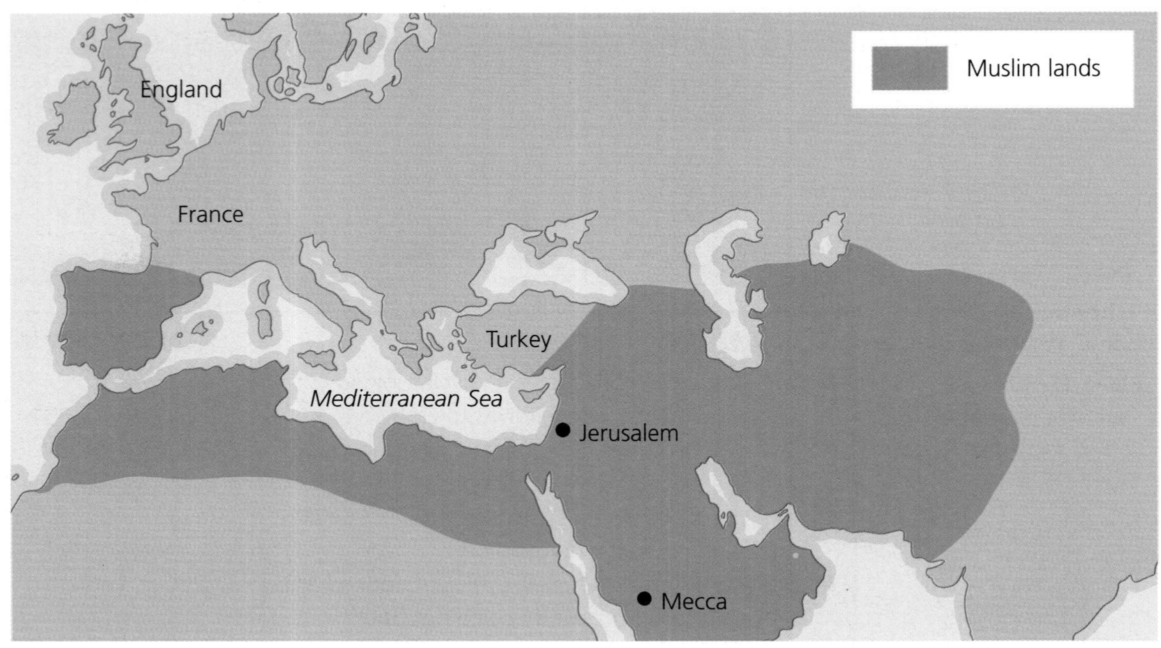

▲ ***Fig 2*** *Muslim lands in Europe and Asia in the thirteenth century.*

Jerusalem

For a long time, the Muslims allowed Christians to visit Jerusalem as pilgrims, and many thousands made the journey from Europe. Then, in 1071, a group of fanatical Turkish Muslims captured Jerusalem. They would not tolerate Christians and began to ill-treat them.

Q4 What happened in 1071?

Pope Urban II calls for a crusade

Pope Urban II heard of this and in 1095 called a mass meeting in France of all the knights of **Christendom**. He made a passionate speech to them, calling on them to fight against the evil enemy to regain Jerusalem. At the end of his speech, thousands surged forward, shouting that they were ready to fight and die for Christ.

The First Crusade 1096

The next year they set off on the First Crusade. There were about 30,000 foot soldiers and 10,000 knights on horseback, among them Robert, the eldest son of William the Conqueror. They made their way through Europe and into Turkey, finally reaching Jerusalem three years after they set off. They took Jerusalem, and held the city and the land around it for the next 87 years.

The meaning of the effigy

▲ ***Fig 3*** *The effigy (sculpture) of a knight from a church tomb.*

Position of feet:

- resting on a lion – died on crusade;
- resting on a dog – died peacefully;
- ankles crossed – went on one crusade;
- knees crossed – went on two crusades.

Key words

Christendom – all the land in Europe where Christians lived

Christian – a follower of Christ

Holy Land – the land where Jesus Christ lived

Muslim – a follower of Muhammad

SUMMARY

- A crusade was an expedition to fight for Christ.
- Muhammad founded a great religion that dominated many lands around the Mediterranean.
- Muhammad's followers are called Muslims.
- Fanatical Muslims captured Jerusalem in 1071.
- In 1095 Pope Urban II called for a crusade to drive the Muslims from Jerusalem.

SUMMARY *activity*

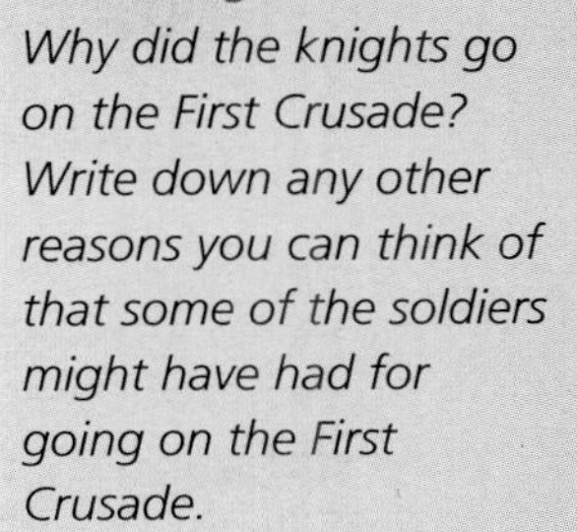

Why did the knights go on the First Crusade? Write down any other reasons you can think of that some of the soldiers might have had for going on the First Crusade.

18 Richard I and the Third Crusade

In this section of the book you will learn the following things:

- Richard I went on the Third Crusade;
- Saladin was the leader of the Muslim armies;
- there were several more crusades.

Henry II and Richard I

Henry II was supposed to go on a crusade for three years as a **penance** for bringing about the murder of Thomas Becket, but he managed to change this penance to building three monasteries instead. However, his son, Richard I, was much more interested in fighting than in running the country, so no sooner was he King than he was off to join the Third Crusade in 1189.

Q1 Why was Henry II supposed to go on a crusade?

Why did men go on crusades?

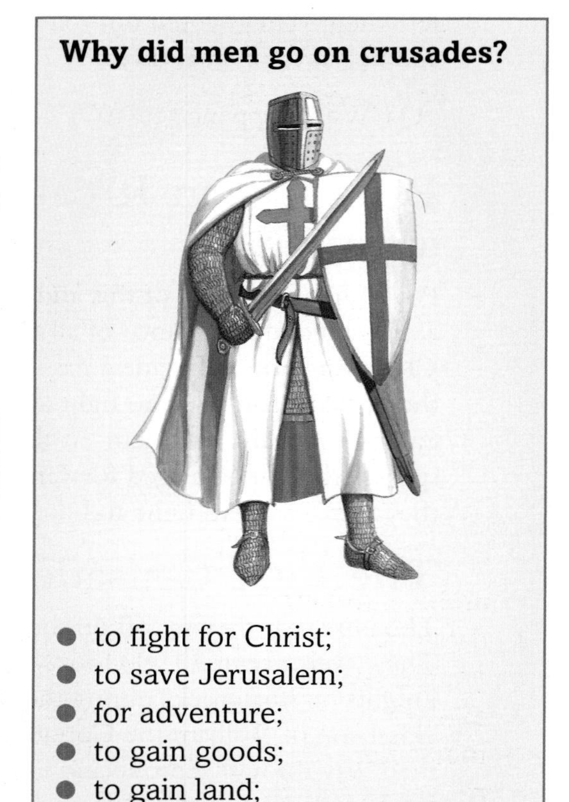

- to fight for Christ;
- to save Jerusalem;
- for adventure;
- to gain goods;
- to gain land;
- for honour and glory;
- to gain forgiveness for their sins.

▲ *Fig 1*

The siege of Acre

Richard journeyed overland to the south of France, then by sea and land to join the King of France and the Duke of Austria at the city of Acre. The Crusaders had been **besieging** this fortified city for two years without success. When Richard arrived, things changed. He was a skilful soldier, very brave and a good leader. Within a short space of time, the Crusaders took the city of Acre. Richard was not an easy man to work with, however, and soon the other two leaders left him to continue the fight. Besides, the King of France wanted to get home because he saw a chance to raid the English lands in France while Richard was so far away.

Richard and Saladin

Richard stayed and marched towards Jerusalem, pursued by the Muslim armies under their great leader, Saladin. Richard got within 12 miles of Jerusalem and even rode with a small war group to look at the walls. However, he knew he did not have the army or the time to take it. He came to an agreement with Saladin that Christian pilgrims could visit the holy city of Jerusalem in safety, then withdrew and made his way back to England.

The end of the crusades

There were several more crusades, including the Children's Crusade in 1212, when thousands of French and German children set out to save Jerusalem and the Holy Land. Most died of cold or starvation on the way or were taken and sold into slavery. In 1291, however, the Muslim Turks retook the city of Acre and the crusades ended.

What did Europe gain from contact with the Muslim East?

Knowledge

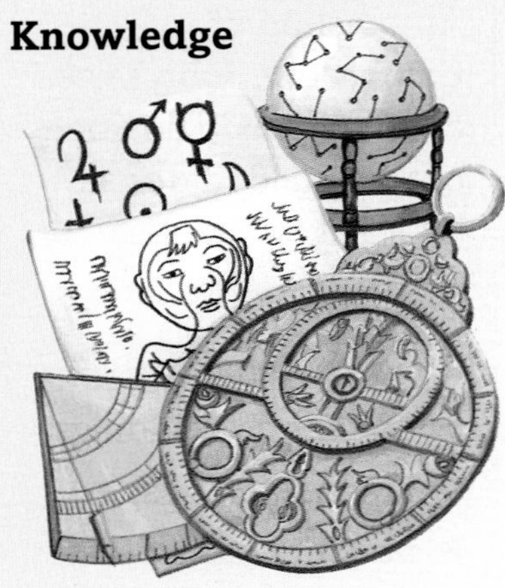

- arabic numbers;
- decimals;
- geometry;
- algebra;
- medicine;
- military science;
- biology;
- astronomy.

New farming ideas and animals

- windmills;
- mules;
- donkeys;
- Arab horses.

New goods from the East

- cotton;
- **muslin**;
- **damask**;
- figs, plums, apricots, melons;
- dates;
- spices;
- oils;
- perfume.

▲ *Fig 2*

Q2 Do you think the Muslim people were more advanced in learning than the English? Give reasons for your answer.

Key words

besiege – attack a castle for a long period of time

damask – heavy, patterned cotton, called after the city of Damascus

muslin – fine cotton, called after Muslims

penance – doing something good to make up for doing something bad

SUMMARY

- Richard I became King of England in 1189 and went on the Third Crusade immediately.
- He was a good soldier and helped to take the city of Acre.
- He made an agreement with Saladin that Christian pilgrims could go to Jerusalem in safety.

SUMMARY *activity*

Write an account of Richard I and the Third Crusade.

19 King John and Magna Carta

In this section of the book you will learn the following things:

- why King John was unpopular;
- he was forced to sign Magna Carta in 1215.

John made himself unpopular

When Richard I died in 1199, his younger brother John came to the throne. John was not a good soldier and he lost most of the land that England owned in France. The wars were expensive and he asked for taxes over and over again, which made him even more unpopular. John also resented the ever growing power of the Church and argued with the Pope about who should be Archbishop of Canterbury.

Q1 Why was John unpopular?

▶ ***Fig 1***

King John and the Pope quarrelled over who should become Archbishop of Canterbury. John seized church lands. The Pope put England under an interdict for six years.

This meant:

- no church burials;
- no church weddings;
- no christenings;
- no church services;
- no services for the dying.

Murder of Arthur 1202

By the year 1202 John's unpopularity increased even more when his nephew died in suspicious circumstances. This nephew was John's main rival to the throne, and though his murder by John was never proved, many people were prepared to believe the worst of the King.

◀ ***Fig 2*** *King John (1199–1216).*

The barons and Magna Carta 1215

John was not only unpopular with his barons, they were also powerful. In 1214, they drew up a list of complaints against the King, saying that he was ruling unfairly. When John refused to change, the barons raised an army and captured London. Now John had to listen. He agreed to meet the barons at Runnymede, by the River Thames, where they made him sign an agreement called the Great Charter or **Magna Carta**. Within a month it was written up, signed by 25 important barons and the King had set the **Great Seal of England** on it.

What did Magna Carta say?

There were 61 sections to Magna Carta. A lot of them dealt with the barons' grievances about what they had to do for the King – paying taxes and fighting for him. Some dealt with the freedom of the Church and a very few with the rights of freemen. The barons forced John to sign Magna Carta for their own selfish ends. They were not concerned with the rights of ordinary English men and women. The Church, too, wanted to safeguard its own power. So why is Magna Carta important?

Q2 What were the barons' grievances?

Q3 What did the Church want?

The importance of Magna Carta

Magna Carta said that a freeman could travel wherever he wanted and that no freeman was to be imprisoned, **outlawed** or punished except by the law of the land. The King could not override the law. Many years later Magna Carta became important to prove that kings could not override the law.

▲ ***Fig 3*** *A page of Magna Carta.*

Key words

Great Seal of England – an imprint in sealing wax that only the King could make

Magna Carta – Great Charter

outlawed – put outside the protection of the law so anyone can harm you and you can do nothing about it

SUMMARY

- John was unpopular because he lost England's lands in France, charged high taxes, argued with the Church and may have murdered his nephew.
- The barons hated paying taxes and thought John ruled unfairly.
- The barons forced King John to sign Magna Carta at Runnymede in 1215.
- Magna Carta dealt with many of the barons' grievances, such as taxes, with the freedom of the Church and with the legal rights of freemen.

SUMMARY *activity*

What is Magna Carta? Why is it so important in the history of England?

20 Towns

In this section of the book you will learn the following things:

- **the size and number of towns in England at the time of the Domesday Book;**
- **how towns were organised.**

The growth of towns

The Domesday Book named just over 100 small towns in 1086. Very few had a population of over 10,000 people. However, as England settled down after the Norman Conquest, the population increased and so towns grew. England became more peaceful, a greater number of people had money to spend, so more goods were made and bought and sold in towns. The townspeople wanted to rule themselves and often managed to persuade the King to sell them a **charter** so they could have their own town council.

Some facts about Colchester in 1300

There were:

- 8 butchers;
- 15 shoemakers;
- 95 ale-brewers (70 of them were women).

▲ *Fig 1*

The guild and the apprentice

There were many different trades in the town. Each one organised itself into a guild. When a boy wanted a job in a certain trade, such as shoemaking, his parents or guardian signed an agreement with a master shoemaker in the town. The boy became an apprentice for seven years. He was unpaid but lived with his master's family free and was taught the trade. At the end of the seven years he became a **journeyman**, until he could make a **masterpiece** and buy his way into becoming a master. Then he could have apprentices of his own.

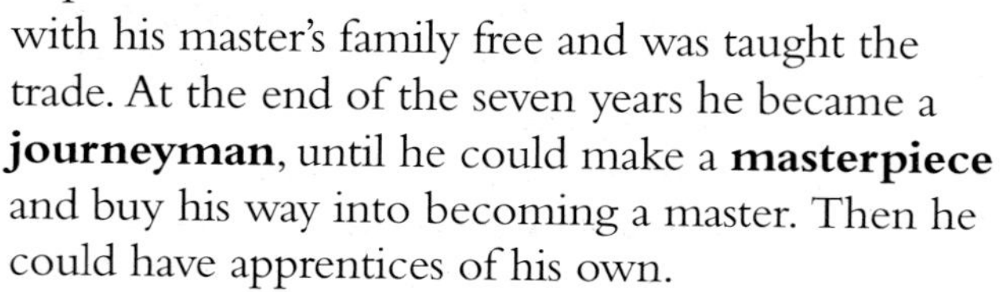

▲ ***Fig 2*** *Selling fish.*

Q1 What were the three stages of training in a guild?

Q2 For how long did an apprentice train?

Inside the town

Medieval towns had narrow streets which were noisy, crowded and dirty. The houses on each side of the streets were the homes of guild members. They made their goods in the back rooms and sold them in their shops at the front. Sometimes streets were called after the craftsmen in them, such as Baker Street. Streets where butchers were found were often called The Shambles because of the mess of offal, bones and fat in the middle of the roadway. There were no sewers, no running water in the houses and no rubbish collection. So there was a great deal of filth and disease.

Repairing streets

Pavage was a tax to pay for paving streets in towns. The people most likely to be charged were 'outsiders' driving carts into the town to market (particularly carts with iron rims on the wheels).

▲ *Fig 3*

Markets and fairs

In addition to the ordinary shops, most towns had markets. Men and women from the villages around the town brought in their goods such as butter, cheese and eggs to sell at market stalls. In some places markets grew much bigger than just trading in local goods. The very biggest were the great annual fairs, where merchants from all over Europe displayed their goods. There were silks and spices from the East, wines, cloth, furs and jewels. Only rich people could buy these goods, but even the poor enjoyed the street entertainments such as **bear-baiting**, wrestling and dancing.

Q3 How did townspeople entertain themselves?

◀ ***Fig 4*** *A medieval street market.*

Key words

bear-baiting – a bear put to fight with dogs
journeyman – qualified member of a trade who was paid by the day (from *jour*, French for a 'day')
masterpiece – article made by a journeyman to show he was good enough to be a master
charter – agreement sold to a town by the King, Church or local lord, allowing the townspeople to run the town themselves

SUMMARY

- Towns increased in size as the population and trade grew.
- Guilds governed the different trades in the town.
- The towns were crowded and filthy.
- There were markets and fairs in the towns.

SUMMARY *activity*

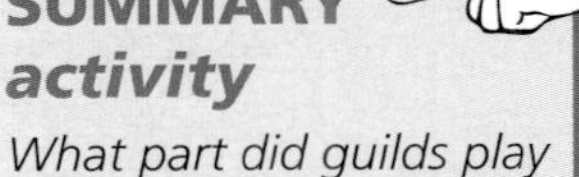

What part did guilds play in the life of a town ?

21 Henry III and Parliament

In this section of the book you will learn the following things:

- **Simon de Montfort led a rebellion against Henry III;**
- **Simon de Montfort called the First Parliament.**

Henry III 1216–1272

Henry III was childlike, vain, **pious** and occasionally charming. However, none of these attributes made him a good king. He gave enormous amounts of money to the Church and allowed himself to be governed by the relations of his wife, Eleanor of Provence. This did not please the barons and the increasingly powerful town merchants of England.

Q1 Who was not pleased with Henry III as King?

Simon de Montfort 1208–1265

Simon de Montfort was a much respected baron. In 1258, he led the other barons in a rebellion against Henry to force him to rule properly. Henry agreed to do this but then went back on his word. De Montfort left England feeling that the other barons were not supporting him. A few years later, however, some of them asked him back and, in 1264, de Montfort defeated Henry III at the Battle of Lewes.

Q2 Who was Simon de Montfort?

Q3 What happened in 1258?

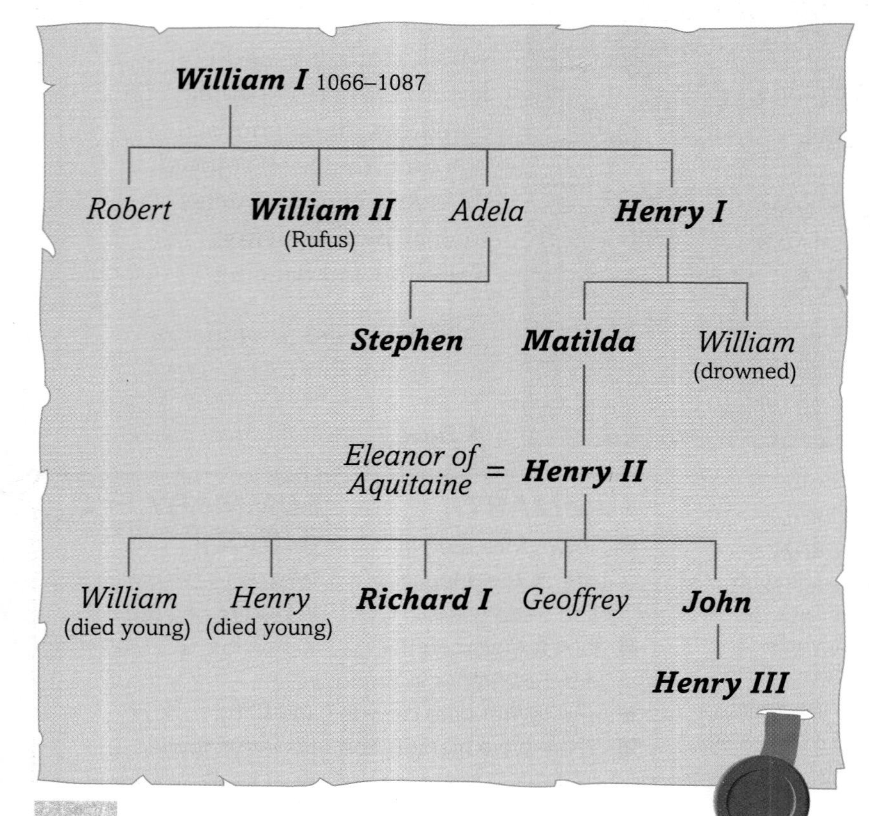

◄ ***Fig 1*** *The family tree of Henry III.*

The First Parliament 1265

For a short time, de Montfort was the real ruler of England. To make sure he was well supported he summoned a Great Council made up of:

- barons;
- knights;
- men from certain towns.

Why the Council or Parliament was important

This was the first time that men other than barons and knights had been called to a **King's Council**. It was the beginning of **Parliament**. Although de Montfort was soon defeated and killed at the Battle of Evesham, the custom of calling men from the towns, as well as knights from the country, and barons, continued.

▲ ***Fig 2*** *The houses of Parliament today, built in Victorian times.*

Medieval parliaments

Edward I called several parliaments. In 1297, he agreed that he would not demand taxes unless he had the consent of all the **realm**. This meant that he had to call Parliament and ask it to agree to give him money to fight wars and for other expenses. The merchants from the growing towns were now as wealthy and powerful as many knights and barons. This is why, from this time on, men from the towns were always included in parliaments.

Q4 Why were men from the towns included in parliaments after 1297?

Key words

King's Council – group of men to advise the King
Parliament – made up of the King and important men; a place to talk (from the French *parler,* 'to talk')
pious – very religious
realm – area or country ruled by a king; the kingdom

SUMMARY

- Henry gave money to the Church and was governed by his wife's foreign relations.
- The barons rebelled against Henry under Simon de Montfort.
- De Montfort wanted Henry to rule properly, so he called a Council or Parliament of the important men of England.

SUMMARY *activity*

Why was Simon de Montfort's First Parliament important?

22 Edward I and Wales

In this section of the book you will learn the following things:

- William the Conqueror set up the Welsh Marches;
- Edward I defeated Llewellyn of Gwynedd;
- Edward built castles and reorganised Wales.

The Marcher Lords

William the Conqueror set up the three earldoms of Chester, Shrewsbury and Hereford, which were known as the **Marcher** Lordships. These earls had special powers from the King to rule the borders of Wales. This was to make sure the Welsh did not invade England. As the years went by these Marcher Lords were strong enough to attack Wales, and by the time Edward I became King in 1272 all of south Wales was under their control.

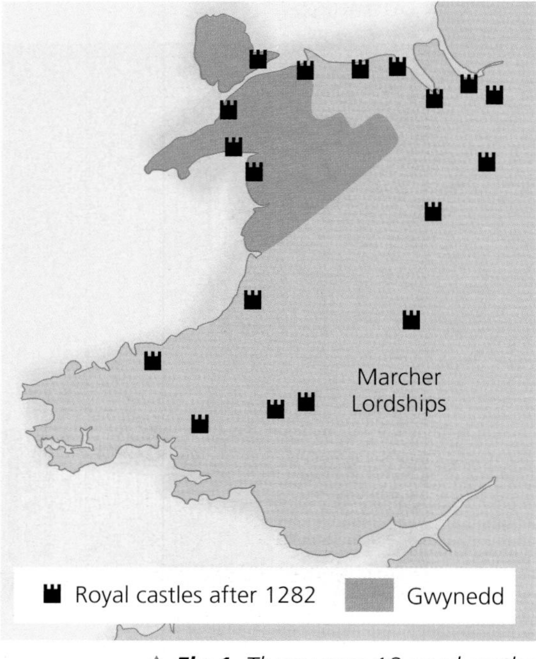

▲ *Fig 1 There were 18 royal castles in Wales after 1282.*

North Wales and Llewellyn 1277

North Wales was mountainous and much harder to conquer. It was ruled by a powerful prince called Llewellyn of Gwynedd. He refused to do homage to the new King, so Edward decided to invade Wales. By sending English armies to surround Llewellyn and cut off his food supplies from Anglesey, Edward forced him to surrender.

Q1 Why was north Wales much harder to conquer than south Wales?

Q2 How did Edward force Llewellyn to surrender?

▲ *Fig 2 Caernarfon Castle.*

Rebellion again 1282

Llewellyn and his brother, David, had not given up. They rebelled again in 1282. Again Edward sent troops and Llewellyn was killed in battle. His brother was executed. After this Edward wanted to make sure there were no more rebellions.

Edward I and castles

Edward built a chain of castles around north Wales. They were the strongest castles ever built by the English and could withstand all the siege weapons used at that time. Thousands of **masons**, carpenters, labourers and **smiths** worked on the castles for a number of years.

Reorganising Wales

Edward passed a law for the reorganisation of Wales under English rule:

- Wales was divided into five counties (the rest was ruled by the English barons).
- English law replaced Welsh law.
- The English language replaced the Welsh language.
- The English clergy were put in charge of the Welsh Church.

Prince of Wales

In 1301, Edward made his son, who had been born in Wales, the Prince of Wales, in the hope that this would help unite the Welsh and the English.

Q3 Why did Edward make his son Prince of Wales?

▲ ***Fig 3*** *Building in the fourteenth century. Masons travelled a great deal in the Middle Ages because their skills were in such demand.*

Key words

Marches – land on the borders between England and Wales

masons – stoneworkers

smiths – metalworkers

SUMMARY

- William the Conqueror established three Marcher Lords to control the borders of Wales and England.
- By the time of Edward I, south Wales was under English control.
- Edward I defeated Llewellyn in north Wales in 1282.
- Edward built castles and reorganised Wales under English rule.

SUMMARY *activity*

In what ways did Edward I reorganise Wales?

23 Edward I, II, III and Scotland

In this section of the book you will learn the following things:

- English kings tried to make Scottish kings accept them as overlords;
- the Scots often rebelled;
- the Scots gained independence at the Battle of Bannockburn.

Scotland and the English kings

The English kings always had worries about the Scots making raids across the border into England. They tried various ways of dealing with the problem. By the time of Edward I, England was growing stronger. Edward I hoped to unite the two countries by marriage and arranged for his son to marry the heiress to the Scottish throne, but unfortunately she died at the age of six. Scotland was in **turmoil**, however. There was no one to inherit the throne once the little princess had died. No less than 13 Scots claimed the right to be king. In 1286 they agreed to ask Edward to choose the next king.

Henry III 1216–1272
|
Edward I 1272–1307
|
Edward II 1307–1327
|
Edward III 1327–1377

▲ ***Fig 1*** *The heirs of Henry III.*

William Wallace

Edward chose William Wallace as the next king and this led to trouble between the English and Scots. William Wallace led a rebellion and drove the English from Scotland in 1297. Edward sent an army and defeated Wallace at Falkirk. Wallace went into hiding but was betrayed to the English and executed. Edward I became known as the 'hammer of the Scots'.

Q1 How did William the Conqueror deal with the problem of Scotland?

Q2 Write down what Henry II and Richard I did.

Q3 What was Edward I's plan and how did it go wrong?

Relations between England and Scotland from William I to Edward I

William I	said he was the overlord of the Scottish King
William II, Henry I, Stephen	too involved in England to become embroiled in Scottish affairs
Henry II	said he was the overlord of the Scottish King
Richard I	sold overlordship to the Scottish King for money for the crusades
John	too involved with French wars, the barons and Magna Carta to concern himself with Scotland
Henry III	too involved with fighting Simon de Montfort and the barons to become involved with Scotland
Edward I	planned to marry his son to the Scottish princess, but she died

▲ ***Fig 2***

The Hundred Years War

Edward III ruled for 50 years. He started the Hundred Years War (1337–1453) with France to further his claim to the French throne. The war was carried on by his successors until 1453 when the French had won back all of France except Calais. Edward III added the French fleur-de-lys to his coat of arms.

▲ **Fig 3** *Edward III's coat of arms.*

Robert the Bruce

The Scots had not given up, however. Robert the Bruce had been one of the 13 Scots who claimed the throne in 1286. In 1305 he was secretly crowned King of Scotland. He seemed to have an impossible task, however, because all the castles were in English hands. Edward I sent English armies to Scotland and Bruce had to go into hiding. Then in 1307 he heard some excellent news. Edward I was dead.

The Battle of Bannockburn 1314

Edward II was a most unwarlike King and **retreated** from Scotland as soon as he could. Bruce captured castles from the English and finally reached the greatest castle of all at Stirling. Edward II could not allow this castle to be taken. He marched north and met Bruce and the Scots for battle at Bannockburn, just south of Stirling. The result was a great success for the Scots.

Edward III

Edward II was murdered in 1327 and his son, Edward III, agreed that Scotland was an independent country from England.

Key words

retreat – to leave, fall back from
turmoil – confusion

SUMMARY

- Partly to deal with Scottish raids on England, the English kings wanted to control Scotland.
- William Wallace led a Scottish rebellion against the English but was defeated by Edward I.
- Robert the Bruce was crowned King of Scotland in 1305 and finally defeated Edward II at the Battle of Bannockburn in 1314.

SUMMARY *activity*

How did the Scots gain independence from England?

24 The Black Death

In this section of the book you will learn the following things:

- how the Black Death came to England;
- what the Black Death was.

How the Black Death came to England

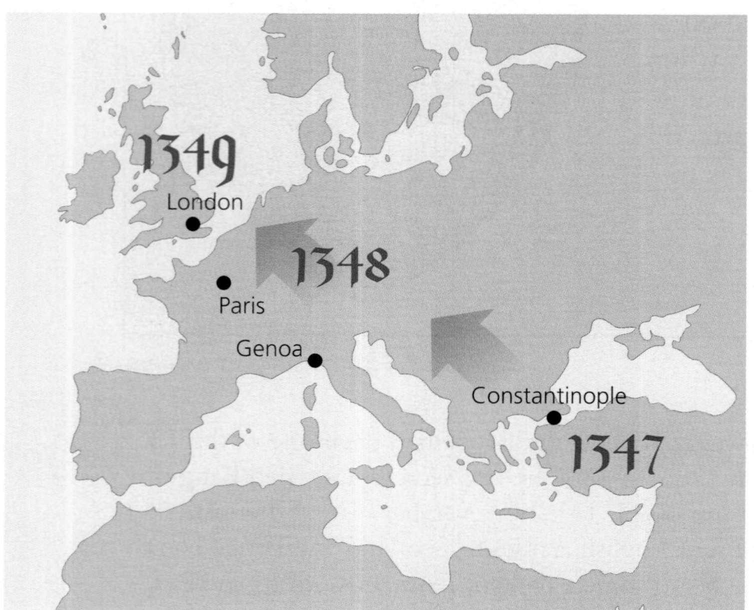

In the summer of 1348, a French ship docked in the small Dorset port of Melcombe. It was one of any number of ships that came and went from England, part of the busy trade with France and the continent of Europe. But this one was different. On board was a French sailor dying of the plague. In no time others were ill with swellings in the armpits and black and red spots on their bodies. Very few recovered.

◄ ***Fig 1*** *The spread of the plague in Europe. Between 1347–49, bubonic plague – the Black Death – spread fr ,m eastern Europe to the north.*

What was the Black Death?

The **Black Death** was the **bubonic plague**. It is an illness carried by the fleas that live on black rats. When the rats died, the fleas often transferred to the nearest human being, who then caught the disease when they were bitten by the flea. Since rats lived on every ship, the plague spread easily from country to country. Since people did not wash very much in those days, fleas lived on every person.

Q1 How did the Black Death reach England?

Q2 What was the Black Death?

Why did people catch the Black Death so easily?

By 1300, the population of England was three times greater than in 1066. More and more people crowded into the growing towns. A few lived in fine houses, but most lived in crowded shacks. Even the people in the fine houses could not avoid the filth of towns that had no sewers and where all rubbish was thrown into the streets. Moreover, the rising population meant that more food was needed, and although more forests and wasteland were being cleared by this time to grow crops and graze animals, many poorer people spent most of their lives without enough to eat. So the Black Death struck a population that some people think was less fit than it had been 300 years before.

What did medieval people think was the cause of the Black Death?

Medieval people did not know about the connection between rats, fleas and the Black Death. They had many theories. Some thought it was a judgement from God because people were wicked. Others thought it came from smells in the air. Still others thought it was to do with astrology. Whatever caused it, everyone saw the terrible effects.

▲ ***Fig 2*** *From a later painting by Brueghel (1568–1625) entitled 'The Triumph of Death', which illustrated the devastation of the plague.*

Burying the dead

At first the dead were buried in coffins. Then there were so many that new cemeteries had to be made outside town walls and bodies were buried in enormous pits. Perhaps as many as one-third of the population of England died. In some villages there were not enough men and women left to look after the animals and the villages ceased to exist. Some monasteries and nunneries were almost wiped out. London's population nearly halved.

Key words

Black Death – so-called because of the black marks on the skin the disease caused

bubonic plague – so-called because the swellings were called buboes

SUMMARY

- The Black Death was brought to England in 1348.
- The disease was carried by the fleas that lived on black rats.
- Medieval people did not know what caused the disease.
- About one-third of the population of England died.

SUMMARY *activity*

Why do you think people in towns, and in monasteries and nunneries, were most likely to catch the plague?

25 Anger amongst the peasants

In this section of the book you will learn the following things:

- life changed for the peasants after the Black Death;
- the peasants became angry about their treatment.

Changes after the Black Death

After the Black Death there were far fewer people. This speeded up the end of the feudal system under which peasants paid for their land by working for some of the week on their lord's land. There were so few peasants left that lords of the manor were forced to pay money to get people to work for them. Although this had been happening slowly for some time, things changed rapidly after the Black Death.

Benefits of the Black Death

- more land to claim;
- higher wages;
- villeins demanded freedom.

▲ *Fig 1*

The Statute of Labourers 1351

However, Parliament was worried by these changes, particularly since many of the men sitting in Parliament were landowning lords of the manor. They passed a **statute** in 1349 ordering labourers to return to the manor where they were born and to which they were tied. In 1351 they passed another law saying that wages must be kept at the same level as they had been before the Black Death. Anyone travelling outside his own village to look for work at higher wages could be branded with a red-hot iron.

Q1 What did the Statute of Labourers say?

Anger at the law

The peasants were angry. They had survived the Black Death and often seen the loss of many family members. Now they had a chance to break free of the old ties and earn a better wage. Not only did the peasants often ignore the law of 1351, but the landowners also did. Otherwise they could not get anyone to work for them.

Q2 Why did landowners often ignore the law of 1351?

The money economy versus the feudal system

Lord of the Manor	→	feudal system	→	reluctant villeins working two days a week for Lord when they wanted to work on their own land
Lord of the Manor	→	money economy	→	labourers working every day for Lord for money. Not distracted by own land

▲ *Fig 2*

Returning soldiers

The peasants' anger might just have gone on simmering if other things had not been happening as well. Some peasants had been soldiers in the wars against France in the 1340s and 1350s. English bowmen had played their part in the great victories at Créçy and Poitiers. When they came home they resented the way they were treated by landowners.

▲ ***Fig 3 Harrowing*** *on an estate in the middle ages.*

John Ball

There was also far more questioning of religion. For years peasants had been told it was God's will that they worked hard and were poor while others never worked and were rich. Now priests like John Ball were making speeches saying this was wrong. Needless to say, wealthy people such as the King, the barons (who were beginning to be called lords) and the Church did not like what John Ball said and he was arrested and put in prison. Only one spark was needed to start off a Peasants' Revolt and that came in 1381.

'When Adam delved and Eve span, who was then a gentleman?'

John Ball, 13 June 1381

▲ ***Fig 4***

Key words

delved – dug
harrowing – breaking up and levelling the soil
span – used a spinning wheel
statute – a law

SUMMARY

- The Black Death speeded up the end of the feudal system.
- The Statute of Labourers of 1351 said wages must be kept at the same level as they had been before the Black Death.
- Peasants and soldiers returning from France were angry at the law.
- John Ball was a priest who questioned whether it was God's will that some people were rich and some poor.

SUMMARY *activity*

Explain John Ball's saying: 'When Adam delved and Eve span, who was then a gentleman?'

26 The Peasants' Revolt

In this section of the book you will learn the following things:

- **the Peasants' Revolt began in 1381 because of the poll tax.**

The poll tax

The spark that ignited the Peasants' Revolt was the **poll** tax. Richard II was fighting wars with France and desperately needed money. So he introduced the poll tax, which everyone had to pay. His officials went round the country collecting the tax in 1377 and 1380. However, the war with France went badly and England lost all but a small amount of land. When Richard's officials started collecting the poll tax again in 1381 there were riots in some places. This was the start of the Peasants' Revolt.

Q1 Why did Richard II introduce the poll tax?

The poll tax

Everyone over the age of 15 had to pay the poll tax.

1377 . . . 4d

1380 . . . 4d

1381 . . 12d

▲ *Fig 1*

The revolt spreads

During the summer of 1381, the rioting spread. In Kent, the rebel peasants attacked several towns including Maidstone, where they chose Wat Tyler as their leader. They forced their way into the cathedral at Canterbury and released John Ball from the Archbishop's own prison. Then they marched towards London. Meanwhile, another army of peasants began marching on London from Essex. The King was in great danger. On 13 June the peasants surged over London Bridge and the gates of the city were opened to them. The King retreated to the Tower of London, from where he could see the flames rising as the peasants ransacked and blew up his uncle's palace. They opened the prisons and let out the prisoners.

Q2 Who was Wat Tyler? **Q3** What happened in London in June 1381?

What did the peasants want?

- to do away with villeinage (when a peasant was tied to a lord under the feudal system);
- to do away with bad laws (e.g. the Statute of Labourers);
- no more lords except the King (everyone else equal);
- the Church to give up all the land it owned to ordinary people.

▲ *Fig 2*

Mile End

Richard, who was only 14 years old, agreed to ride out of the city to Mile End to meet the Essex rebels. When he promised them he would grant their wishes, many returned home. They had no wish to overthrow the King. Meanwhile, however, the Kent rebels had broken into the Tower of London and murdered the Archbishop of Canterbury. Then they began to kill tax collectors, lawyers and foreign merchants. These were people the peasants thought had misled the King and caused the high taxes and harsh laws.

Smithfield

Richard agreed to meet the Kent rebels in the city at Smithfield. Some say that Wat Tyler was deliberately rude to the King, others that the King's companions meant to kill him anyway. After speaking about a **charter** of rights, Tyler was pulled from his horse and stabbed to death. It was a tense moment. The rebels surged forward, but Richard rode to them and said, 'Sirs, will you shoot your King? I shall be your captain and you shall have from me what you seek.' He then led them out of the city and they agreed to go home.

Q4 Why did the Kent rebels agree to go home?

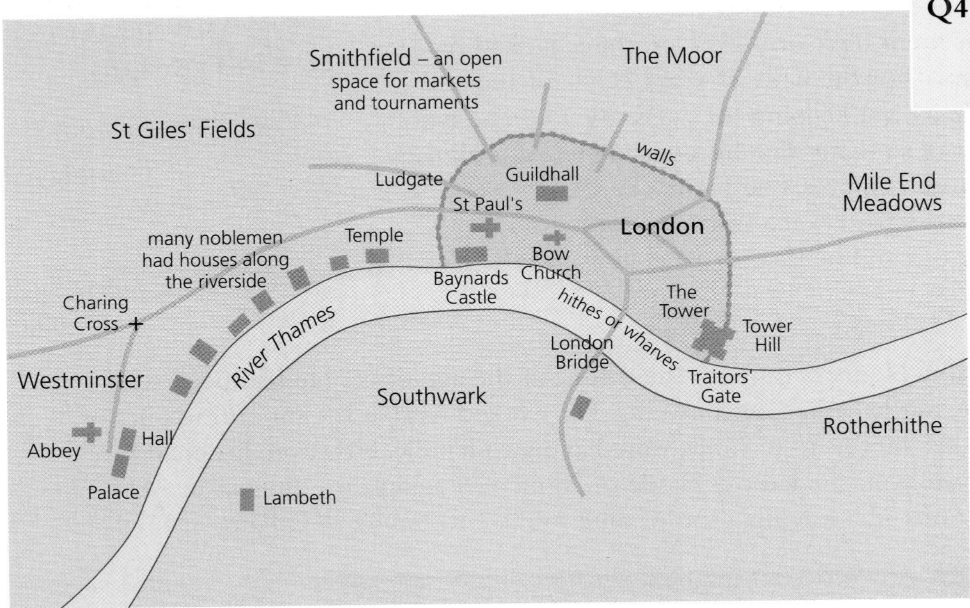

◀ ***Fig 3*** *Medieval London, showing areas where confrontations between the rebels and the King took place. There were seven gates in the city walls.*

The broken promise

Richard did not keep his promise, however. The King's armies rounded up the peasants' leaders and hanged them. John Ball was hanged and his body cut into four quarters. The main rebellion was over. The King had won. However, the poll tax was not tried again until the twentieth century. Wages began to rise and within 100 years peasants were completely free from their lords' control.

Key words

charter – a document agreeing something
poll – head

SUMMARY

- The demands for the poll tax sparked off the Peasants' Revolt in 1381.
- The peasants marched on London and demanded better laws from the King.
- The King promised to grant their wishes, so they went home.
- Later the King went back on his promises.

SUMMARY *activity*

What do you think Richard should have done when he met the rebels, and afterwards?

27 Richard II, Henry IV and Henry V

In this section of the book you will learn the following things:

- Henry IV deposed Richard II;
- Henry V was a warlike King and died young;
- England was growing richer and Parliament more powerful.

Richard II and Henry IV

Richard II had shown great courage when he dealt with the Peasants' Revolt. He was then only 14 years old. However, he went back on all the promises he had made to the peasants. For the next 21 years, Richard angered many people by not keeping his word. By 1399, he had lost the trust of so many that his cousin, Henry, took the throne from him and became Henry IV. Lack of money, wars with France and rebellions at home wore Henry out and he died in 1413 at the age of 47.

'Villeins you are and villeins you shall remain.'

Richard II's words after the Peasants' Revolt was over.

▲ *Fig 1*

Henry V 1413–1422

Henry IV's son, Henry V, came to the throne at the age of 25. He had been wild when young, but became a serious king. He worked hard at the mounting piles of paperwork that, by this time, kings were having to handle. However, his great love was war and he won the famous Battle of Agincourt against the French in 1415. He died of fever in 1422, leaving a son of nine months to be the next King of England.

▲ ***Fig 2*** *The English defeated the French at the Battle of Agincourt in 1415, but they were soon to lose the Hundred Years War.*

Q1 Why did Richard II anger people?

Q2 What problems did Henry IV have?

The growth of the wool trade

Meanwhile, most people in England got on with their lives. The population was slowly recovering after the Black Death and some people were doing well from the growth of trade. Wool was the most important commodity for England. Thousands of sheep grazed in places such as East Anglia, Yorkshire and the Cotswolds. In the early Middle Ages the wool was packed into large bales and sold to places in Europe that specialised in spinning and weaving cloth from the wool. However, by the later Middle Ages, the English had learnt the art of making fine woollen cloth themselves and many cloth merchants grew very rich.

▲ ***Fig 3*** *Merchants counting their money in their office.*

The growth of Parliament

From the time Simon de Montfort and the barons forced Henry III to consult not only barons and knights but also men from the towns, there was no stopping Parliament. The growth of trade throughout the Middle Ages meant that the merchants in towns grew wealthy. Whenever kings, after Henry III, wanted money to fight wars (which they often did), they had to call Parliament. In return for money, the merchants steadily began to demand a say in what the King did. By the end of the Middle Ages Parliament was a force to be reckoned with, as future kings and queens would discover.

Key words

villein – a peasant who had to work for a lord in return for his land

SUMMARY

- Richard II lost the trust of his followers, so Henry IV deposed him in 1399.
- Henry IV had to face lack of money, rebellious subjects and war with France.
- Henry V was a great soldier but died leaving a nine-month-old son.
- England grew in wealth because of the wool trade.
- Parliament grew stronger.

SUMMARY *activity*

What is the link between the constant wars with France, the growth of the wool trade and the growing strength of Parliament?

28 The Wars of the Roses

In this section of the book you will learn the following things:

- from 1454, two groups of nobles went to war with each other as to who should be King;
- one group was the family of Lancaster, the other the family of York.

▲ ***Fig 1*** *The **emblems** of York, Lancaster and the Tudors.*

Henry VI

Henry VI was nine months old when his father died, so others ruled for him for many years. When he was older, it was obvious he was not a strong king like his father and grandfather. As his reign progressed there was more and more trouble. In 1454, two groups of **nobles** went to war. These were the family of Lancaster who supported Henry VI and the family of York who supported the Duke of York's claim to the throne. Both families were descended from Edward III and both felt they had an equal claim to the throne.

Q1 What were the names of the two family groups who fought for the throne?

Q2 Why did both families think they had an equal claim to the throne?

◀ ***Fig 2*** *A nineteenth-century picture of the murdered princes in the Tower. Their bones were alleged to have been found 200 years after their deaths.*

Edward IV and the death of Henry VI

In 1461, Henry VI was overthrown by the Yorkists, now led by Edward, who became Edward IV. Despite the fact that Henry VI was having more and more frequent bouts of madness, his Lancastrian supporters fought to win the crown back for him. This they did in 1470, but not for long. Henry VI was murdered in 1471.

The murder of the young princes and Richard III

Back came the Yorkist king, Edward IV, and all went fairly smoothly for a number of years until he died in 1483. His son, Edward V, was only 12 years old. Nobody is sure exactly what happened then, but the young King and his ten-year-old brother disappeared while staying in the Tower of London. Their uncle said they were dead and forthwith became King himself.

Richard III and the Battle of Bosworth Field 1485

Richard III's Yorkist reign did not last long. His rival, the Lancastrian Henry Tudor, landed in Wales with an army. He marched north-east and met Richard's army at Bosworth. After much hand-to-hand fighting, a large part of Richard's army went over to Henry's side. Richard was killed and his crown found hanging on a thorn bush.

The Battle of Bosworth Field

On 7th August 1485 Henry landed in Wales with a force of only 2000 men, but as he marched into England a number of important men joined him. One of these men was almost certainly Lord Stanley, although this was kept secret.

By the time Henry reached Bosworth, in Leicestershire, on 22nd August, he had an army of around 6000 – about half Richard's army. However, Lord Stanley, who was supposed to be on Richard's side, kept his soldiers back, despite the fact that Richard was holding his son hostage. When Stanley saw that Henry was likely to win he went over to his side. Richard was soon killed (before harm came to Stanley's son).

▲ *Fig 3*

Henry VII: the first Tudor king

Having won the Battle of Bosworth Field, Henry was crowned as Henry VII. He married Elizabeth of York, a daughter of Edward IV. This united the families of Lancaster and York and put an end to the Wars of the Roses.

Key words

emblem – a sign

nobles – known as 'barons' in the early Middle Ages

SUMMARY

- Henry VI was a weak king.
- The Wars of the Roses started in 1454.
- The conflict was between the family of Lancaster (red rose) and the family of York (white rose).
- The Wars of the Roses ended in 1485 when Henry Tudor (Lancaster) defeated Richard III (York) at the Battle of Bosworth Field.
- Henry married Elizabeth of York and put an end to the rivalry between Lancaster and York.

SUMMARY *activity*

Explain why the wars between Lancaster and York are called the Wars of the Roses and why the Tudor rose is red and white.

29 Women

In this section of the book you will learn the following things:

- about the lives of women;
- why women do not appear in histories of the Middle Ages.

Marriage and pregnancy

Most women married and had children. They could expect to have many children and perhaps half of them would die. As well as being pregnant a lot of the time and bringing up children, they ran the home. This was not a simple matter of going to the shops to buy food. Most people grew their own food, prepared it, cooked it and **preserved** as much as they could for winter. Running a home was a highly skilled job and there was very little time for women to be active outside the home.

Farming

Most people lived by farming. Women's work included looking after the hens and ducks, and often the pigs. Women ran the dairies, and frequently did the milking as well as making butter and cheese. In the summer everyone helped with the harvesting, and in the autumn with the slaughtering of animals and preserving of meat.

The question of marriage in 1477

'... my right well beloved Valentine, my lady, my mother hath laboured the matter to my father full diligently, but she can get no more for which I am full sorry. But if that you love me, as I trust truly that you do, you will not leave me therefore; for if that you had not half the livelihood that you have, I would not forsake you...'

Part of a letter from Margery Brews to John Paston in February 1477. Her father will not give her much as a dowry (money, land or goods when a girl married).

All was well. They married later in the year.

▲ ***Fig 1***

▶ ***Fig 2*** *Women working in the fields (fifteenth-century illustration).*

Men and history

Gathering herbs, milking cows, spinning woollen thread and feeding chickens were not exciting tasks. Wars and conquests were. So history was written about the activities of kings and their battles. Moreover, most people who wrote history books were monks because they were some of the few people who could read and write. They wrote about religion, which was run by men, and wars, which were fought by men. The only time they wrote about women was when a woman appeared in a man's world, such as a queen.

▲ ***Fig 3*** *Childbirth: a woman surgeon performing a Caesarean section (fourteenth-century illustration).*

Q1 What did most women do?

Q2 Why were monks some of the only people who wrote history books?

Nuns

A few women did not marry. Some went into nunneries because they wanted to or because their families wished them to. Many found fulfiling lives because of religion itself and because the way of life gave them scope to organise and run things such as hospitals in their own right.

Key words

preserving – making sure food was fit to eat through the winter by salting, pickling, drying etc

SUMMARY

- Women did many different jobs according to who they married.
- Some women did not marry and lived and worked in nunneries.
- Most of the people who wrote things down were monks.

SUMMARY *activity*

How is a housewife's work different today from her work in the Middle Ages?

Kings and Queens 1066–1509

	born	reigned	died
William I (the Conqueror)	1027?	1066–1087	1087
William II (Rufus)	1060	1087–1100	1100
Henry I	1068	1100–1135	1135
Stephen	1094?	1135–1154	1154
Henry II	1133	1154–1189	1189
Richard I	1157	1189–1199	1199
John	1166	1199–1216	1216
Henry III	1207	1216–1272	1272
Edward I	1239	1272–1307	1307
Edward II	1284	1307–1327	1327
Edward III	1312	1327–1377	1377
Richard II	1366	1377–1399	1400
Henry IV	1366	1399–1413	1413
Henry V	1387	1413–1422	1422
Henry VI	1421	1422–1461 1470–1471	1471
Edward IV	1442	1461–1470 1471–1483	1483
Edward V	1470	1483	1483?
Richard III	1452	1483–1485	1485
Henry VII	1456	1485–1509	1509

Note: See the key to the crowns on page 250.

Medieval realms: Timeline 1066–1485

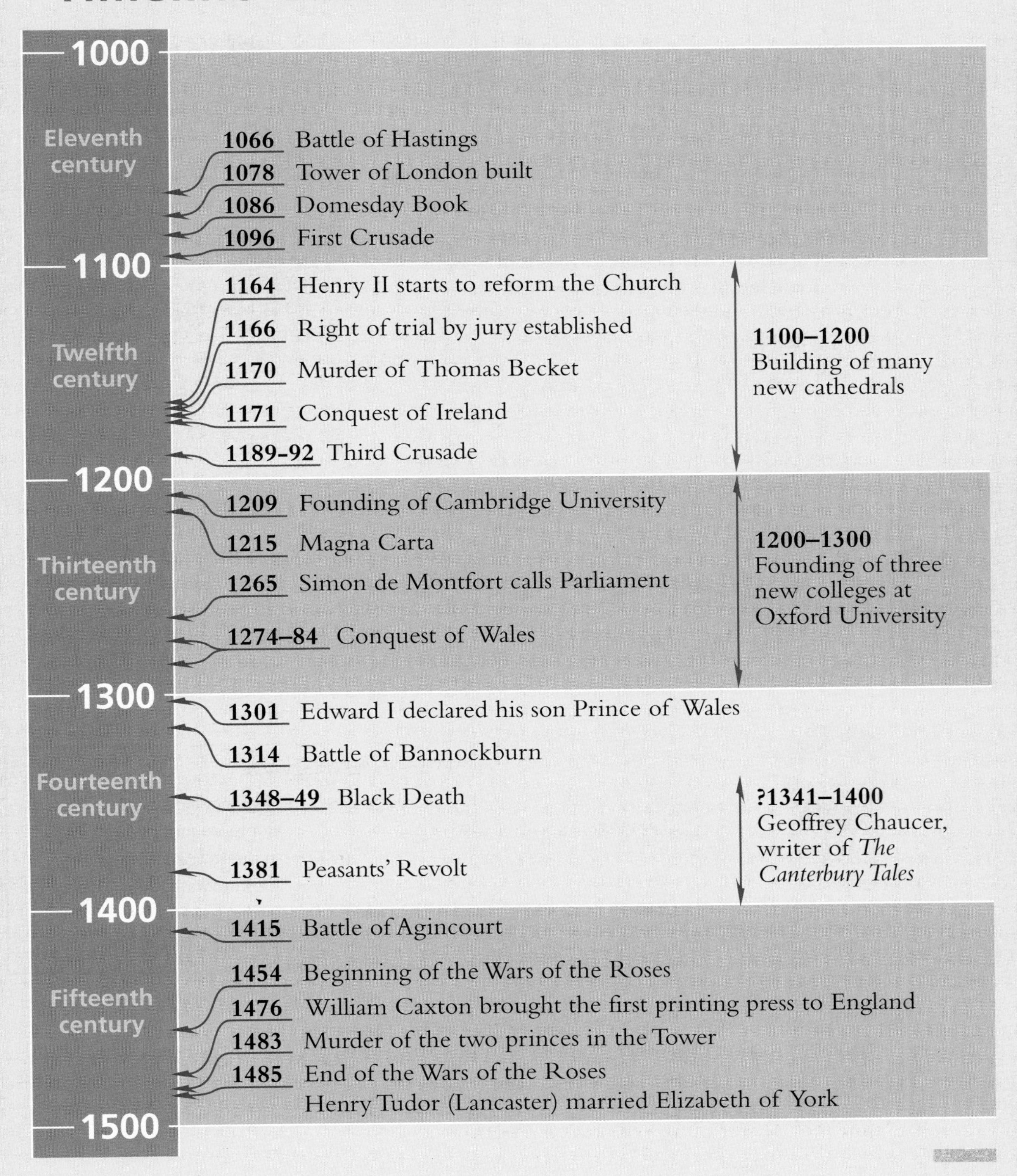

30 Henry VII 1485–1509

In this section of the book you will learn the following things:

- how Henry dealt with the Yorkist threat;
- how Henry dealt with the nobles;
- what Henry did about money.

Henry won the Battle of Bosworth Field 1485

Henry VII was a Welshman. Through his mother, Margaret Beaufort, he was descended from Edward III. However, the most important reason he became King in 1485 was that he had defeated and killed Richard III at the Battle of Bosworth Field. Now he had to prove himself, or the Wars of the Roses would start all over again.

Q1 What was the most important reason Henry VII became King?

▲ ***Fig 1*** *Henry VII.*

▲ ***Fig 2*** *Henry Tudor (Lancaster) married Elizabeth of York to unite the two families.*

Henry dealt with the Yorkist threat

Soon after he was crowned, Henry married Elizabeth of York, a daughter of the Yorkist King, Edward IV. He hoped this would put an end to the feuds between the families of Lancaster and York. To some extent it did. However, there were plots against Henry VII. The Yorkists supported two young men who pretended (claimed) to have a right to the throne.

Threats to Henry VII

Name	*Who he said he was*	*What happened*
Lambert Simnel	Earl of Warwick	Captured and put to work in the King's kitchen
Perkin Warbeck	Duke of York	Captured and beheaded 1499
Earl of Warwick	Earl of Warwick	In the Tower from 1485. Beheaded in 1499

▲ ***Fig 3***

Q2 Which pretender did Henry fear most – Lambert Simnel or Perkin Warbeck? How do you know?

Q3 Why do you think Henry had the real Earl of Warwick beheaded?

Henry and the nobles

The Wars of the Roses had shown how dangerous it was for a king when the nobles got out of hand and fought each other. Luckily for Henry, many of them had been killed in the long wars, but he was taking no chances. He only allowed two of them to be his close advisers. All his other advisers were Churchmen who had no families or men of humble birth who had no land or powerful families behind them.

How Henry gained control

Court of Star Chamber:
Nobles were fined for:
- keeping too many servants in livery (uniform);
- threatening juries.

Council of the North:
- dealt with lawbreaking in the north.

Council of Wales:
- dealt with lawbreaking in Wales.

▲ *Fig 3*

Henry and money

Henry knew that a poor king was a weak king, so he made money where he could. He made his nobles pay enormous fines if they broke the King's laws. Towards the end of his reign, he employed two lawyers, named Empson and Dudley, to **extort** as much money as possible from nobles, merchants or any others who could be made to pay. They were fined hundreds of pounds for things done years before and, if they argued, they were packed off to the Tower of London.

Q4 Apart from making money, why do you think Henry wanted to make his nobles pay huge fines?

Henry and trade

Henry was also interested in England becoming richer from trade. He made a **treaty** with Flanders in 1496 that allowed English wool freely into Flanders, and took a keen interest in shipping, which he knew would help trade.

Henry and foreign countries

Royal marriages cemented royal friendships, so Henry VII looked around for a suitable bride for his eldest son, Arthur. He chose a Spanish princess, Catherine of Aragon. Both sides haggled about the **dowry**, but at last Catherine came to England to marry the young Prince Arthur. Meanwhile, Henry arranged the marriage of his daughter to the King of Scotland.

Key words

dowry – money paid by the bride's parents to the bridegroom's family
extort – gain by force
treaty – agreement

SUMMARY

- Henry VII married Elizabeth of York to unite the families of York and Lancaster.
- Lambert Simnel and Perkin Warbeck were pretenders to the throne.
- Henry kept the nobles out of power by choosing Churchmen or men of humble birth to be his advisers.
- Henry made money and also encouraged trade and shipping.
- Henry cemented a friendship with Spain by marrying his eldest son, Arthur, to the Spanish princess, Catherine of Aragon.

SUMMARY *activity*

Why was Henry VII a successful king?

31 Henry VIII: the man 1509–1547

In this section of the book you will learn the following things:

- Henry VIII became King in 1509 and married Catherine of Aragon;
- Henry spent money on foreign wars;
- Henry was interested in the Royal Navy.

The fateful marriages

The marriages that Henry VII organised for his children had far-reaching effects on English history. His daughter, Margaret, married the King of Scotland and, about 100 years later, their great-grandson became King of England as well as Scotland. However, this was a long way in the future. In 1501, Prince Arthur married Catherine of Aragon, but he died five months later. Henry VII was reluctant to lose her dowry, so he arranged that she should marry his younger son, Henry, instead.

Q1 Who did Henry VII's daughter, Margaret, marry?

Q2 Who did Catherine of Aragon marry?

▲ **Fig 1** *Henry VIII.*

Henry VII = *Elizabeth of York*

Henry VIII

Edward VI

Mary

Elizabeth I

Margaret = *James IV*
of Scotland

James V

Mary Stuart
(Queen of Scots)

James VI
who became
James I
of England

▲ **Fig 2** *Family tree of Henry VII.*

The King is dead. Long live the King.

When Henry VII died the 18-year-old Henry VIII came to the throne. He was tall, good looking and loved sport. He was all set to be a popular king. His first move was to have the hated money extortionists, Empson and Dudley, executed.

Marriage with Catherine of Aragon 1509

His next move was just as popular: he married Catherine of Aragon and two years later she had a son. Sadly, he died within a month. In the next 18 years, Catherine had seven children but only one lived, a daughter, Mary.

Henry VIII: money, glory and war

Henry's chief **minister** was Thomas Wolsey and most of the next 20 years passed with the two of them spending all Henry VII's hard-earned money on foreign wars, without much success or the glory they both wanted.

Henry and the Navy

More serious and successful was Henry's support of the Royal Navy. Like his father he saw the importance of shipping, but Henry VII had been more interested in the Merchant Navy, the ships that carried English goods to sell abroad. These ships had guns on board to use against pirates and carried more in time of war, but they could not carry big guns. Henry VIII saw that if ships were built especially for war, they could carry the new, large cannons. He ordered the latest warships to be built with **portholes** in the sides so the big guns were carried low down in the ship and, firing through the open portholes, delivered a devastating **broadside** to enemy vessels.

▲ ***Fig 3*** *The* Mary Rose.

Key words

broadside – when all the guns along the side of a ship were fired

minister – an adviser and assistant

portholes – small windows in the side of a ship

SUMMARY

- Henry VIII succeeded his father, Henry VII, in 1509.
- Henry married his brother Arthur's widow, Catherine of Aragon, in 1509.
- Catherine only had one child who lived. Her name was Mary.
- Henry spent all his father's money on wars.
- Henry thought ships were important and ordered modern ships with big guns to be built.

SUMMARY *activity*

In what ways was Henry VIII different from his father and in what ways was he similar?

32 Explorations

In this section of the book you will learn the following things:

- explorers sailed west as well as east to find a route to India;
- the Spanish and Portuguese started large empires;
- Henry VII was interested in trade.

▲ *Fig 1 Christopher Columbus.*

Christopher Columbus and the route to India 1492

The reason that Henry VII and Henry VIII were so interested in ships was that men were starting to explore the world. No longer did people think of the world as a flat saucer. By the 1500s, many people believed it was a **sphere**. Therefore, if a ship sailed either west or east, eventually it would come back to where it started. This was the thinking that drove men such as Christopher Columbus to sail westwards. He wanted to find a new way to reach India. In fact, after five weeks of sailing, he landed on islands close to America. He thought he had reached islands off India, so the islands came to be called the West Indies.

Q1 How did the islands of the West Indies get their name?

▲ *Fig 2 John Cabot.*

John Cabot

John Cabot also wanted to sail west to find a way to India and China. He asked Henry VII to allow him to sail in an English ship from Bristol in 1497. Although over the next few years, John and his son Sebastian Cabot made three voyages westward, they never found China or India. What they did find was North America, but no one was interested in these great forested lands then.

My master hath willed me to write thanking you all the parcels which he received being 12 lbs pepper, 1 lb cloves, ½ lb maces, 1 lb grain, 1 lb nutmegs, 2 lb ginger, 1 lb cinnamon, a box fruit in sugar

▲ *Fig 3 Letter to a merchant in 1542 about spices from the East. (1 lb = 450 g)*

Why explorers wanted to reach India, China and the East Indies

Q2 What luxury goods did people in Europe want from the Far East?

Explorers wanted to find routes to India, China and the East Indies because all the luxuries such as spices, silks and precious stones came from there. Spices could be bought in the Far East very cheaply, then sold in England and the rest of Europe for huge amounts of money to flavour rich people's food. The same rich people wanted silk for their clothes and precious stones for their jewellery. It was easier and safer to bring these goods by ship than by the dangerous, overland route to the East.

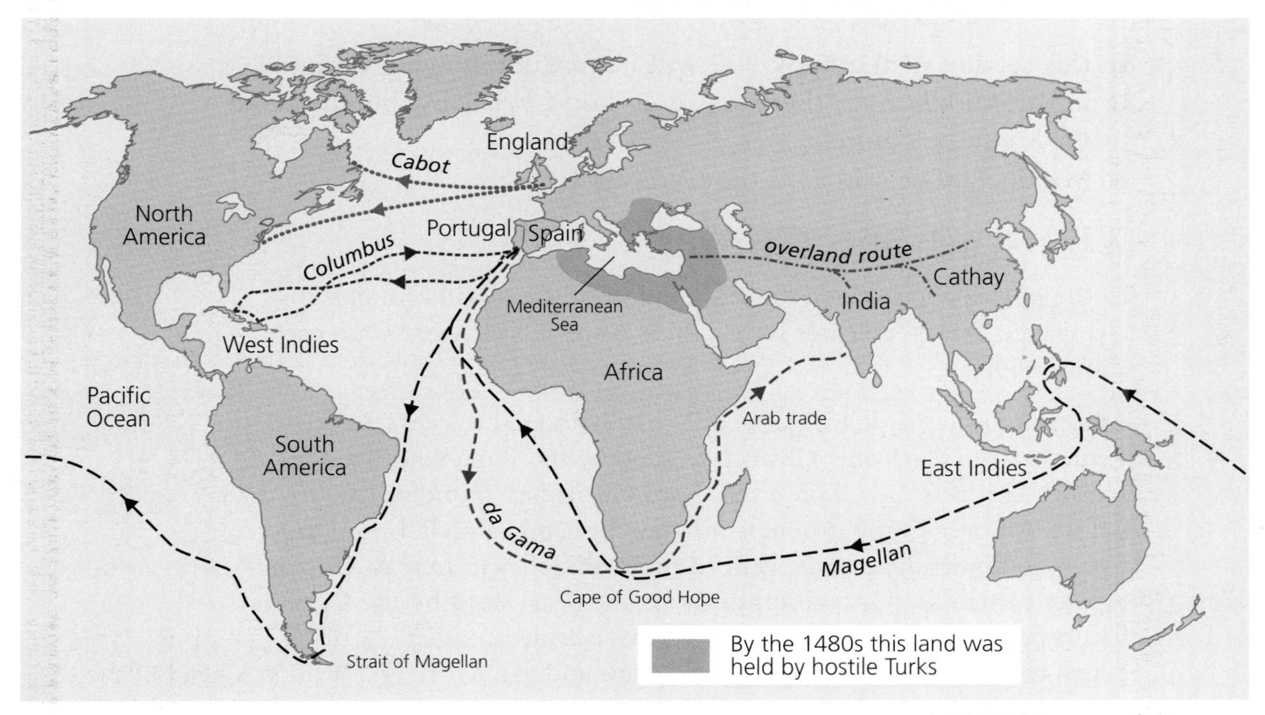

▲ ***Fig 4*** *Voyages of discovery.*

The Spanish and Portuguese

Gradually, people realised there was a whole new land in the west between Europe and India. It might be valuable itself. The Spanish found silver and gold in the Americas. Meanwhile the Portuguese sailed round Africa to start trading with the East. In this way **empires** were started.

England's trade in Europe

Trade around the world grew slowly. Of more interest to Henry VII in the early 1500s was the local trade between England and Europe. He made treaties with Italian states and with Denmark that made sure more and more English ships carried goods from foreign ports to England. He passed a law saying that wines from Bordeaux in France must be carried in English ships.

Key words

empire – group of countries controlled by another, more powerful state

sphere – ball shape

SUMMARY

- Explorers wanted to find a new sea route to India and the East, so some sailed west and some east.
- Traders wanted to bring the luxuries of the East to Europe by a sea route that was safer than the overland route.
- The Spanish and Portuguese were the most successful explorers at first.
- Henry VII was interested in encouraging English shipping and trade.

SUMMARY *activity*

You need a blank map of the world and an atlas. Then mark on it all the places mentioned in this spread. Also mark on it the routes shown on the map in this spread.

33 Religion and change

In this section of the book you will learn the following things:

- **in the Middle Ages there was only one Christian Church, called the Catholic Church;**
- **Martin Luther criticised the Catholic Church.**

The Catholic Church

In the next few centuries, the exploration of the world brought great changes to Europe. Nearer home, there were also changes. One was about religion.

All through the Middle Ages people had belonged to one Christian Church – the **Catholic Church** headed by the Pope who lived in Rome. This was the Church that Jesus Christ had founded 1,000 years before. All over Europe there were churches and cathedrals in villages, towns and cities. Everyone went to these churches to pray to God and to take part in the local community. As the years went by, the Church had become rich and powerful. Ordinary people began to criticise it. They said the bishops and priests were lazy and wanted money and the Popes were not good men; they sold jobs in the Church for money. All these criticisms might have come to nothing if it had not been for a man called Martin Luther.

Q1 Who was head of the Catholic Church?

Q2 Why did some people criticise the Church?

▲ ***Fig 1*** *A later painting showing the church at Wittenberg after Luther had nailed a list of his arguments against the Church to the door.*

Martin Luther 1483–1546

Martin Luther lectured in **theology** at Wittenberg University in Germany. He was disgusted by the behaviour of many men in the Church. This came to a head in 1517 when a monk named Tetzel came to Wittenberg selling **indulgences**. In a fury, Luther wrote out 95 **theses** or arguments about the Church and nailed them to the church door at Wittenberg. They caused an uproar. Within three years, people were arguing not just about indulgences but whether there should be a Pope at all.

◀ ***Fig 2*** *Martin Luther.*

Q3 What was an indulgence? (look at the Key words section)

What was Luther saying?

In 1521, Luther was ordered by the Church to go back on what he had said. He replied that he dared not act against what the Bible said and against his conscience. In this way he set both the Bible and a person's conscience against what the Catholic Church said was right. This was the beginning of the Protestant religion.

▶ ***Fig 3*** *The sale of indulgences raised money for the Church. At its best, the indulgence was a certificate showing you were truly sorry for doing wrong. At its worst, you paid money for an indulgence and did what you liked.*

Key words

Catholic Church – Christian Church that everyone belonged to

indulgence – a piece of paper that a person could buy saying that God forgave him for the bad things he had done

theology – the study of religion

theses – a statement that people can debate or argue about

SUMMARY

- Everyone belonged to the Catholic Church, headed by the Pope in Rome.
- Towards the end of the Middle Ages some people criticised the Church for being too rich.
- Martin Luther spoke for many people who were angry about the sale of indulgences.
- Luther said he must act on what the Bible said and what his conscience told him was right, not on what the Catholic Church told him to do.

SUMMARY *activity*

What made Protestants different from Catholics?

34 Marriage and monasteries

In this section of the book you will learn the following things:

- **Henry wanted a son to be King after him;**
- **Henry broke away from the Pope;**
- **Henry closed down the monasteries;**
- **Henry was married six times.**

Henry VIII and his wife, Catherine of Aragon

Henry VIII was a **devout** Catholic. Yet it was he who broke away from the Catholic Church for one very important reason. By 1527, Catherine of Aragon had had seven children but only one had lived – a daughter called Mary. Catherine was too old to have any more children, but Henry was desperate for a son to become King after him. He asked the Pope for a divorce and the Pope refused. By this time Henry had fallen in love with the young, black-haired Anne Boleyn and more than ever wanted a divorce. In 1533, he discovered that Anne was pregnant. It was now important to marry her before the baby was born so the baby would be Henry's heir.

Q1 What was Henry and Catherine's daughter called?

Henry became Supreme Head of the Church in England 1534

Henry decided to ignore the Pope and told the Archbishop of Canterbury to grant him a divorce. The next year, he got Parliament to make him Supreme Head of the Church in England. No longer was the Church ruled by a foreign Pope; Henry, alone, was in charge. This suited him very well. He liked the power and he needed money. He knew that the 850 or so monasteries and nunneries owned about a quarter of the land in England. Once Henry became head of the Church, despite opposition, particularly in the north, he **dissolved** the monasteries and took all their land and buildings, which he sold off.

Q2 What did Parliament make Henry?

Q3 Why did Henry dissolve the monasteries?

The rise and fall of monasteries and nunneries

- many founded in about AD 1100;
- monks and nuns lived simply;
- by 1450 many were rich from land and money given to them;
- monks and nuns often lived well and had servants;
- by the 1530s many people criticised the way monks and nuns lived.

▶ *Fig 1*

What happened to Anne Boleyn?

Henry and Anne had a daughter called Elizabeth. Although Henry was disappointed, he still hoped for a son, but Anne's next baby died. By this time Henry was tired of Anne. He accused her of being unfaithful and a witch and she was beheaded. He then married Jane Seymour, who died after giving birth to a son called Edward. After this he married three more times but had no more children.

Henry VIII married six times. This is what happened to his wives

Name		*Children*
Catherine of Aragon	divorced	Mary
Anne Boleyn	beheaded	Elizabeth
Jane Seymour	died	Edward
Anne of Cleves	divorced	–
Catherine Howard	beheaded	–
Catherine Parr	survived	–

◀ *Fig 3*

▲ ***Fig 2*** *Anne Boleyn – a portrait painted in the nineteenth century.*

Henry: Catholic or Protestant?

While all these things were going on in England, the **Protestant** movement, which had been started by Martin Luther, was getting under way in the rest of Europe. The Pope was trying to crush the new Protestants, who wanted to do away with the Pope and the Catholic Church. Now here was Henry VIII getting rid of the Pope in England. Did that make Henry a Protestant? It certainly did not. Henry wanted to be head of the Catholic Church in England, not to get rid of it.

Key words

devout – very religious
dissolved – closed down
Protestant – name given to the people who protested when they were not allowed to follow Martin Luther's ideas on religion

SUMMARY

- Catherine of Aragon, Henry's first wife, only had a daughter, Mary.
- Henry divorced Catherine by breaking from the Pope.
- Henry became Supreme Head of the Church in England.
- Henry married Anne Boleyn who had a daughter, Elizabeth.
- Henry dissolved the monasteries to make money.
- Henry married six times and had two daughters and a son, Edward.
- Henry remained a Catholic.

SUMMARY *activity*

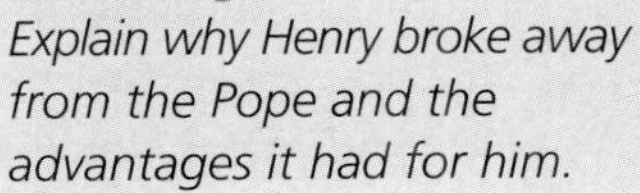

Explain why Henry broke away from the Pope and the advantages it had for him.

35 Edward VI and Protestantism

In this section of the book you will learn the following things:

- **Edward VI was King from 1547–1553;**
- **Lord Protectors ruled while he was young.**

Edward VI: King at nine

Henry VIII died in 1547. He was a strong King and had been able to keep the two religious parties – Catholics and Protestants – apart. However, the new King, Edward VI, was only nine years old. Everyone was very respectful to him but it was obvious that someone would have to rule for him until he was old enough to take control. This was exactly what happened.

▲ ***Fig 1*** *Edward VI.*

The first Lord Protector: Duke of Somerset

The Duke of Somerset was the King's uncle and became Lord Protector from 1547–1549. He was a Protestant and had many good ideas, such as being fairer to the peasants who were suffering from rising prices and the **enclosure** of land for sheep farming. However, he was not above profiting from the destruction of the monasteries and was able to build a beautiful London house on the money he made from gaining Church land. He was overthrown and, by 1551, the new Lord Protector, the Duke of Northumberland, had shown his true colours.

Reasons for discontent 1547–1553

- rising prices;
- enclosures;
- taking treasures from churches;
- end of 'holy' days to celebrate Church festivals (holidays for farmworkers);
- new Protestant Prayer Book had to be used in every church.

▲ ***Fig 2***

The second Lord Protector: Duke of Northumberland

Northumberland was unscrupulous and self-seeking. It suited him to be Protestant: He led the attack on all the remaining Church property. Local churches were sacked of everything from gold crosses and candlesticks to lead roofing. The money from **guilds** and **chantries** was meant to go to build new schools, but only a small amount did. The rest went into the pockets of the government (which was always short of money) and the new rich men who built lovely houses all over the country.

Q1 What were the reasons for discontent between 1547 and 1553?

Q2 What sort of things were taken from the churches?

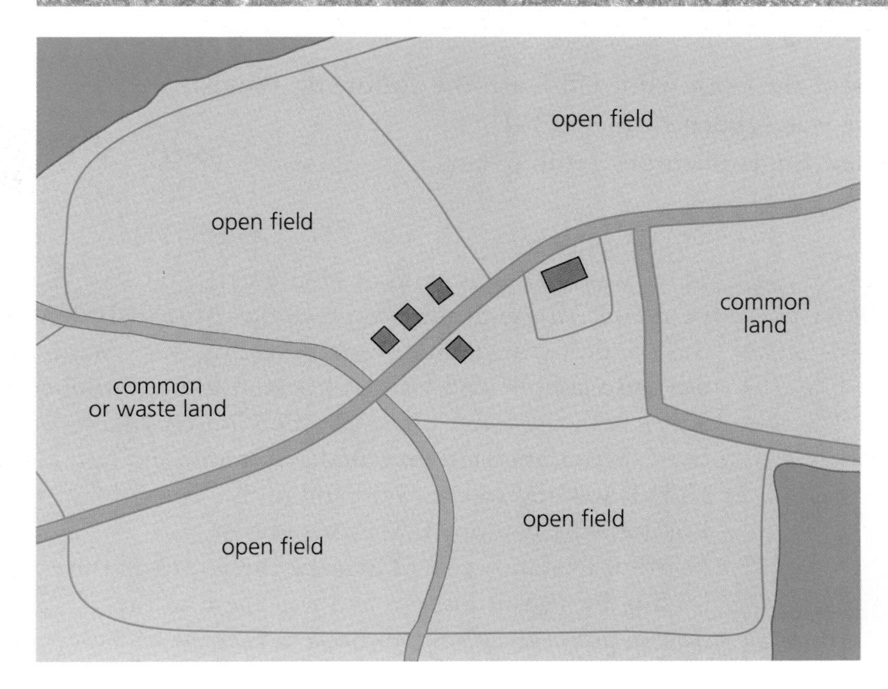

◄ *Fig 3 The old medieval open field village. Many lords of the manor or new rich men wanted to make money from the booming wool trade. They enclosed (fenced) common land or waste land in the old villages. Some even began to enclose the open fields. This was called enclosure.*

Q3 What is enclosure?

The illness of Edward VI

Northumberland had his rival, the Duke of Somerset, executed, but he could only remain in power if the young King continued to support him. However, Edward had always been delicate and it became obvious by 1553 that he was going to die. This was a disaster for Northumberland. He persuaded Edward to make a will saying that the crown would go to his second cousin, Lady Jane Grey. Northumberland then married his son to Lady Jane Grey.

Queen for nine days

As expected, Edward died, in July 1553, and Northumberland declared Lady Jane Grey Queen. However, Henry VIII's daughter, Mary, was on her way to London. The streets were full of cheering people and even the late King's Council declared for Mary. The game was up for Northumberland.

Key words

chantries – chapels where prayers were said for dead people. Rich people often endowed (gave) them their money.

enclosure – fencing of land

guild – group of people belonging to a particular trade in the Middle Ages

SUMMARY

- The Lord Protectors, Somerset and Northumberland, ruled for the young Edward VI.
- Both Protectors made England more Protestant and gained from taking Church property.
- Edward agreed that Lady Jane Grey should be the next Queen.
- Mary, Henry VIII's daughter and Edward's half-sister, was declared Queen in 1553.

SUMMARY *activity*

Explain why the reasons for discontent from 1547–1553 were so important to peasants in England.

36 Mary Tudor 1553–1558

In this section of the book you will learn the following things:

- Mary Tudor was Queen from 1553–1558;
- Mary wanted England to be Catholic again.

▲ ***Fig 1*** *Queen Mary I.*

Mary comes to the throne

Mary was the eldest child of Henry VIII. She was 36 years old. Although she was greeted **rapturously** by the London crowd, there were problems. Mary was a **devout** Catholic and wanted England to be Catholic again, with the Pope as head of the Church. Mary had Northumberland executed as a traitor and put Lady Jane Grey and her husband in the Tower of London. She pardoned everyone else in Northumberland's plot. Then she threw out all the leading Protestant bishops and sent them to the Tower, putting Catholic bishops in their place.

Q1 What did Mary do to Protestant bishops at the beginning of her reign?

Q2 What did she do with Catholic bishops?

Mary's marriage

Mary got her way on the next matter despite the fact that both Parliament and many people in England did not like it: she decided to marry King Philip of Spain. Not only was he a Catholic, but he was also a foreigner. Many English people feared that once he was King, Philip (and after him any son who became King) would use English money and power to do what Spain wanted. Bad feeling came to a head when Sir Thomas Wyatt led a rebellion against Mary. The idea was to put her sister, Elizabeth, on the throne instead. The rebellion was **quashed**, Mary put Elizabeth in the Tower and had Lady Jane Grey executed. She felt safer.

Q3 Why were so many people upset about Mary marrying King Philip of Spain?

Q4 Why do you think Mary did not execute Elizabeth at this time?

▲ ***Fig 2*** *A later picture of the execution of Lady Jane Grey.*

◀ *Fig 3 The burning of the Protestant Archbishop Cranmer.*

Mary triumphant

Philip II came to England and married Mary. At the same time she managed to persuade Parliament to make the Pope head of the Church in England again. She was delighted. Her only defeat was that Parliament refused to return all the Church land to the Church again. The 40,000 families that had shared in the plunder held on tightly to the lands they had gained.

Mary makes England Catholic again

- Catholic church services;
- sacked Protestant priests;
- married the Catholic King of Spain;
- persuaded Parliament to make the Pope head of the Church;
- important Protestants burned to death.

▲ *Fig 4*

Bloody Mary

From 1555, Mary began to persecute Protestants and continued to do so until her death. About 300 Protestants were burned as **heretics**. In spite of this, however, Protestantism was not wiped out and Mary became more and more hated. When she died, childless, in 1558, all the church bells in London rang out to celebrate her death.

Key words

devout – holy, serious
heretic – someone who does not believe the accepted religion
quashed – put down
rapturously – very happily

SUMMARY

- Mary wanted to make England Catholic with the Pope as head of the Church.
- Mary married the Catholic King Philip II of Spain.
- Mary put down Wyatt's rebellion and put her sister, Elizabeth, in the Tower.
- From 1555, Mary began to persecute Protestants.
- Mary died childless in 1558.

SUMMARY *activity*

People cheered when Mary came to the throne in 1553 and cheered when she died in 1558. What had happened in between?

37 Elizabeth I 1558–1603

In this section of the book you will learn the following things:

- Elizabeth I reigned from 1558–1603;
- the Elizabethan Settlement set up a moderately Protestant Church of England.

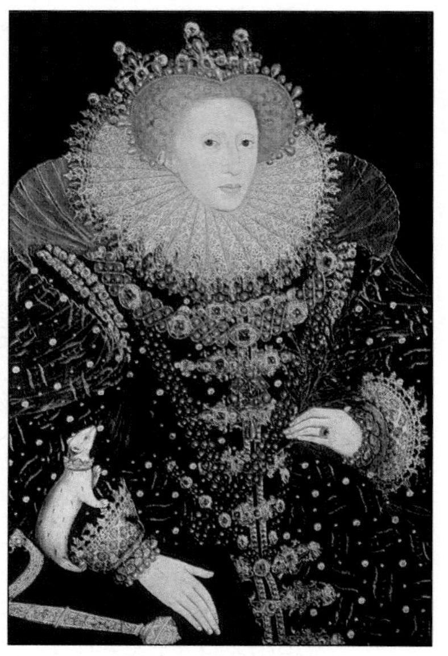

▲ ***Fig 1*** *Queen Elizabeth I.*

Who was Elizabeth?

Elizabeth I was the daughter of Henry VIII and Anne Boleyn. She came to the throne when she was 25 years old, an attractive, red-haired woman with a strong personality. She needed to be strong. Her half-brother, Edward VI, had been a weak young King and her half-sister, Mary, had become very unpopular because of her persecution of Protestants. Would Elizabeth do any better?

Elizabeth, Parliament and the Elizabethan Settlement

Elizabeth did not like extreme Catholics or extreme Protestants (known as **Puritans**). Many of the 460 members of Parliament wanted England to be very Protestant. The Queen did not. In the end there was a compromise known as the Elizabethan Settlement, under which England became Protestant again. A law was passed in Parliament stating that the Queen was the Supreme Governor of the Church. All English **clergymen** had to swear loyalty to the new Church of England. If they refused, they lost their jobs.

Q1 What was the Elizabethan Settlement?

Q2 What happened to clergymen if they did not swear loyalty to the Church of England?

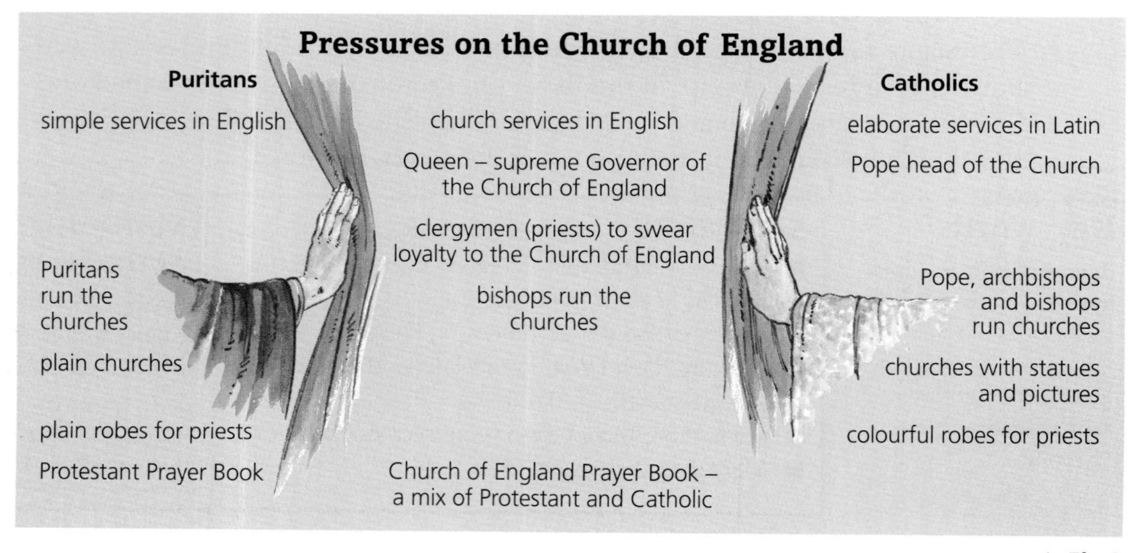

▲ ***Fig 2***

No 'window on men's souls'

▲ *Fig 3* *A 'window on men's souls'.*

Elizabeth did not want to have a 'window on men's souls', which meant she was willing to turn a blind eye to Catholics as long as they were loyal to her. They had to put their loyalty to the Queen and England before their loyalty to the Pope and the Catholic Church. That was the most important thing to Elizabeth.

Q3 What was the most important thing about religion to Elizabeth?

Q4 What does not having a 'window on men's souls' mean?

Trouble and triumph for Elizabeth's Church of England

However moderate Elizabeth was, she had trouble with religion on and off through her long reign. In 1570, the Pope said she was not the true Queen of England and that Catholics should replace her with a Catholic monarch. In support of this, some extreme Catholics, called **Jesuits,** were training priests in France. These priests then travelled secretly to England to persuade more English people to become Catholics. Protestants in England became angry about this and Parliament insisted on passing harsher laws against Catholics. Despite trouble from Catholics and Puritans, by the time Elizabeth died most people in England belonged to the moderate **Anglican Church**.

▲ *Fig 4* *The dilemma of English Catholics.*

Key words

Anglican Church – Church of England

clergyman – a priest of the Church of England

Jesuit – extreme Catholic priest

Puritan – extreme Protestant

SUMMARY

- Elizabeth did not like extreme Catholics or extreme Protestants (Puritans).
- The new Church of England (the Anglican Church) was moderately Protestant.
- The Queen was Supreme Governor of the Church of England.
- At the end of Elizabeth's reign most people belonged to the Church of England.

SUMMARY *activity*

How was the Church of England a middle way between the Puritans and the Catholics?

38 Elizabeth I and politics

In this section of the book you will learn the following things:

- about the Queen and Parliament;
- about Mary Queen of Scots.

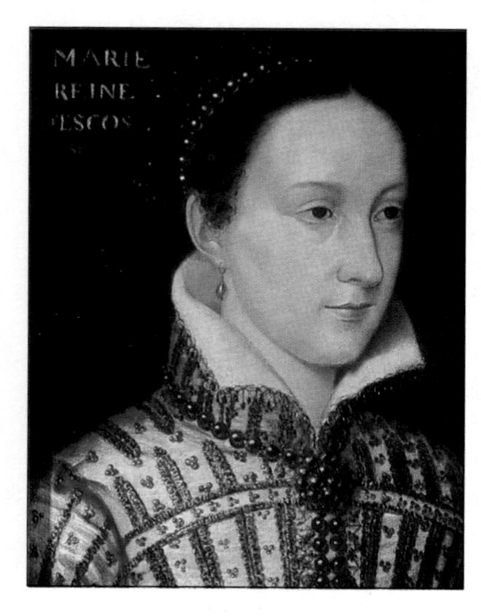

Elizabeth, Parliament and marriage

Religion was not Elizabeth's only problem. As soon as she came to the throne **Parliament** pressed her to marry. She told them to mind their own business. The trouble, as she saw it, was that if she married a foreign king, then a foreign country would control England. If she married an English noble, all the other nobles would be jealous of his power. She solved this dilemma by staying unmarried, but the question of who would be King or Queen after her remained.

◄ ***Fig 1*** *Mary Stuart, Queen of Scots.*

Parliament's power

Parliament was not easily put off. There were 460 members of the House of Commons and their job was to pass laws and grant money if the Queen needed it. Therein lay their power. The Queen was supposed to live on her own money, but she often needed much more if there was a war. The Commons could refuse to grant money unless the Queen agreed to such things as changes in religion, whether she should marry or whether to go to war. This infuriated Elizabeth, and she dealt with it in a number of ways.

▼ ***Fig 2***

All three parts of Parliament had to agree for a law to be made

- the Queen;
- the House of Lords;
- the House of Commons.

Q1 What were the three parts of Parliament?

Q2 How did Elizabeth deal with Parliament?

How Elizabeth dealt with Parliament

- many of her privy councillors were MPs in the House of Commons;
- she lived on her own money, only calling Parliament 13 times in 44 years;
- she appointed the Speaker (chairman) of the House of Commons;
- she imprisoned MPs who criticised her too openly;
- she could be gracious and give all the MPs a Christmas holiday.

▲ ***Fig 3***

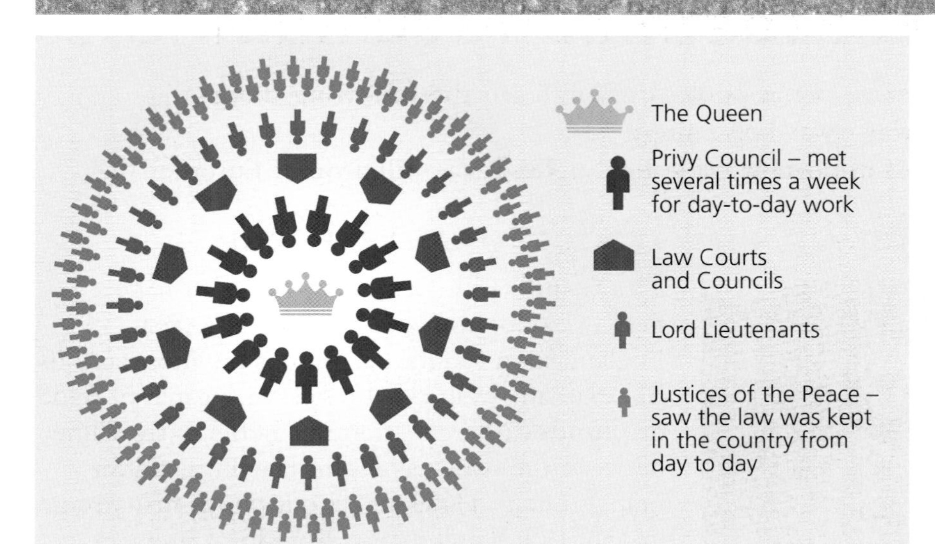

◀ ***Fig 4*** *Running the country from day to day.*

Who would be the next monarch?

In 1562, Elizabeth had smallpox. This was the situation Parliament dreaded. If she died, who would be the next monarch? The answer was her cousin, Mary Queen of Scots, who was a devout Catholic. Elizabeth recovered, but Parliament remained nervous. Then in 1568, there was a rebellion against Mary in Scotland, partly about religion and partly about the murder of Mary's husband, which many Scots thought she herself had planned. Mary fled to England.

Death of Mary Queen of Scots

What was Elizabeth to do? If she handed Mary back to the Scots, they might put her to death for the presumed murder of her own husband. Elizabeth did not like the idea of people putting queens to death. If Mary stayed in England, however, she might try to become Queen of England. Elizabeth decided to keep Mary in comfortable captivity in the north of England. Over the next 20 years, Mary was the centre of several plots to **depose** Elizabeth. Finally, in 1586, Elizabeth's spies had clear evidence that Mary had taken part in a plan to murder her. Elizabeth set up a court and Mary was found guilty. Elizabeth tried to avoid signing Mary's death warrant, but in 1587 she did so. Parliament and most Protestants in England were very relieved.

Key words

depose – remove from power

Parliament – from *parler,* meaning 'to speak' in French. It was the place where the government of the country was discussed.

SUMMARY

- The House of Commons granted money to the Queen. They wanted a say in her decisions.
- Parliament was worried about who would be King or Queen after Elizabeth. They wanted a Protestant.

SUMMARY *activity*

Why was Parliament so keen for Elizabeth to marry?

39 Elizabethan trade and riches

In this section of the book you will learn the following things:

- **world trade was beginning;**
- **the most important trade for England was still around Europe.**

Exploration and trade: John Hawkins

▲ ***Fig 1*** *Sir Francis Drake.*

Q1 Why was Hawkins' last voyage a disaster?

The Spanish and Portuguese were first in the field of exploration and trading. However, England soon caught up. Two of the most famous Elizabethan voyagers who sailed in search of trade or **plunder** (there was often a rather narrow line between the two) were John Hawkins and Sir Francis Drake. Hawkins set out on his first voyage in 1562. He bought slaves from local rulers in Africa and sailed to the West Indies to sell them to the Spanish settlers. His next voyage was even more successful. Having sold slaves again, he sailed north and bought fish in Newfoundland to bring back to England to sell. His third and last voyage was a disaster, however. The Spanish settlers in the West Indies were coming more firmly under the control of the King of Spain and could not trade with Hawkins.

Sir Francis Drake

Very able, very daring and less tactful than Hawkins, Francis Drake emerged as the new English hero. He sailed round the world between 1577 and 1580, exploring, plundering and trading. Like Hawkins, he found **shareholders.** This meant that two or more people put up the money for the expedition. When the expedition returned, they shared in the profits. Merchants, and even the Queen herself, invested money in Drake's long voyage. He returned in 1580 with profits beyond their wildest dreams. For £1 a shareholder had invested, he or she received £47 in return. Apart from genuine trading in goods such as spices, Drake had captured a Spanish silver **bullion** ship off the west coast of South America. The scene was being set for a great growth in trade in the next centuries.

▲ ***Fig 2*** *A sixteenth-century merchant in his office.*

Q2 How long did it take for Drake to sail round the world?

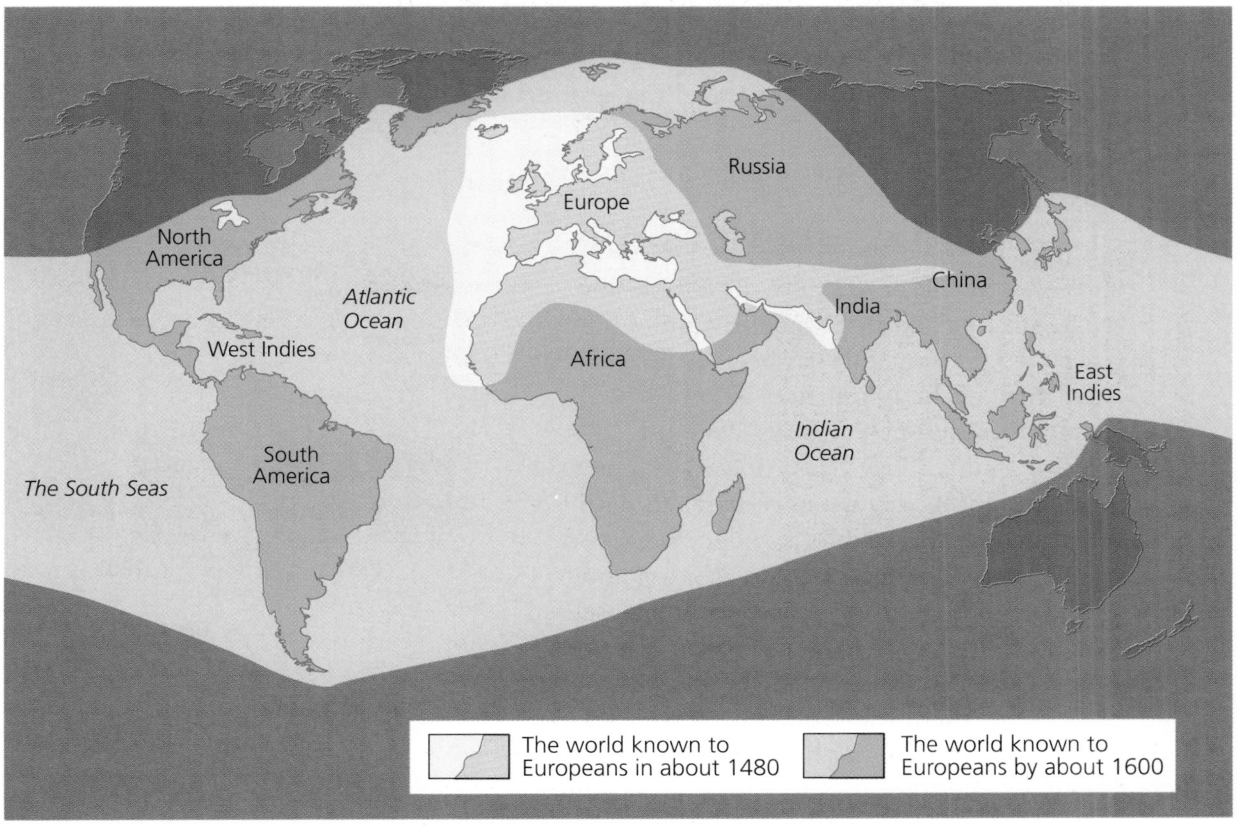

▲ ***Fig 3*** *Changes in European knowledge of the world between about 1480 and 1600.*

Nearer home

However, most trade still took place around Europe. England exported woollen cloth as far afield as Russia, and imported goods such as wines from France and Spain, glass from Venice, iron from the Baltic, carpets from Turkey, spices, silk and sugar from the East that came overland into Europe, furs from Russia and many other goods as more and more ships plied back and forth across the Channel to and from big ports such as London.

Key words

bullion – precious metal, usually gold or silver

plunder – steal, often by force

shareholders – people who invest money in a company and share in the profits (or losses)

SUMMARY

- Two of the most famous English traders were John Hawkins and Francis Drake.
- They got shareholders to invest money in their expeditions and share profits (or losses) at the end.
- Drake sailed round the world in three years, trading and plundering.
- Most English trade still took place around Europe, with goods coming to and from ports such as London.

SUMMARY *activity*

Why were the voyages of all the explorers and traders, including Hawkins and Drake, important?

40 Poverty and rogues

In this section of the book you will learn the following things:

- **more poor people were travelling around looking for work by Elizabethan times;**
- **new Poor Laws were introduced in 1598.**

The Patchingham family

It is easy to talk of the growth of trade and riches in England in Elizabethan times but not everyone grew rich. It has been estimated that one-third of the population did not have enough to eat. Such a family were the Patchinghams. They had a one-room cottage with a mud floor and a roof thatched with reeds. There was a table, two benches, a bed with a straw mattress and a log for a pillow. The village they lived in had been enclosed, so the Patchinghams had lost their land and relied on working on the new enclosed farms. In good years there was work, but when rain ruined the harvest, the Patchinghams and thousands of other people who lived on the edge of starvation, crept nearer to it.

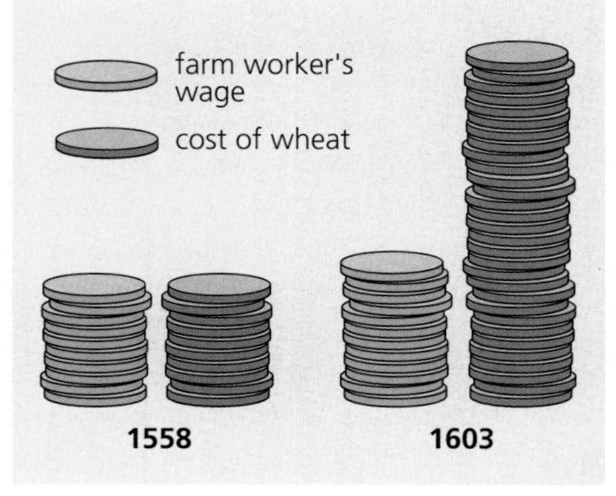

▲ ***Fig 1*** *Rising prices.*

The 'wandering poor'

When times were bad, hundreds of people left their homes and travelled around looking for work, begging or stealing. The laws about the 'wandering poor' made no allowance for people who wanted to work but could not do so because there were no jobs. Punishments were harsh and included whipping, boring a hole in the ear and death.

◀ ***Fig 2*** *One of the 'wandering poor' begs for money.*

Why there were more 'wandering poor'

By the 1590s, the problem had worsened. Both wandering people and crime were rising. Enclosure was only part of the problem. A downturn in the woollen cloth trade meant there were many out-of-work **spinners** and **weavers**. Food prices kept rising. The population of England had nearly doubled since the beginning of Tudor times. Worst of all, it rained. It rained all through the summer of 1594, so the crops were ruined. Then it rained the next year and the next. By 1596 there was near-starvation. It became obvious that many people who really wanted to work could not get jobs. Something had to be done.

Q1 What sort of punishments were there for the 'wandering poor'?

Q2 Make a list of all the reasons why there were more and more poor people in the 1590s.

The Poor Laws

The Elizabethan Parliament was concerned about the problem of the 'wandering poor', mainly because they were a threat to law and order. The first **Acts** Parliament passed were all to do with punishing any able-bodied person who was found wandering around without a job and was therefore considered a rogue. Some effort was made to help old and disabled people. Then in 1598, there was a big change in thinking. A law was passed to help find work for able-bodied people who genuinely could not find work. This law remained the basis of how to treat the poor for several hundred years.

Helping the poor: a law of 1598

Money was collected in each parish to help disabled and aged poor.

Some of this money was used to buy materials to give work to the genuinely unemployed.

▲ ***Fig 3***

Key words

an Act – a law
spinners – people who spun wool into thread
weavers – people who wove thread into cloth

SUMMARY

- About one-third of the population was very poor.
- Wandering poor people were classed as rogues or criminals.
- The Poor Laws of 1598 recognised that some able-bodied wanderers could not help being out of work.

SUMMARY *activity*

What did Parliament do about the 'wandering poor' in 1598?

41 Life in country and town

In this section of the book you will learn the following things:
- **farming was changing;**
- **farmers and merchants were making money;**
- **the guilds were losing power to Parliament.**

Why things were changing

Just as in the Middle Ages, most people in Tudor times lived and farmed in the country. Things were changing, however. The population of England doubled between 1485 and 1600. This meant a lot more mouths to feed and there were more people to buy things. Prices went up. Clever, forward-thinking farmers saw a chance to make money.

Old and new ways of farming

The old open field system of farming was wasteful. New enclosed fields meant better weeding and manuring and **selective breeding** of cows and sheep. This meant that more food could be grown and sold at a good price to the growing number of people living in towns. Moreover, everyone wanted English woollen cloth, so sheep farming was very profitable. Many landowners and farmers wanted to fence off the old common lands and even the open fields, to make smaller fields for their flocks of sheep.

Q1 What was better about the new enclosed fields?

Q2 Why was sheep farming profitable?

New building in the country

Although wool prices did not rise so much in Elizabethan times, many landowners, merchants and farmers made money. They spent it building and improving their houses. One of the biggest improvements for the very rich was moving out of cold, draughty castles into comfortable houses with glass in the windows. Even for ordinary farmers, adding one of the new chimneys to a farmhouse made a big difference to daily comfort.

▶ ***Fig 1*** *Hardwick Hall was built by Bess of Hardwick in the grand Elizabethan manner. Notice the enormous amount of glass used.*

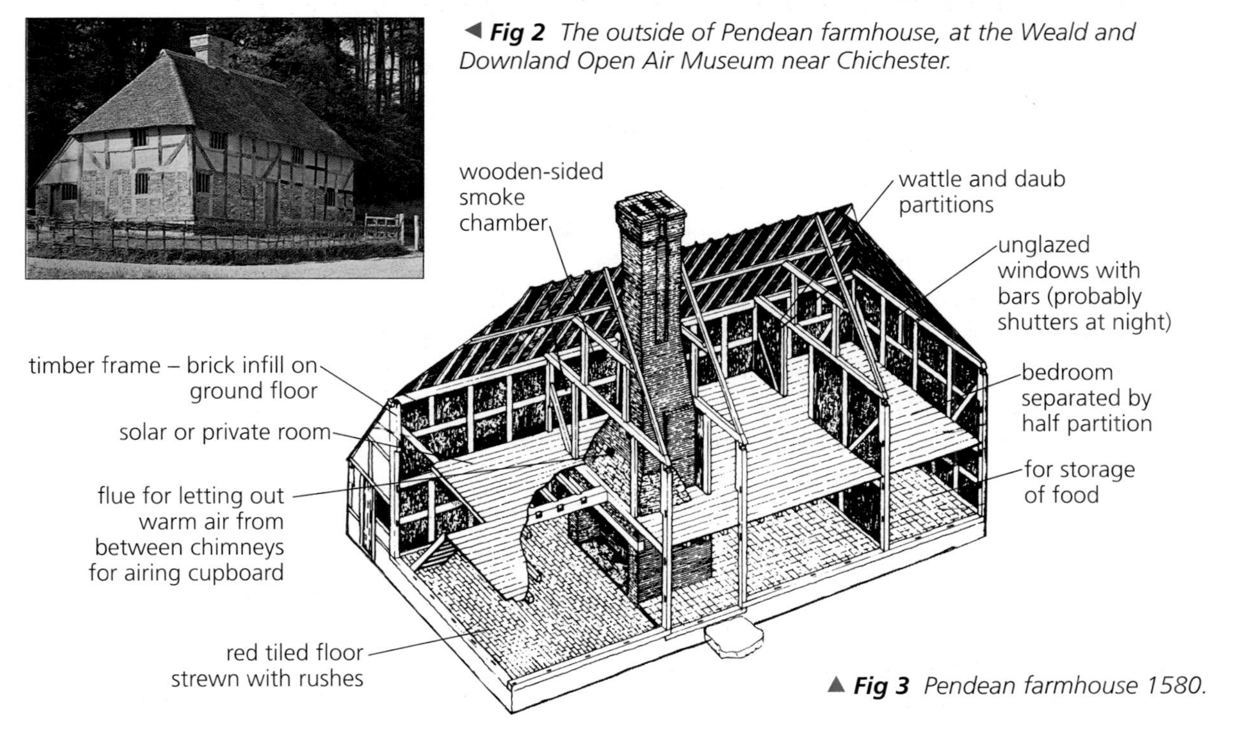

◀ ***Fig 2*** *The outside of Pendean farmhouse, at the Weald and Downland Open Air Museum near Chichester.*

▲ ***Fig 3*** *Pendean farmhouse 1580.*

Merchants and guilds

In the towns, merchants were making money from the growing trade in England and beyond. They were also building new houses. In London these might be as much as five storeys high, with a shop on the ground floor and workshops or storage behind. The family lived above. The **guilds** still controlled many crafts such as those of goldsmiths, glovemakers and so on, but they were losing their power. One of the reasons for this was that Parliament was taking over much of the making of rules and regulations for the whole country. For instance, the **Statute** of **Apprentices** 1563 was a law which laid down a seven-year apprenticeship for all crafts. In the Middle Ages it would have been the guilds who made those sort of rules.

Key words

apprentice – someone learning to do something from a master craftsman
guilds – groups of members of one craft who kept control of that craft in a town and helped each other
selective breeding – breeding the best animals together
statute – law

SUMMARY

- The population of England doubled between 1485 and 1600.
- Some landowners and farmers were enclosing land for better farming and to make money.
- Rich lords moved out of castles and built comfortable homes.
- Farmers built better houses.
- Merchants benefited from the growing trade in England and abroad.

SUMMARY *activity*

What things showed that England changed between 1485 and 1600?

42 The Spanish Armada

In this section of the book you will learn the following things:

- **Philip II of Spain wanted to crush Protestantism;**
- **Philip sent the Spanish Armada to invade England in 1588.**

Philip II of Spain and Elizabeth I of England

Most people in England were content with the Church of England and its moderate Protestant religion. However, Philip II of Spain was a different matter. Philip had been married to Mary Tudor and they were both devout Catholics. At first Philip was on good terms with Elizabeth I and even thought of marrying her. As the years went by, however, it became obvious that England and Elizabeth were going to remain Protestant. Philip was having continual trouble with the part of his empire called the Spanish Netherlands, where Protestantism was very strong. Now the Netherlanders turned to England for help.

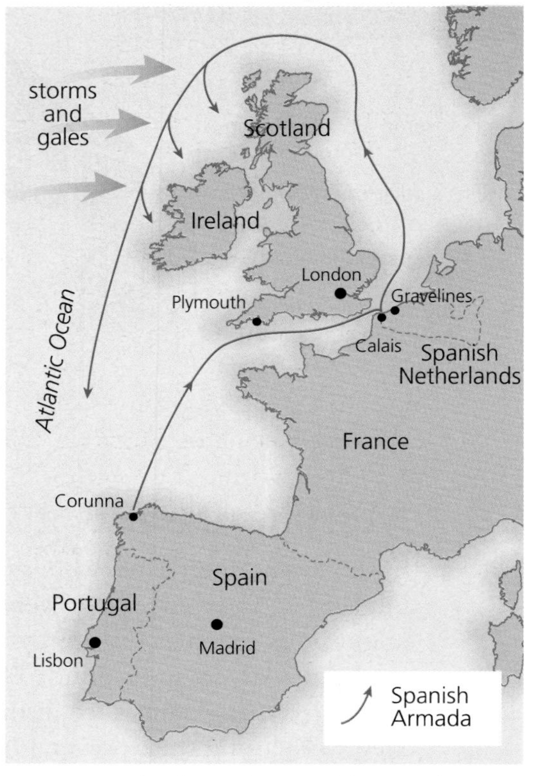

▲ ***Fig 1*** *The Spanish Armada 1588.*

Philip decided to invade England 1588

For Philip this was the last straw. For years Elizabeth had turned a blind eye to Francis Drake and other English sailors raiding Spanish ships. Then, in 1587, the Catholic Mary Queen of Scots had finally been beheaded on Elizabeth's orders. Philip felt this was the time to crush the Protestant menace of England once and for all. He prepared a great fleet of ships to invade England. They set sail in May 1588.

England prepares for invasion 1588

- All Catholics were arrested.
- All able-bodied men were called on to defend their country.
- The fleet was prepared.
- Watchers were stationed at high points along the coast and on hills inland.
- When the Armada was sighted, the watchers lit beacons (bonfires) on hilltops, so the message was passed across England.

▲ ***Fig 2***

Q1 What were the three reasons Philip had for wanting to invade England?

Q2 What did the English do to make ready for an invasion?

The Spanish Armada 1588

The English first sighted the Spanish **Armada** off Cornwall. The fleet left Plymouth on 18 July and, for nine days, it followed the Spanish slowly up the Channel. The Spanish kept tightly together and the English could not break them up. The Spanish, on the other hand, could not stop as they had hoped to do, and capture a port on the Isle of Wight. The running fight (almost in slow motion) lasted until the Spanish fleet anchored at Calais on 27 July. The English saw their opportunity. At night they sent six unmanned **fireships** sailing into the midst of the Spanish fleet. Terrified, sailors on most of the ships cut their cables and drifted away into the darkness. At daybreak only three or four Spanish ships remained at anchor. Somehow the commander grouped them together and the Battle of Gravelines followed. The Spanish ships took a terrible battering from the English guns. Then a storm broke up the battle and the Spanish ships fled north. The danger to England was over.

▲ ***Fig 3*** The Ark Royal *was built for Sir Walter Raleigh in 1587 and then sold to the Queen for £5 000. It weighed 800 tonnes and carried a crew of 400 men.*

The war with Spain dragged on until 1603, but despite scares of new invasions, England was not directly threatened.

▼ ***Fig 4***

Comparison of ships

English	***Spanish***
• low, slim ships;	• tall, heavy ships;
• long-range guns to fire broadsides from a distance;	• short-range guns. Aim: to get close, board enemy ship and fight hand to hand;
• well-trained crews of seamen.	• a mixture of seamen and soldiers.

Key words

armada – an armed fleet of ships

fireships – unmanned ships that were set on fire and floated towards the enemy

SUMMARY

- England remained Protestant under Elizabeth I.
- King Philip II of Spain felt threatened by Protestantism and in 1588 decided to invade England.
- The Spanish Armada fought the English fleet at Gravelines, but was scattered by a storm.
- This was the end of the threat of invasion for England, although the war dragged on until 1603.

SUMMARY *activity*

What advantages did the English have in fighting off the Spanish Armada?

43 James I 1603–1625

In this section of the book you will learn the following things:

- **James VI of Scotland became James I of England in 1603;**
- **James I faced two problems: Parliament and religion.**

James I

Elizabeth reigned until 1603. When she died, her cousin, James VI of Scotland, became James I of England. He was the son of Mary Queen of Scots, but had been brought up as a Protestant. Religion was one of the two problems he faced when he came to the throne. Parliament was the other.

▲ ***Fig 1*** *James I.*

Parliament

In the past kings and queens had relied mostly on landowners to be their advisers. Now this was changing. **Merchants** and **industrialists** had become wealthy. Now that England was a trading nation, they wanted more say in how the country was run. Many of them became members of the House of Commons. They began to want more power for the Commons. The scene was set for Parliament to clash head on with the King.

Q1 What two problems did James face when he came to the throne?

Q2 On whom had kings and queens relied to be their advisers in the past?

Q3 How had this changed by James I's time?

The King's income

- rent from his own lands;
- money from taxes such as customs duties;
- money granted by Parliament.

▲ ***Fig 2***

Religion

By far the most difficult problem for James, however, was religion. He had been brought up as a Protestant in Scotland, where the extreme Protestants (Puritans) were very powerful. He felt he had been bullied enough. He was not going to be bullied by the Puritans in England. He stood by the Church of England and sacked clergymen who would not accept bishops and the *Book of Common Prayer*. In 1611, he also brought in the Authorised Version of the Bible, that had to be used by all.

The Gunpowder Plot 1605

Now he was King, James did not feel he needed support from Puritans or Catholics. So the Catholics also felt angry. A group of them planned to blow up the King when he opened Parliament. The plotters rented a house which had a cellar running under the House of Lords. They packed in 36 barrels of gunpowder. Meanwhile, one of the conspirators had second thoughts. He wrote to Lord Monteagle, who was a Catholic, warning him not to attend Parliament. When James was shown the letter, he was horrified. His mother and father had died violent deaths. He ordered that the cellars around Parliament be searched. At 11 o' clock on the night of 4 November, the gunpowder was discovered together with Guy Fawkes, who was on guard. Under torture, he revealed the names of the other conspirators. They were all executed.

▲ *Fig 3 The Gunpowder Plot conspirators.*

▼ *Fig 4*

The Pilgrim Fathers

Many Puritans left England in James I's reign. Some went to Holland, some went to America.

The most famous were the Pilgrim Fathers, who sailed on the *Mayflower* on 6 September 1620 to found the first of the New England colonies in America.

The end of James I's reign

Once the Gunpowder Plot was **foiled**, James did not continue to dislike Catholics. His daughter had married a Protestant and he felt it would be a good idea for his son to marry a Catholic. Parliament objected to a Catholic and told him so. The only way James could stop Parliament arguing was by telling them to go home (called **dissolving** Parliament). Tired and ill, he died in 1625.

Q4 How do you know that James was tolerant about religion?

Key words

dissolve – to close down or dismiss

foil – prevent from succeeding

industrialists – people who make goods to sell

merchants – people who buy and sell goods

SUMMARY

- James I supported the Church of England. He would not help Puritans or Catholics.
- Many Puritans left England. Some Catholics planned to blow up the King and Parliament.
- Merchants and industrialists were richer and wanted more say in running the country. Many became members of the House of Commons.

SUMMARY *activity*

By 1600 it was much more expensive to run the country than it had been in 1066. How did this make Parliament stronger and the King weaker?

44 Charles I 1625–1649

In this section of the book you will learn the following things:

- **Charles I needed money and could not agree with Parliament;**
- **Charles believed in the Divine Right of Kings.**

The failure of the raid on Spain

When Charles came to the throne, England was at war with Catholic Spain. This pleased Parliament, but unfortunately the war went badly. A raid on Spain, led by the handsome but incompetent Duke of Buckingham, failed completely, and the English fleet returned to Plymouth in a terrible state. Starving sailors were dying in the streets of Plymouth. Watching this, furious and saddened, stood a man called Sir John Eliot.

▲ ***Fig 1*** *A portrait of Charles I by a famous artist, Van Dyck.*

Divine Right of Kings

James I and Charles I believed that God had made them King. Their subjects had to obey them.

▲ ***Fig 2***

Parliament and the Petition of Right 1628

Eliot was a Puritan. He represented Cornwall in the House of Commons. When Charles called Parliament in 1626 to ask for more money for the war, he was met by a storm of complaints from the House of Commons, led by Sir John Eliot. Charles got nothing and dissolved Parliament. He still needed money, however, so he forced merchants and landowners to lend him money; any who refused were imprisoned. The war continued to go badly, and when Charles met Parliament to ask for money again, the members were ready for him. They agreed, but only if he signed the **Petition** of Right.

Petition of Right 1628

- no soldiers were to be billeted on private citizens;
- no civilians were to be tried by army law;
- the King could not raise taxes without Parliament's consent;
- no man was to be imprisoned without good reason.

▲ ***Fig 3***

Q1 What did the Petition of Right say?

Charles and the Earl of Strafford 1629–1640

Charles was furious, but decided to do without Parliament. He spent the next 11 years enjoying family life, encouraging great artists to come to England and, best of all, having nothing to do with Parliament. He relied on Thomas Wentworth, Earl of Strafford, to run the country. He advised the King that there were all sorts of old laws that could be dredged up to make rich merchants and landowners pay money to the King. One of these laws was about taxing people in coastal towns to provide money for ships. Charles levied ship money on people living inland – and without Parliament's permission.

▶ *Fig 4*

The coat of arms of the Stuart kings.

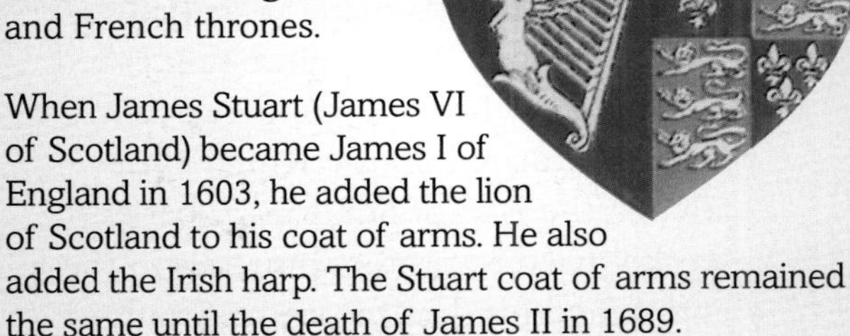

The golden lions of England and the fleur de lys of France made up the coat of arms of the Tudor kings and queens, reflecting their claims to the English and French thrones.

When James Stuart (James VI of Scotland) became James I of England in 1603, he added the lion of Scotland to his coat of arms. He also added the Irish harp. The Stuart coat of arms remained the same until the death of James II in 1689.

The fleur de lys remained on the coat of arms of British monarchs until 1801, when the French insisted that all English claims to the French throne should be surrendered.

Charles and William Laud 1629–1640

The other man who helped the King was William Laud, the Archbishop of Canterbury. He ran the Church of England and **reinstated** all the beautiful robes, the ceremony and the music that Puritans hated. Charles liked this so much that he decided to make the Church in Scotland the same. This was too much for the strongly Puritan Scots. There were riots and war. The Scottish army routed the English and overran Northumberland and Durham. Charles had no money, so he called Parliament, hoping it would support him against the Scottish invasion.

Q2 How did Charles get money during the 11 years he ruled without Parliament?

Key words

petition – a document asking for something
reinstate – to bring back

SUMMARY

- Charles I needed money to fight a war with Spain, but Parliament would not give him any unless he agreed to listen to its complaints.
- Charles dissolved Parliament, but was forced to call it in 1628, when it made him sign the Petition of Right.
- Charles ruled without Parliament from 1629 to 1640 by raising money from using old laws.

SUMMARY *activity*

Why was Parliament likely to be very angry with the King by 1640?

45 Charles I and the Civil War

In this section of the book you will learn the following things:

- **Parliament and the King could not agree, so a Civil War started in 1642;**
- **Parliament won the Civil War.**

The Long Parliament 1640–1642

The Puritan merchants in the Commons felt more sympathy with the Scots than with Charles. Moreover, they were angry that so many years had passed without Parliament being called. They put Archbishop Laud in prison and then turned on the King's close adviser, the Earl of Strafford. Charles weakly tried to protect him, but in the end signed his death warrant. Strafford was executed on Tower Hill amidst a vast cheering crowd.

The two sides in the Civil War

King	***Parliament***
• many great landowners;	• many merchants and industrialists;
• Catholics;	• Puritans;
• Church of England.	• the navy (sailors were hardly ever paid by Charles).

▲ ***Fig 1***

New laws

With Strafford out of the way, the Commons, led by John Pym, passed laws saying the King could not dissolve Parliament or get money in taxes without its consent. It passed a law which did away with the law courts that had supported the King and passed another which said Parliament had to be called every three years. It would only grant money to Charles to pay the Scots to leave England once he had signed all these laws. Many members of the Commons felt they had gone far enough. Others wanted to make the Church more Puritan. Charles would never agree to this, so he set off for Parliament with a troop of soldiers to arrest John Pym and the other four leaders of the House of Commons, but they escaped.

Q1 What four laws did Parliament make and insist the King signed?

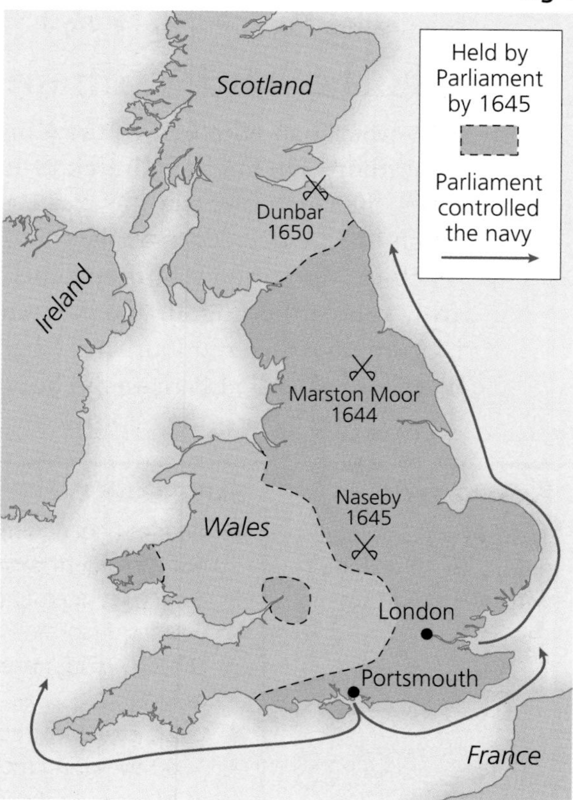

▲ ***Fig 2*** *The Civil War.*

Beginning of the Civil War

Now the Commons was really annoyed. Members decided they must gain control or the King would break them. They took over the army and the King left London. The country was divided. The King raised an army and for the next two years there were many small battles. Then in 1644, Parliament's army, led by Sir Thomas Fairfax and Oliver Cromwell, with the help of the Scots, defeated the **Royalist** army at Marston Moor. A year later Parliament raised a new, well-trained, well-paid army, which smashed the Royalists at the Battle of Naseby. The next year Charles was a prisoner.

▶ ***Fig 3*** *A New Model Army soldier (Roundhead).*

Q2 What two important battles did Parliament win?

Charles in prison 1647–1649

Charles hoped to get the Scots, Parliament and the army to fall out with each other. The Scots were annoyed because the army was blocking their scheme for a more Puritan religion. So Charles managed to do a deal with the Scots behind Parliament's back and arranged for a Scottish army to invade England. Parliament was furious. It could not trust Charles an inch. After the Scots' army was defeated, it decided Charles had to be dealt with once and for all.

▶ ***Fig 4*** *A Royalist soldier (Cavalier).*

Key words

civil war – a war in which citizens of the same country fight against each other

Royalist – on the King's side

SUMMARY

- Parliament was angry with the King for ruling without Parliament.
- It made him sign laws giving Parliament more power.
- Charles thought Parliament had gone far enough and went to arrest five members of the House of Commons.
- This started the Civil War in 1642, which was finally won by Parliament in 1649.

SUMMARY *activity*

What evidence is there that Charles was not very trustworthy?

46 The Commonwealth

In this section of the book you will learn the following things:

- Charles I was beheaded on 30 January 1649;
- Cromwell, as leader of the army, eventually took control.

▲ ***Fig 1*** *The execution of Charles I.*

Death of the King 30 January 1649

It was difficult to try Charles I for **treason** because he said he was the King and was responsible to no one but God. The Parliamentarians decided to get it over quickly. He was pronounced guilty and his death warrant was signed by 59 judges. Two days later Charles was beheaded in public, outside his palace of Whitehall. Who would rule now?

▼ ***Fig 2***

How shall we run England?

Royalists

- bring back Charles II;
- bring back the House of Lords;
- bring back the bishops.

Moderates

- bring back Charles II;
- bring back the House of Lords (maybe);
- no bishops.

Radicals

lots of different ideas, e.g.:

- House of Commons elected by one man one vote;
- do away with all private property;
- Puritan religious ministers to run the country

Cromwell, Ireland and Scotland

The army was now in charge. Since Fairfax had retired it was led by Oliver Cromwell. For a year or two the army was **occupied** with rebellions in Ireland. Having crushed these, Cromwell took land from the Catholics and gave it to Protestants, so that England would always have some allies in Ireland. After this there was the question of Scotland. The Scots were furious with the English for executing Charles I, who was King of Scotland as well as England. They crowned his son, Charles II, as King. Cromwell was having none of this. He invaded Scotland and defeated the Scots at the Battle of Dunbar in 1650. Next year, however, the young Charles II led another Scots army into England. Cromwell defeated the King at the Battle of Worcester and Charles escaped abroad.

Q1 What happened in Ireland?
Q2 What happened in Scotland?
Q3 What happened to Charles II?

Cromwell dismisses Parliament 1653

Meanwhile in England things had changed. The House of Lords was abolished, so was a Church run by bishops and the country was run by a few Puritans in the House of Commons who were friends of the army. However, very little was being done about running the country properly. Cromwell was impatient. He marched into the House of Commons in 1653, turned the members out, saying they were useless, and locked the doors.

▼ ***Fig 3*** *Oliver Cromwell.*

Oliver Cromwell as the Lord Protector 1653–1658

The King was gone. Parliament was gone. Cromwell had all the power in his hands. He ruled England for the next five years, until his death. He had far more power than Charles I had ever had, and was King in all but name. He even named his son, Richard, to succeed him. To be fair, he tried to set up Parliament several times, but he could never put up with the members' bickering and inefficiency, and always sent them away.

Key words

dismiss – to send away
occupied – busy with
radicals – people who want to change things a great deal
treason – a crime against the state

SUMMARY

- Charles I was beheaded on 30 January 1649. His death warrant was signed by 59 judges.
- The army was then in charge. It was led by Oliver Cromwell.
- The Scots crowned Charles I's son, Charles II, King, but Cromwell defeated him and he fled abroad.
- Cromwell **dismissed** Parliament in 1653 and ruled on his own until his death in 1658.

SUMMARY *activity*

How would you have run England after the death of the King? Give reasons for your answer.

47 Charles II 1660–1685

In this section of the book you will learn the following things:

- Charles II was invited back to be King in 1660;
- he was careful to keep on fairly good terms with Parliament.

The return of Charles II

In 1660 most people felt that ruling without a monarch had failed. Parliament invited Charles II back to be King and he rode into London amidst cheering crowds. He was 30 years old, tall and dark with a heavy face, but he was good humoured and most of all he was intelligent. He agreed that Parliament would decide who to punish for rebelling against his father and it would control the country's finances. Indeed, Parliament was so happy to have him back it granted him £1 million a year, far more than his father, Charles I, ever had.

▶ **Fig 1** *Charles II.*

A Catholic King to follow?

Charles had no wish to 'go on his travels again' so, for the most part, his reign went smoothly. He only ran into trouble when he tried to be lenient to Catholics. The whole question of Catholics was a very touchy one. Charles was outwardly a Protestant, but he had no legitimate children. Therefore his brother, James, would be King when Charles died. James was a Catholic. This made the Protestants in England very nervous, particularly the ones who owned lands that Henry VIII had taken from the Catholic Church.

Q1 What religion was Charles II?

Q2 What religion was his brother, James?

▼ **Fig 2**

What Parliament settled when Charles II became King

- granted Charles £1 million a year;
- disbanded Cromwell's huge army;
- brought back the Church of England;
- forbade all forms of worship except the Church of England.

Titus Oates

Matters came to a head in 1678 when a curious looking man called Titus Oates and a mad Protestant clergyman called Israel Tonge told a magistrate of a plot to murder the King and put his Catholic brother, James, on the throne. This story ran and ran despite many sensible men, including the King, disbelieving it. Catholics accused of being part of the plot were arrested. To crown everything, the magistrate was found strangled and stabbed in a ditch. London was in an uproar. Several Catholics were tried and hanged. Then Oates went too far: he accused the Queen and her doctor of plotting to murder the King. When the case came to court, the judge tore the evidence to pieces. Oates was sent to prison.

Q3 What did Titus Oates tell the magistrate?

Q4 How did Oates go too far?

The Titus Oates affair

Charles II speaking to the Earl of Essex, who had told the King that he believed a Catholic was innocent of plotting to kill the King:

'Then, my lord, be his blood on your own conscience. You might have saved him if you would. I cannot pardon him because I dare not.'

▲ *Fig 3*

The Exclusion Bill

In the midst of the **furore**, Parliament passed a **Bill** saying that the Catholic James could not become King. Charles refused to sign the Bill, so it did not become law, but he was worried. He knew his brother would want to favour Catholics when he became King and that England would not stand for that. On his deathbed, Charles declared himself a Catholic and received the **last rites** from Father Huddleston, the old priest who had saved his life after the Battle of Worcester, 34 years earlier.

Key words

Bill – a draft of a law or Act of Parliament. A Bill has to pass the Commons, the Lords and be signed by the monarch to become law.

furore – public excitement

last rites – last blessing before death

SUMMARY

- Parliament invited Charles II back to become King in 1660.
- Charles had no legitimate children so the next King would be his Catholic brother, James.
- The Titus Oates affair showed how anti-Catholic many English people were. They did not want the next King to be Catholic.
- Charles only declared he was Catholic on his deathbed.

SUMMARY *activity*

Explain why Charles II could not pardon the Catholic. Why might he have wanted to?

48 London after 1660

In this section of the book you will learn the following things:

- **London was a growing city;**
- **the Plague and the Great Fire were two disasters for London.**

London when Charles II became King 1660

By this time London was a huge city of tall houses and narrow cobbled streets. The air was thick with smoke from the factories and from the coal fires in the houses. The streets were noisy with street sellers shouting their wares, such as rabbits from the country, oranges from abroad, hot pies and song sheets. The cobbles were filthy because there was no sewerage system or rubbish collection. Everything landed in the gutter in the middle of the street. It is hardly surprising that disease was rife. The bubonic plague visited London in most summers but was particularly devastating in the summer of 1665.

The Plague 1665

It is now known that the plague is carried by the fleas that live on black rats – and rats were everywhere. When rats died of the plague the fleas looked for a new home and this could be a human being. The first symptoms were shivering and vomiting, followed by a fever and the growth of **buboes** in the armpits and groins. Sometimes these burst and a person recovered, but more often they did not. Once someone had the plague the whole house was shut up. No one was allowed in or out. This usually meant that everyone died. As the hot summer went on, more and more people died. There were so many they were buried at night in huge plague pits. Many fled from the city, often taking the plague with them. Even when the weather became cooler, the plague did not slow down. It was not until the next year that life began to return to normal in London. Then another disaster struck.

▼ ***Fig 1***

Population of London in 1665: ***about 460 000.***
Deaths from plague in London in 1665: ***about 70 000.***

Q1 What were the symptoms of the plague?

▼ ***Fig 2*** *Londoners fleeing the city in the hope of avoiding the plague 1665.*

▲ *Fig 3 London on fire, showing the extent of the fire and the flames fanned by the easterly wind.*

London amusements 1660s

theatres;
taverns;
fairs;
executions;
cockfighting;
music;
dancing.

Most of these had been banned during the Puritan Commonwealth.

▲ *Fig 4*

London industries 1660s

ship building;
silk weaving;
paper making;
brewing;
soap making;
brick making;
cloth weaving.

▲ *Fig 5*

The Great Fire 1666

Shops reopened after the plague and people returned to London, enjoying a long hot summer. By September the timber houses with their thatched roofs were as dry as tinder and when fire struck it spread in moments. The fire began at a baker's shop in Pudding Lane in the early hours of 2 September. The wind was blowing from the east, and burning thatch blew from house to house. People panicked, stacked their goods on handcarts and fled, while the fire raged for three days. Then the wind dropped and it was possible to put out the remaining fires. A large part of London was destroyed, however. When it was rebuilt, the government insisted houses were made of brick and tiles not wood and thatch; Sir Christopher Wren rebuilt many city churches, including St Paul's Cathedral, and London was all set to grow again.

Q2 How did the fire start?

Q3 Why did it spread?

Key words

buboes – black swellings

SUMMARY

- London had doubled in size since early Tudor times. It was dirty and noisy.
- The Plague killed about 70,000 people in 1665.
- The Great Fire destroyed a large part of the city of London in 1666.

SUMMARY *activity*

Describe London before and after the Great Fire. Why do you think the Plague might not return?

49 James II and his children

In this section of the book you will learn the following things:

- James II wanted to help Catholics in England;
- several leading Protestants invited William of Orange and Mary to rule.

▲ ***Fig 1*** *James II.*

James II and his children: Mary and Anne

James II came to the throne in 1685. At first he was popular. People didn't even mind that he went to Catholic church services. They knew that he was quite old and had only two daughters, both of whom were Protestants. The younger one was Anne and the elder was Mary. Not only was Mary a Protestant, but she was married to the important Dutch leader, a Protestant called William of Orange. Soon Mary would become Queen.

The warming pan baby

When James II's wife gave birth to a son there was a rumour that the Queen had not had a boy. The rumour went that a baby boy had been smuggled into the Queen's bedroom inside a warming pan.

A warming pan was a copper or brass container that could be filled with hot water and used to warm the bed, like a hot-water bottle today.

▲ ***Fig 2***

James as a Catholic King

James really wanted to make England Catholic. He enlarged the army and began to appoint Catholic rather than Protestant officers, even though this was illegal. When Parliament protested, James dissolved it. He said that everyone, including Catholics and **Nonconformists**, could worship as they liked. He arrested bishops who protested and sacked judges he did not trust. If all this wasn't worrying enough, in 1688 his wife gave birth to a son. This meant that when James died the next King would be Catholic. Several important Protestants decided to act. They wrote to William of Orange and asked him to bring an army to England.

Q1 What did James do that was worrying to Protestants and Parliament?

Q2 What happened in 1688?

Q3 Who do you think would spread the story about the warming pan baby?

William and Mary

William landed in Devon and was welcomed. Some of James's best soldiers went over to him and even James's younger daughter, Anne, escaped from her father's palace in London, jumped in a **hackney coach** and rushed off to join her sister and husband. James went abroad and the next year William and his wife were jointly proclaimed King and Queen by Parliament.

The Glorious Revolution 1688

This was a bloodless **revolution** but it was nevertheless a revolution. Parliament had made William and Mary King and Queen. Parliament could unmake them. Never again did a King or Queen try to rule without Parliament.

The Glorious Revolution
(new laws for William and Mary)

Parliament:

- controlled judges;
- only voted money for one year to the monarch;
- put the army under Parliament's control;
- said Kings and Queen's must be Protestant;
- said Kings and Queen's must marry Protestants;
- said the monarch must hold elections for Parliament every three years;
- said only Parliament could collect taxes and control spending.

▶ ***Fig 3***

Key words

hackney coach – a seventeenth-century horse-drawn taxi

Nonconformists – Protestants who did not conform to (accept the rules of) the Church of England

revolution – a complete change

SUMMARY

- James II was a Catholic; his two daughters were Protestant.
- His elder daughter, Mary, was married to a Dutch Protestant leader called William of Orange.
- When James's wife had a son in 1688, William and Mary were invited to become King and Queen.
- This was known as the Glorious Revolution.

SUMMARY *activity*

What laws did Parliament pass to make sure that future kings and queens were kept under the control of Parliament?

50 Ireland and England

In this section of the book you will learn the following things:

- **England attempted to conquer Ireland;**
- **James I set up colonies of English and Scottish settlers in places such as Ulster;**
- **the Irish were suppressed after the Battle of the Boyne in 1690.**

Tudor times

Serious efforts were made in Tudor times to conquer Ireland. Religious differences now divided the two countries. When England tried to introduce a Protestant Prayer Book, the Irish turned to Philip of Spain for help. Rebellions simmered on for years and were ruthlessly **suppressed** by the English.

Ulster

James I carried on the policy of conquering Ireland. He took land in places like Ulster from the Irish and gave it to Protestant Scottish and English settlers. For instance, the town of Derry was given to the City of London. Londoners settled there and called it Londonderry. Charles I's trusted **deputy**, the Earl of Strafford, continued stern rule in Ireland. When Strafford fell from power and was executed, however, the 'iron hand' was lifted. Irish Catholic grievances surfaced in a massacre of Protestants.

Oliver Cromwell

When Cromwell came to power he wanted to subdue the Catholic Irish. He landed in Ireland in 1649, took towns and killed anyone opposing him. He settled former soldiers and gave them land, but many in the south married Catholic wives and became Irish. Nevertheless, the ruthlessness and suffering meted out to the Irish was one more bitter memory in Irish-English relations.

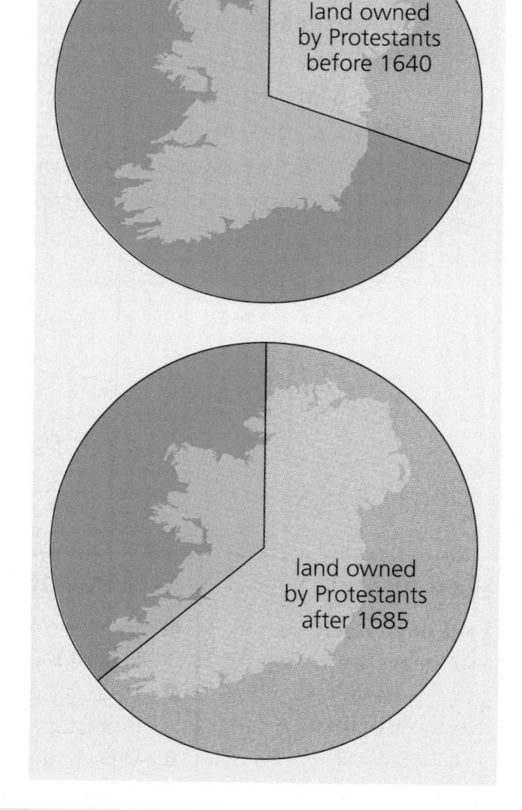

▶ ***Fig 1*** *Land facts in Ireland.*

Q1 What differences divided England and Ireland in Tudor times?

Q2 What did James I do in places such as Ulster?

James II and Ireland

James II fled and William and Mary were accepted as King and Queen in England but not in Ireland. Most people in Ireland were Catholic and had flourished under James II, who had let them worship freely. In 1689, James fled from England to Ireland with a French army lent to him by the King of France. He quickly gained the support of the Irish, who passed laws in their Parliament taking land back from the English and Scots settlers of Cromwell's time. There was only one part of Ireland that James could not take. That was Ulster. James laid siege to the city of Londonderry and cut off all food supplies.

▶ ***Fig 2*** *William of Orange (William III).*

The Battle of the Boyne 1690

William, now King of England, saw the danger of letting the French get a foothold in Ireland, so he sent warships to take food to Londonderry. In 1690 he went to Ireland himself and won the Battle of the Boyne. Once again James fled, this time to France. The Protestants were in control, but most of the population were Catholic. The Protestants brought in more laws against Catholics, with the aim of destroying the power of the Irish landowners. Soon Protestants had taken most of the land.

▶ ***Fig 3***

Laws against Irish Catholics

A Catholic could not:

- be a Member of Parliament;
- vote in an election;
- go to university;
- be a lawyer;
- be a teacher;
- be a soldier (officer);
- sit on a jury;
- have a job in the Government;
- buy land from a Protestant;
- own a horse worth more than £5.

Key words

deputy – someone who acts in the place of someone else

suppress – to keep down

SUMMARY

- From Tudor times the English kept trying to conquer Ireland.
- The Irish were Catholic while most of the English were Protestant.
- The Protestant King William defeated the Catholic James II and the Irish at the Battle of the Boyne in 1690.

SUMMARY *activity*

Explain how the laws against Catholics kept the Irish poor and resentful.

51 Scotland and England unite

In this section of the book you will learn the following things:

- **England and Scotland became united;**
- **some Scots supported James III and his son, Bonnie Prince Charlie.**

Why England and Scotland wanted to unite Parliaments

A Scottish King had become King of England in 1603, but the two countries had kept separate Parliaments. By 1707 things were changing, however. England was becoming wealthier because of the growth of overseas trade. The Scots merchants of the Lowlands wanted a share in this trade. At the same time the English wanted to unite with Scotland, at least partly to make sure the Scots would agree to have the same monarch as the English. This was important because by 1707 it was becoming obvious that Queen Anne was probably not going to have any surviving children.

Highlands
Lowlands
Scotland
Glasgow
Edinburgh
Ireland
Wales
England

▲ ***Fig 1*** *The division between Highland and Lowland Scots was strong. The Lowlanders often had more in common with the English than with the Highlanders.*

◀ ***Fig 2*** *Bonnie Prince Charlie.*

The Act of Union 1707

The Scots agreed to the Act of Union in 1707. They abolished their Parliament and instead sent Scots lords and MPs to Parliament in London. All seemed well and the two countries were set to prosper, but there was a fly in the ointment.

Q1 What was agreed in the Act of Union 1707?

Jacobites

William and Mary had no children and Anne died childless in 1714. There were two possibilities for the next King, either George of Hanover (German and Protestant) or the would-be James III (Stuart and Catholic). The Highland Scots, who were Catholic, were unhappy at seeing the end of the Scottish Stuarts on the throne. There were many **Jacobite** plots and two rebellions, one in 1715 and one in 1745. Both failed, mainly because James and later his son, Bonnie Prince Charlie, remained firmly Catholic.

Q2 What was the main reason that James Stuart and Bonnie Prince Charlie did not win support in most of Scotland and England?

The '45

The most successful rebellion was led by James III's son, known as Bonnie Prince Charlie. At the head of 5,000 Highlanders, he took control of much of Scotland. He decided to march on London. He got as far as Derby when it became obvious that the English were not going to join him. He went back to Scotland, pursued by an English army under the Duke of Cumberland. Bonnie Prince Charlie was cornered at Culloden. His Highlanders made two brave charges uphill against an army double their size and were cut to pieces. Bonnie Prince Charlie escaped.

Laws against the Highland clans
- not allowed weapons;
- not allowed to wear tartan;
- not allowed clan names;
- schools set up to teach in English only.

▲ *Fig 3*

After the rebellion

The government was determined such rebellions would never happen again. Laws were passed to destroy the power of the **clan** chiefs, but the English were also far more intelligent in their treatment of the Highlanders than of the Irish. For instance, within 15 years Highland regiments were raised and rapidly became among the leading soldiers of the British Army.

Key words

clan – the extended family or tribal system of the Highlands of Scotland

Jacobite – from the Latin *Jacobus*, meaning 'James'

SUMMARY

- The English and Scottish Parliaments united in 1707.
- Some Scots (and a few Catholic English) supported James III's claim to the throne in 1715.
- In 1745, Bonnie Prince Charlie (James III's son) led 5,000 Highlanders to claim the throne.
- Bonnie Prince Charlie was defeated at the Battle of Culloden and the Highland clans were suppressed.

SUMMARY *activity*

Why did the Jacobite rebellion of 1745 fail? Think of as many reasons as you can.

52 Growth of trade and empire

In this section of the book you will learn the following things:

- trade and empires grew;
- the European sea powers were the ones who gained empires.

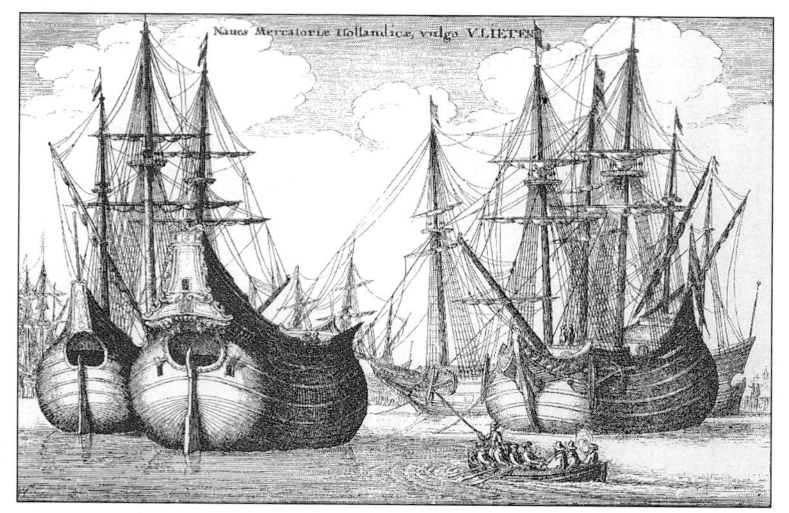

▲ **Fig 1** *Seventeenth-century Dutch merchant ships.*

Explorations

In the Middle Ages the world known to Europeans was very small. Then, in 1492, Christopher Columbus sailed to the West Indies. He was followed by other explorers and, 100 years later, men had sailed right round the world. Soon trade was flourishing, goods poured into European ports from all over the world and people rushed to buy them. There was tea from India, sugar and tobacco from America and the West Indies. There were fortunes to be made – and to be lost too.

How trading expeditions turned into trading companies

Four merchants put up money to fit out a trading ship.

The ship comes home and the merchants share the profits.

Next time, the four merchants decide to leave some of their profits in a 'pool' to pay for another ship, or two or three … .

Beginnings of shareholders and trading companies

It was expensive to buy and fit out ships for trade. They might be gone for months or years, they might be captured or sunk. To spread the cost, several merchants and rich people joined together to put money into an expedition. If the ship was lost, they had each only lost a little. If it came home with a rich cargo, they shared plenty of money. All this started in Elizabeth I's reign and very quickly one expedition became a regular trading company.

◄ **Fig 2**

Q1 When did merchants first start to become **shareholders** in trading expeditions?

Q2 How did these trading expeditions turn into trading companies?

Beginnings of colonies and empires

Some parts of the world were already well-organised trading countries. America, the West Indies and Africa, however, were inhabited by people living mainly by hunting and farming, with no developed trade for Europeans to link into. The temptation for Europeans armed with guns and soldiers was to take over their land. European people went to settle in places such as the Americas and parts of Africa. These were called **colonies**. They then produced goods to sell to the home country, as well as clearing the land to farm.

▼ ***Fig 3*** *Trade routes to Europe in 1750.*

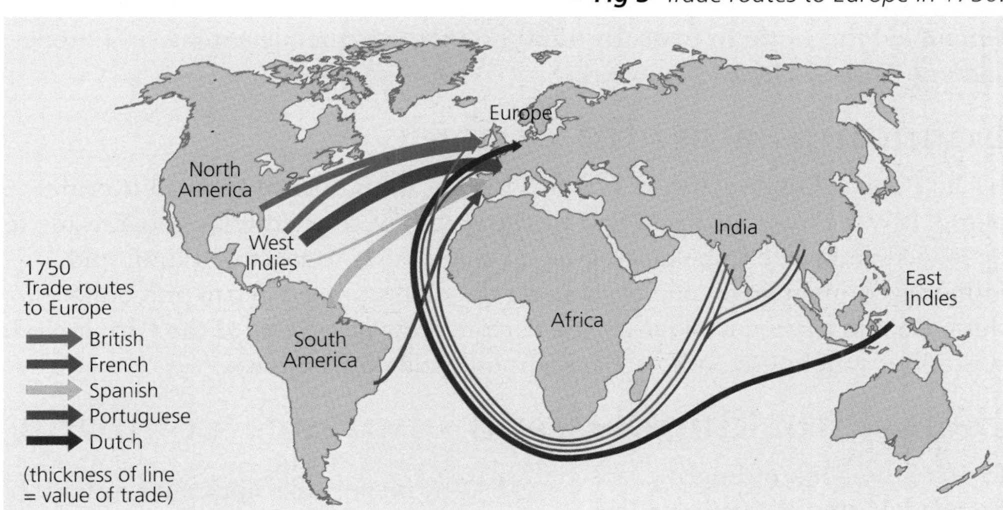

The sea powers of Europe gained empires

These colonies became the basis of overseas **empires** for Europeans. The main European countries with empires were the five sea powers of Europe: Portugal, Holland, Spain, France and Britain. The first two were the weakest and soon dropped out of the main race. The other three spent most of the eighteenth century fighting it out as to who should be 'top dog'. From about 1650 it was clear that the colonies were bringing in an excellent profit and helping to make Britain rich. Nearly every war from then on had something to do with the empire.

Key words

colony – land or country taken over, settled in and run by a more powerful nation, often far away
empire – a collection of colonies
shareholder – someone who puts money into an expedition and therefore holds a share of the profits (or losses)

SUMMARY

- Trade was growing and trading companies were formed with regular shareholders.
- Europeans took over (colonised) land in places such as America.
- The five European sea powers had empires; the French, British and Spanish were the most powerful.

SUMMARY *activity*

Look at a map in an atlas. Explain why France, Spain, Portugal and Holland were just as likely as Britain to gain overseas empires.

53 Britain grows rich 1650–1750

In this section of the book you will learn the following things:

- Britain was gaining a large empire;
- London was a centre of trade;
- new industries were beginning.

The British Empire

Fighting it out with the French and Spanish, the British empire grew and Britain became richer. British merchants were trading with about 14 million people in the British Empire and, with the biggest number of merchant ships, Britain led the world in trade. By 1750 London was the biggest city in Europe and one of the richest in the world.

London as a centre of trade

In the Pool of London, below London Bridge, ships docked from all over the world. It was a forest of masts, and the quaysides were piled with goods, some to be loaded and some to be taken away to warehouses to be stored until sold. Hundreds of men were employed along the docks to load, repair and build the ships. Behind these quaysides lay the narrow, crowded streets of the City itself. It was full of warehouses, offices, banks, houses and coffee houses.

Banks, stockbrokers and insurance companies

In 1694 the Bank of England was founded. It proved so reliable that with other new banks it made it easy for merchants to borrow money. The trading companies that had sprung up when a few merchants invested money fitting out a ship now threw their net much wider. Anyone with money to invest could go to a **stockbroker** and buy shares in a trading company. To encourage merchants to invest in risky things like ships, **insurance** companies were started in the 1690s. The most famous one was called Lloyd's, because the men who started it met in Lloyd's Coffee House. London was not the only successful port. Bristol, Liverpool and Glasgow grew rich on the trade in cotton, tobacco, sugar and slaves.

Q1 Why were banks important to trade?

Q2 What did a stockbroker sell?

► ***Fig 1*** *A London coffee house.*

Beginnings of industry

Industry was beginning to grow as well, but the really large expansion would take place after 1750. In 1710, Abraham Darby invented a new way to make clean coal, called coke, which he could use to make cast iron. This meant a great increase in the making of iron. In 1711, Thomas Newcomen made the first successful steam engine to pump water out of Cornish tin mines. Coal and shipbuilding were growing industries. Woollen clothmaking was widespread and linen was a new industry in northern Ireland. Another new industry was sugar refining.

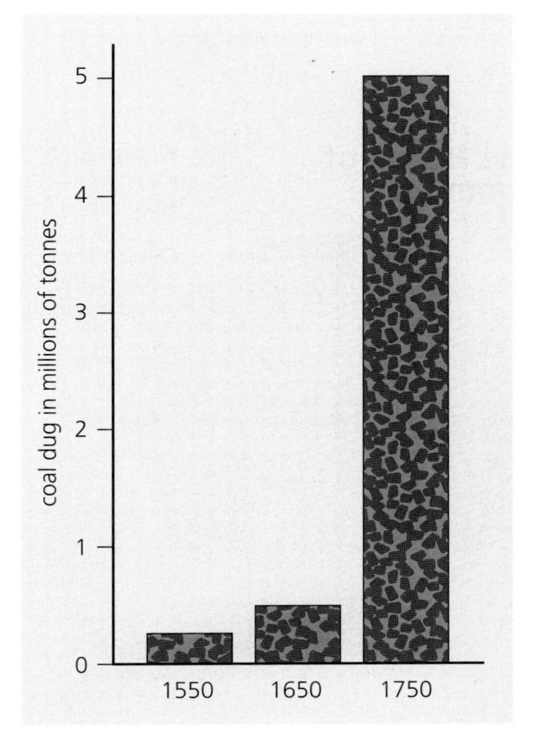

▲ ***Fig 2*** *The growth of the coal industry.*

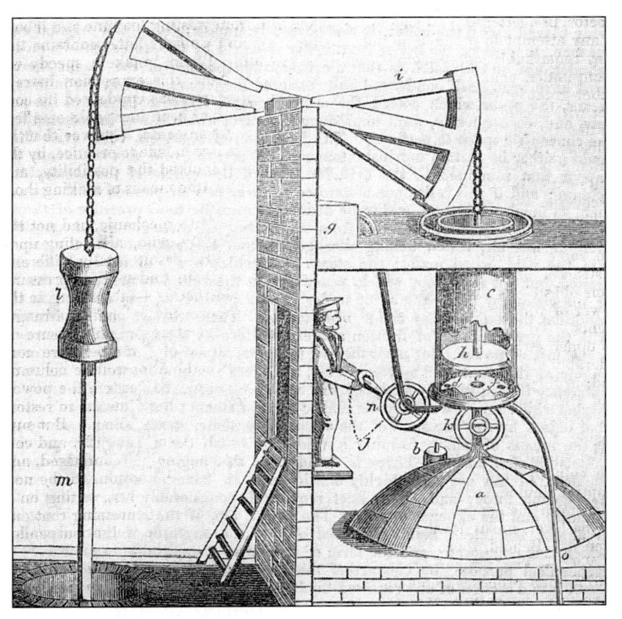

▲ ***Fig 3*** *Newcomen's engine.*

Key words

insurance – many people pay a small sum of money to insure their houses, ships or anything else. If one person's property is destroyed, the insurance company which collected the money, pays out the value of the house, ship etc

stockbroker – someone who buys and sells shares (sometimes called stocks)

SUMMARY

- Britain was gaining a large empire and leading the world in trade.
- London was at the centre of Britain's trade, with its banks, stockbrokers and insurance companies helping trade to grow.
- Old industries (such as coal) were growing and new industries (such as sugar refining) beginning.

SUMMARY *activity*

Why were both trade and industry growing so much at this time?

54 George I and George II

In this section of the book you will learn the following things:

- George I became King in 1714;
- he left the work of running the country to the Cabinet and Sir Robert Walpole.

George I 1714–1727

George I became King in 1714 at the age of 54. He was a cold man whose private life was a scandal. He had quarrelled with his wife and condoned the murder of her lover. Then he shut her up in a German castle for 30 years until she died. Lacking a Queen, George brought over two women friends, the Countess of Kielmansegge and the Countess of Schulenberg. George knew nothing of English politics, could not wait to get back to Hanover in Germany and only spoke German. So how was he going to be King of England?

The Cabinet

Both George I and his son, George II, with whom he was not on speaking terms, used English nobles and gentry as ministers to run the country, just as previous King and Queens had done. A group of the most important advisers or ministers were now known as the **Cabinet**. Since George would not and could not take charge of these Cabinet meetings, someone had to do it for him. This person then had to report back to the King and get his agreement to all the matters that had been decided. Thus was born the job of Prime Minister or 'first among ministers'. The other job the Prime Minister had to do was to get the House of Commons to agree to what was done, because it voted the money to pay for everything.

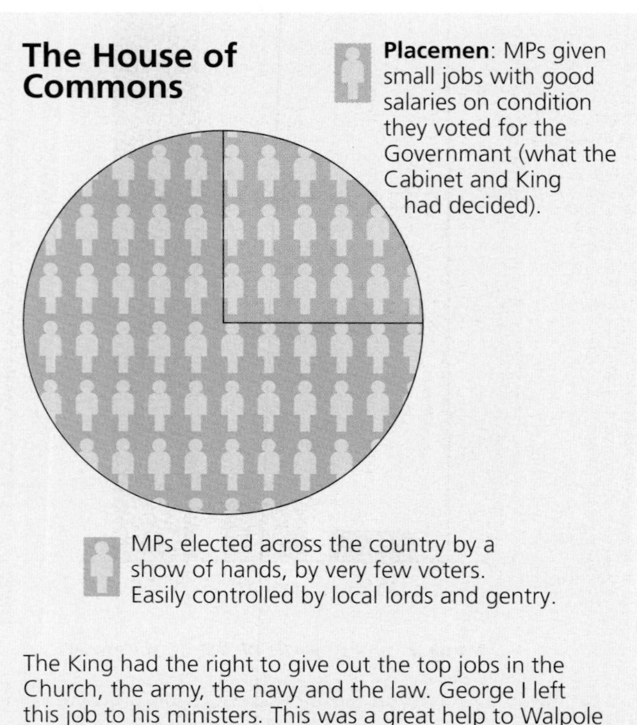

▲ ***Fig 1*** *How to control the House of Commons in the 1720s–40s.*

Q1 Who did George I and George II use to run the country?

Q2 What were the most important ministers known as?

Sir Robert Walpole

By chance a remarkable man appeared on the scene: Sir Robert Walpole, who was first or Prime Minister from 1721–1742. He was a wealthy Norfolk countryman who loved hunting and country sports, but he also enjoyed his work as the King's minister. He was good at managing the King and was outstanding at managing the House of Commons. When George I died, George II was prepared to hate his father's trusted minister, but Walpole had wisely befriended the new Queen and also persuaded the Commons to grant a rise in money to the new King. So Walpole continued on his way.

▲ **Fig 2** *Sir Robert Walpole.*

◀ **Fig 3** *Number 10 Downing Street, built for Walpole in 1736.*

▼ **Fig 4** *How Walpole managed the Government.*

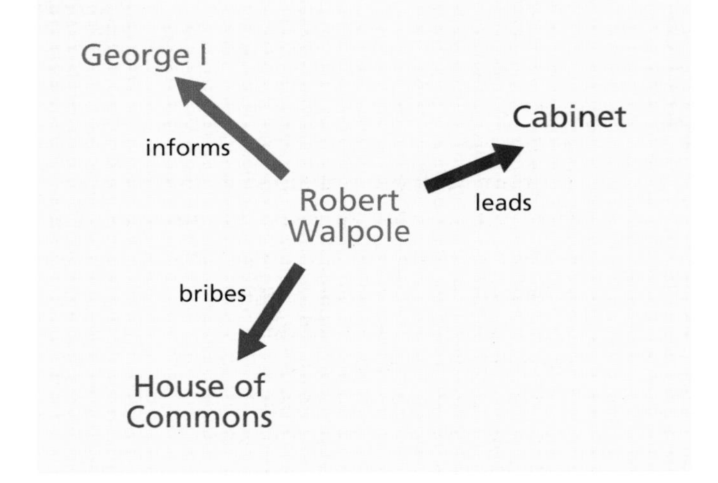

Q3 What three jobs did the Prime Minister do?

Key words

Cabinet – called after the small private room in the palace where ministers had started to meet in previous reigns

placemen – MPs who were given jobs or positions as long as they voted for the Government (in those days MPs were not paid for being MPs)

SUMMARY

- George I left the running of the country to the Cabinet.
- This meant that one minister had to report to the King and manage the House of Commons.
- Sir Robert Walpole became the first Prime Minister (although this was not an official title).

SUMMARY *activity*

Walpole controlled the House of Commons by giving jobs to MPs and jobs to the nobles and gentry who controlled the election of MPs. Where did Walpole get these jobs from?

55 Empire: India and America

In this section of the book you will learn the following things:

- trading companies were founded with regular trade to places such as India;
- Britain gained colonies in North America;
- there were frequent wars between the great powers about colonies and empires.

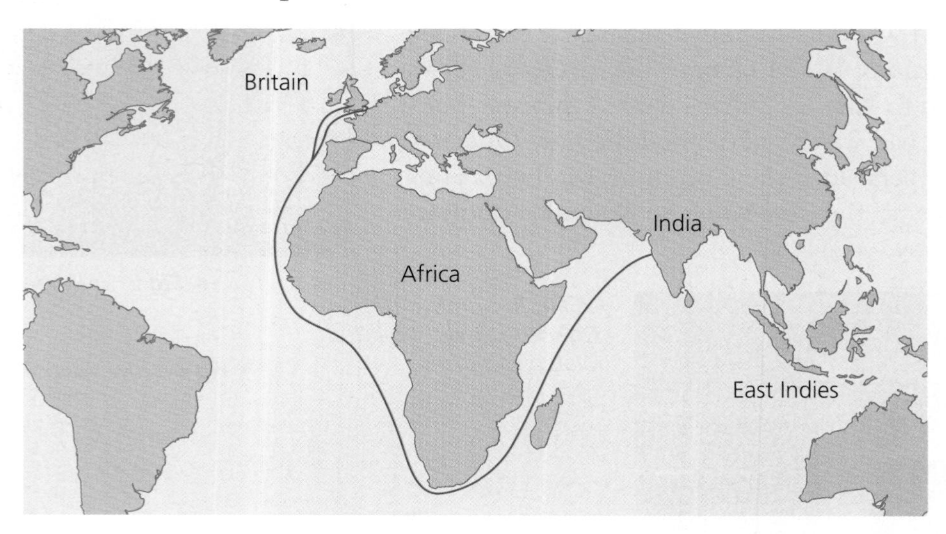

◀ *Fig 1 The main trade route of the East India Company.*

India

Q1 What was the most famous British trading company?

Q2 Where did it do most of its trade?

Robert Walpole remained as the King's first minister for 21 years. He prospered and so did Britain. All the great powers wanted more trade and they fought each other on and off all through the 1600s and 1700s. The most famous British trading company was called the East India Company. It was founded in Elizabeth I's reign and after failing to force the Dutch to allow it to trade in the East Indies, the East India Company turned its attention to India itself.

▶ *Fig 2 The directors of the East India Company watched the money roll in as ships unloaded cargoes of cotton, tea and spices at Bristol and London, then sailed back for more.*

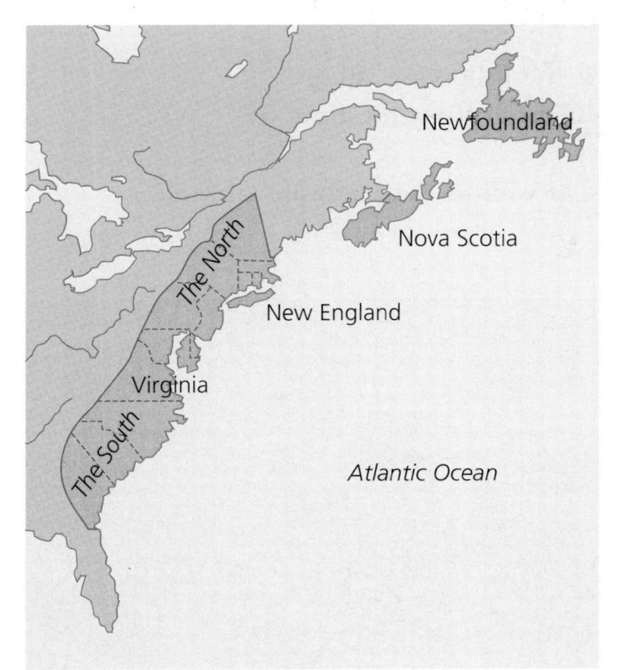

▲ ***Fig 3*** *English colonies in America in the early 1700s.*

America

By the 1730s there were 13 **colonies**. The colonists needed workers. Any native people who had not been wiped out by European disease were not suited to farm work. At first Britain sent over convicts, but they were not used to the climate in the south and died quickly. The answer was found by a merchant who landed in Africa and bought some prisoners from an African chief. He shipped them to America and sold them to the colonists to work on their **plantations**. This was the beginning of the slave trade. The situation was different in the northern colonies; the climate did not suit large plantations of tobacco and cotton, so the settlers had smaller farms to work.

Q3 How did the slave trade begin?

The War of Jenkins' Ear

Some British traders wanted to trade freely with the colonies of other countries. One of them was called Captain Jenkins. He insisted on trading illegally with Spanish colonies, and this so enraged the Spanish that his ship was boarded and searched and Jenkins' ear was cut off in the struggle. Outraged, he sailed for England, with his ear in a box. He demanded that Britain should go to war with Spain. Walpole had no sympathy with Jenkins and prophesied that the war would not go well, but when Jenkins showed his ear to the House of Commons there was a howl of protest against Spain and Britain rushed to war.

▲ ***Fig 4*** *A Spanish treasure ship in the 1600s.*

Key words

colony – land or country taken over, settled in and run by a more powerful nation, often far away

plantation – a huge farm in the southern colonies in North America, growing tobacco or cotton

SUMMARY

- Britain increased trade with India via the East India Company.
- Britain had gained 13 colonies in North America by the early 1700s.
- Slaves from Africa worked on the plantations of the most southern of the 13 colonies.
- Some British traders broke agreements about trading with other countries' colonies and this led to war.

SUMMARY *activity*

Why do you think the House of Commons was so keen for Britain to rush into war with Spain?

56 Religion by 1750

In this section of the book you will learn the following things:

- **the Church of England was the main Church from the time of Henry VIII;**
- **there were other Protestant Churches, as well as the Catholic Church.**

Questioning religion

Since Henry VIII had broken with the Pope and become head of the Church in England, the issue of religion had appeared to be settled. This was far from the case, however. Once Martin Luther had questioned the authority of the Catholic Church and the Pope, the way was open for a lot more questioning.

▲ ***Fig 1*** *An execution. Despite strong feelings about religion, the eighteenth century was a violent time. Public hangings were frequent.*

Cromwell and religion in the Commonwealth

This questioning reached its height during the Commonwealth (1649–1660). With the King of England put to death, the world was turned upside down. Cromwell himself was tolerant; he was in favour of allowing everyone to worship as they pleased. He even allowed Jews freedom of worship – the first time this had been allowed since 1290. Most of his advisers were less tolerant, however, so Catholics were banned.

Q1 Who opened the way for a lot more questioning of religion?

Q2 What was Cromwell in favour of?

Different Protestants

Most other Protestants were allowed to worship freely and many sects sprang up: there were Anabaptists and Adamites, Fifth Monarchists and Ranters. Most did not last very long, but one group that did were the Quakers, who believed that every person could get in touch with God, so therefore no one person was any more important than any other. One Quaker horrified the nobles by not taking his hat off in the presence of the King.

Q3 Why do you think the nobles were horrified that the Quaker did not take his hat off in the presence of the King?

The Church of England and others

Once the Church of England settled back into place when Charles II came to the throne, it was not really threatened again. After 1689 Catholics and **Nonconformists** were allowed to worship, but were not allowed to hold jobs in the government, be Members of Parliament or go to university. The trouble with the Church of England was that it had life too easy. Younger sons from well-off families looked on becoming a clergyman as a good job at a nice church in the country. By the mid-1700s they were losing touch with the working people, particularly in the fast growing cities.

A Church of England clergyman, James Woodforde

income:	£400 a year;
servants:	5;
horses:	3;
occupation:	preaching a sermon once a week, helping the poor;
amusements:	dancing, going to the theatre, fishing and dining.

▲ ***Fig 2***

◀ ***Fig 3*** *John Wesley.*

John and Charles Wesley and the founding of Methodism

John and Charles Wesley wanted to bring God to working people. They travelled around the country preaching to crowds. They often ran into trouble, but equally often people listened to them. They preached non-violence and the love of God, but even so the Church of England did not like such activities going on outside churches. The **Methodists** broke away to found their own Church.

Key words

Methodists – members of a Nonconformist Church founded by John and Charles Wesley

Nonconformists – Protestants who did not conform to (accept the rules of) the established religion, i.e. the Church of England

SUMMARY

- The Church of England was established under Henry VIII and survived threats from Catholics and others.
- During the Commonwealth, many different religious sects flourished.
- After 1689 Catholics and Nonconformists could worship but could not hold important jobs.

SUMMARY *activity*

Why was it sensible to be a member of the Church of England if you wanted to get on in life?

57 Science moves on 1500–1750

In this section of the book you will learn the following things:

- about Galileo and his observations;
- about the founding of the Royal Society;
- about some famous scientists.

Galileo and new ideas

In 1500 knowledge was still based on the ideas of the Ancient Greeks rather than on experiment. One of the first to speak out against this was Galileo in 1609. He looked at the planets through a telescope and said that the work of the Polish **astronomer**, Copernicus, some years before, was correct. Far from being the centre of the universe, the earth went round the sun. There was an outcry from old-fashioned scholars and the Church but, despite this, Galileo's ideas spread. This was mainly because they were printed as a book, so anyone could read about them.

▼ Fig 1

New ways for old

The Ancient Greeks said:
the sun goes round the earth.

The Church said:
the sun goes round the earth.

The new scientists said:
Look through a telescope.
Believe what you see.

Before the printing press:
books had to be copied by hand.

After the printing press:
books were printed mechanically.

Result:
far more books were produced.

The printing press was invented in Germany by Gutenberg in the 1400s and brought to England by William Caxton in 1476.

▲ Fig 2

The Royal Society

After Galileo, other people also carried out experiments: that is, they observed things, noted them down and then drew a conclusion. A group of British scientists, fired by these ideas, formed the Royal Society, supported from 1662 by Charles II, who often came to meetings. All sorts of things were discussed, from breathing ('how it is managed by nature and what use it is') to watching experiments with magnets. Soon similar societies were founded in other countries.

Q1 Why did Galileo's ideas spread?

Q2 Who formed the Royal Society?

Q3 Who supported the Royal Society?

Robert Boyle

Robert Boyle was born in 1627 and by his experiments founded modern chemistry. He rejected the old vague ideas of everything being made of the elements of fire, water, earth and air, and carried out detailed experiments to show such things as how the volume of a gas decreases in proportion as the pressure increases.

The Royal **Observatory** at Greenwich was built in 1676. Charles II appointed an Astronomer Royal. His job was to work out the position of stars observed from Greenwich. Sailors anywhere in the world could observe the same stars which would help them to work out their position in relation to Greenwich.

▲ *Fig 3*

Q4 What other scientific institution did Charles II support?

Isaac Newton

Like Boyle, Newton was a member of the Royal Society and was a genius. Among many discoveries, he put forward the theory of gravity, revolutionised the study of mathematics and discovered that light is made up of a mixture of colours. A professor at Cambridge, he then became President of the Royal Society.

▲ ***Fig 4*** *Sir Isaac Newton.*

Key words

astronomer – a person who studies the stars and planets
observatory – a building from which to look at the stars and planets

SUMMARY

- Galileo supported the ideas of Copernicus that the earth moved round the sun.
- Other scientists observed and experimented too; some British scientists founded the Royal Society in 1662.
- It was supported by Charles II.
- Two famous members of the Royal Society were Robert Boyle and Isaac Newton.

SUMMARY *activity*

Could the Royal Society have existed in the Middle Ages? Give reasons for your answer.

58 Women

In this section of the book you will learn the following things:

- why women do not appear in history books;
- about running a house and having children.

Why don't women appear in history books?

Very few women appear in history books. There are two main reason for this. One is that until recently men wrote all the history books, and wrote about events and changes that were important to men. The only women who appeared were women who took part in a man's world, such as Elizabeth I. The second is that because of their domestic tasks women rarely had much time to do anything in the active, outside world.

▲ **Fig 1** *Rich and fashionable women in the sixteenth (left) and eighteenth (right) centuries.*

▼ **Fig 2**

Tudor women

The widow of a merchant could carry on his business.

Widow Jane Rawe – travelled between London, France and Antwerp dealing in foreign exchange

Widow Rose – dealt in heavy woollen cloth

Widow Fayrey – dealt in many different woollen cloths

Widow Ann Baynham – farmed hundreds of acres near Calais, in France, and dealt in wool, wine and herrings

What did women do?

Running a house was not just a question of turning on the washing machine and putting a ready-made meal in the microwave. It meant everything from growing food, to preparing it, cooking it and preserving it for the winter. Even in small households the housewife kept chickens and ran the kitchen vegetable garden. She made clothes and bed linen, baked bread and brewed **ale.** She prepared and cooked the food, and cleaned. Bigger households preserved food by pickling, smoking, drying, salting and **candying**. The housewife made cheese, grew herbs and made herbal medicines for coughs and other complaints. In good weather in the spring, she had gigantic washes of the winter bed linen that was then hung on bushes to dry. In between all this she might have up to ten or more pregnancies, from which she could expect only about half the children to live beyond the age of five.

Q1 How many ways of preserving food are listed?

Q2 How is food preserved nowadays? List all the ways you can think of.

Help in the house

The good thing was that women were not usually left on their own to do all these things. On big farms there would be several maidservants and a cook. They would do all the work with the housewife, which would include feeding the men who worked on the farm, so around 20 people would sit down to eat each day.

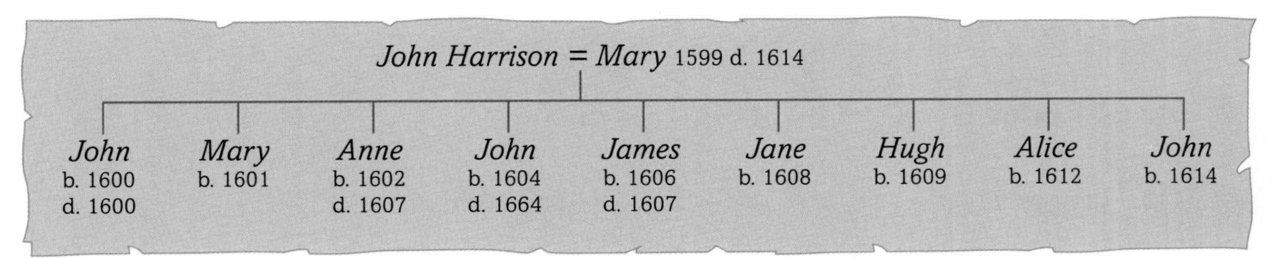

▲ ***Fig 3*** *Forty-five per cent of better-off women died before they were 50. Half of these died of complications from childbirth. Poor people died younger than the better off.*

Having children

Many women could expect a pregnancy a year and to die young. Although very young marriages did take place, most caring parents did not like to see their daughters marry before 19 or 20 years of age. They listed dangerous births, stunted growth and shortened lives as the effects of marriage under 16 years of age. Among less well-off people marriage was often later than this. Couples waited until they had enough to live on before marrying.

Key words

ale – weak beer (drunk by most people; dirty water was too dangerous to drink)

candying – preserving in sugar

SUMMARY

- Women were too busy having children and running a house to be very active outside the home.
- A few women did do jobs in a man's world.

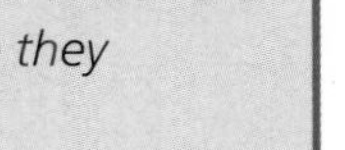

SUMMARY *activity*

Which jobs are the same today in running a house? Which are different? Why are they different?

Kings and Queens 1485–1760

	born	reigned	died
Henry VII	1456	1485–1509	1509
Henry VIII	1491	1509–1547	1547
Edward VI	1537	1547–1553	1553
Mary	1516	1553–1558	1558
Elizabeth I	1533	1558–1603	1603
James I	1566	1603–1625	1625
Charles I	1600	1625–1649	1649
Commonwealth		*1649–1660*	
Charles II	1630	1660–1685	1685
James II	1633	1685–1688	1701
William and Mary	1650 1662	1688–1702 1688–1694	1702 (William) 1694 (Mary)
Anne	1665	1702–1714	1714
George I	1660	1714–1727	1727
George II	1683	1727–1760	1760

Note: See the key to the crowns on page 250.

Making of the United Kingdom: Timeline 1516–1742

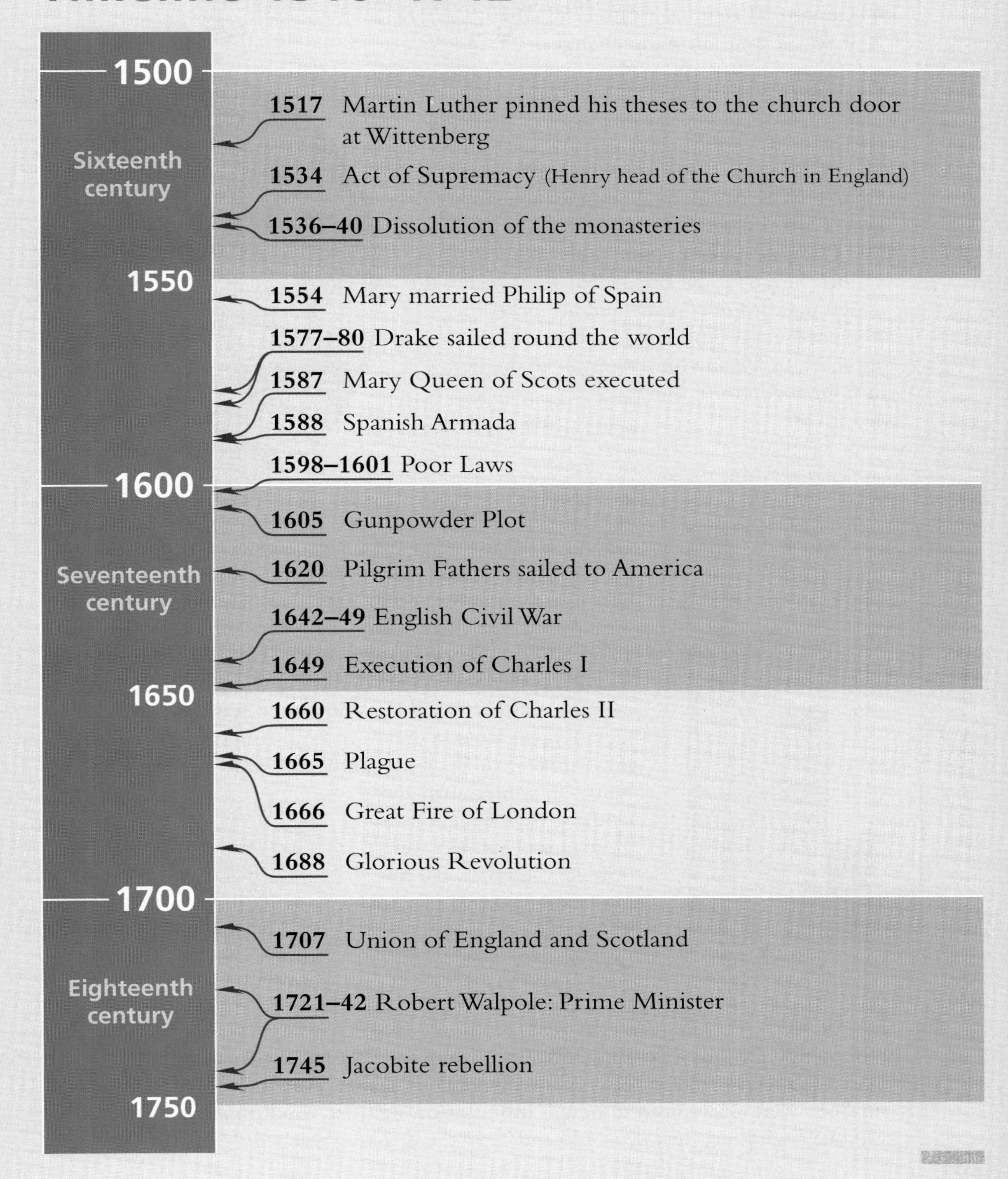

59 Britain in 1750

In this section of the book you will learn the following things:

- **George III reigned from 1760–1820;**
- **it was a time of many changes.**

George II 1727–1760 and George III 1760–1820

In 1750, George II was King; ten years later George III began his long reign, which lasted from 1760–1820. George III, unlike the previous two Georges, spoke English as his first language and felt himself to be British. He was a man with a high standard of conduct and his nickname, 'Farmer George', indicated his down-to-earth approach to life and his interest in all the new farming methods of the time.

► ***Fig 1*** *George III.*

Population (millions)
16
14
12
10
8
6
4
2
0
1086 1500 1700 1750 1800

◄ ***Fig 2*** *Growth of population.*

Falling death rate

George III's long reign saw many changes. The population was growing fast because the death rate was falling. Before this time most people could expect to have many children but up to half of them would die before the age of five. From about 1750, there were fewer deaths. This appears to be due to a better diet and living conditions, which strengthened people's resistance to illness. More food was produced, including potatoes (a discovery from America), cheese and meat; more coal was being produced, which meant warmer homes in winter; soap and clothing were being made more cheaply and so were iron pots and pans. All this meant more cleanliness and less illness.

Q1 Write down the improvements in diet and living conditions in the second half of the eighteenth century.

Gin drinking

Not that everything was wonderful. There were no great improvements in medical science. Dysentery, typhus, tuberculosis, scarlet fever and smallpox were widespread, although **inoculation against smallpox** was just beginning. Between 1720 and 1750 gin drinking reached a peak, leading to many health problems. In 1751, the Government put a heavy tax on all spirits and controls on their sale. From then on the problem lessened.

Q2 What did the Government do about gin drinking in 1751?

Gin

sulphuric acid
oil of almonds
oil of turpentine
spirits of wine
(raw alcohol)
sugar
lime water
rose water
alum
salt of tartar

A landlord's recipe for gin in the 1700s. Good gin would have been bad enough, but many landlords used anything alcoholic they had to hand. Brews like this led to blindness, insanity and death.

▲ ***Fig 3***

▲ ***Fig 4*** *Gin Lane, a 1751 engraving by William Hogarth.*

Other changes

Other changes in George III's reign included the loss of the American colonies, but the growth of an empire in India. Empire or not, trade increased around the world. At home, there were changes in agriculture leading to more food being produced; the towns and cities grew because trade and industry were growing. The industries that expanded most were coal and iron and the new cotton industry. Transport began to improve as better roads were built and canals carved across the country to carry heavy goods. All these developments led to demands to change the ways in which the country was run, particularly after the French Revolution in 1789.

Key words

inoculation against smallpox – taking a little pus from a smallpox scab and rubbing it into a cut on a healthy person's arm. They then got the disease mildly, which gave them immunity (protection) in the future.

SUMMARY

- After 1750 the population rose because of better food and living conditions.
- The American colonies were lost, but Britain gained land in India.
- There was great growth in trade and industry.
- Agriculture changed so that more food was produced.
- Better roads and canals meant better transport.
- All these developments led to changes in the way the country was run.

SUMMARY *activity*

Write out a list of the changes in George III's reign. What did they lead to?

60 Empire in 1750: India

In this section of the book you will learn the following things:

- **the British and French were rivals for trade in India;**
- **the British East India Company became the world's supreme trading company.**

Britain and France

By 1750 the rivalry between Britain and France was growing. There were two main areas of conflict: one was India, the other America. Both countries had trading posts in India and, at first, trade was all they were interested in. However, India was in turmoil because of the break-up of the old **Mogul empire** into a number of independent states. Some states were weaker than others. Whoever controlled the weak states would control their trade, and here lay the temptation for the French and British. The French attempted to control parts of southern India but were challenged by the British, who were led by Robert Clive.

Q1 Why was India in turmoil?

Q2 Why were the French and British tempted to control weak states in India?

Robert Clive and the French

Clive had come out to India as a clerk in the East India Company. The company controlled all British trading with India and acted more or less as though it was the British Government. Clive led a small force of soldiers against the French, who made peace. Not for long, however. Fighting broke out again and did not end until 1761. A treaty was signed between the British and French, which stated that France was not allowed to have an army in India. The way was open for the British East India Company to expand.

▲ ***Fig 1*** *Robert Clive.*

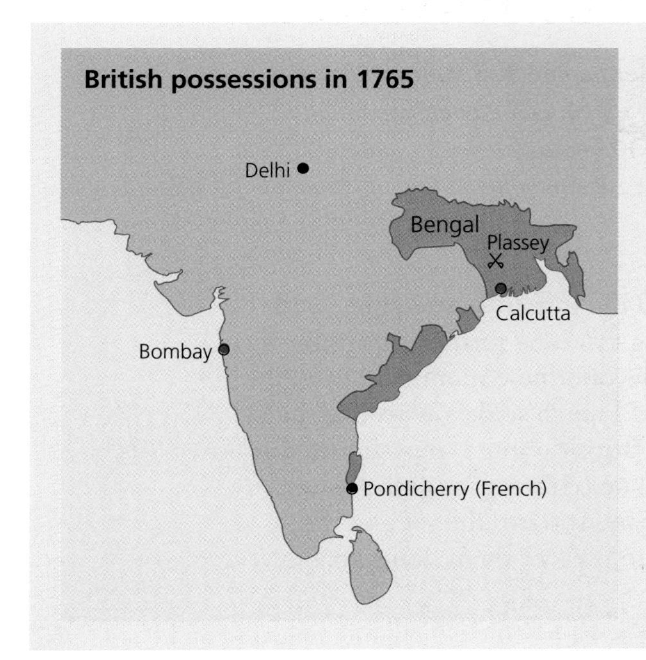

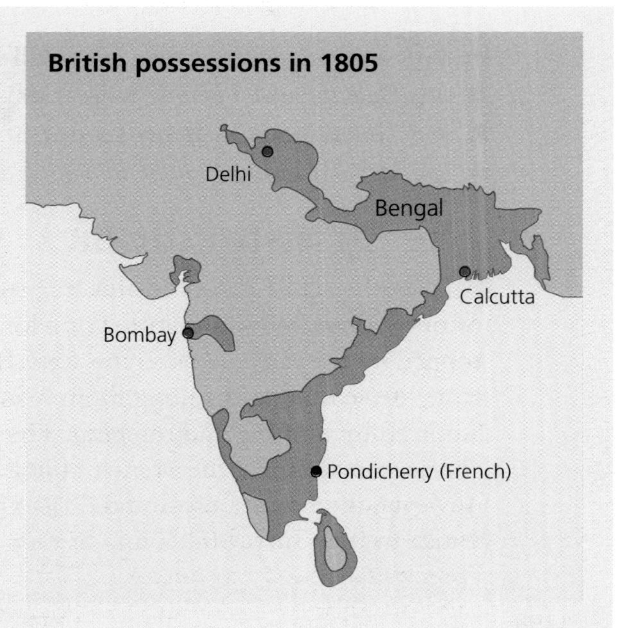

▲ ***Fig 2*** *The growth of British power in India.*

Clive and India

Clive went on to take control of Bengal at the Battle of Plassey in 1757. He then left India and the merchants of the East India Company made fortunes in trade, but **corruption** was **rife**. Clive was sent back to India in 1765 to stop the corruption. He forbade members of the company to accept presents (bribes) and forbade **private trading**, but raised the salaries of the men working for the company to compensate them. Things improved overall and the East India Company traded for many years before the British Government took over its control. Clive returned to England where his enemies accused him of taking bribes himself, years before. Two years later, after a lot of illness, he committed suicide.

Q3 What did Clive do to try to sort out corruption in the East India Company?

Q4 Why do you think private trading might be a bad thing for members of the East India Company to do?

Key words

corruption – not dealing fairly, i.e. taking bribes
Mogul empire – an empire that had controlled most of India for 200 years
private trading – men employed by the East India Company also traded in their own right to make their own profits
rife – widespread

SUMMARY

- The French and British were rivals in trade.
- The British gained control of trade in India.
- Robert Clive reformed the British East India Company to keep corruption under control.

SUMMARY *activity*

In what way was Robert Clive a founder of the British Empire in India?

61 Empire in 1750: America

In this section of the book you will learn the following things:

- **the British and French were rivals in North America;**
- **the Seven Years War broke out in 1756;**
- **the British gained most at the end of the war.**

The British colonies

In 1750, the 13 British **colonies** hugged the east coast, stretching inland for only about 240 kilometres. For a long time any further expansion was stopped by the mountains to the west. Beyond these mountains lived the native Americans and among them many French settlers who, like them, also lived by hunting and trapping. The British wanted to push into this land to start farming; the French built a line of forts to stop them. However, the French also wanted to expand towards the sea and the British in their turn, built a line of forts to prevent them doing so.

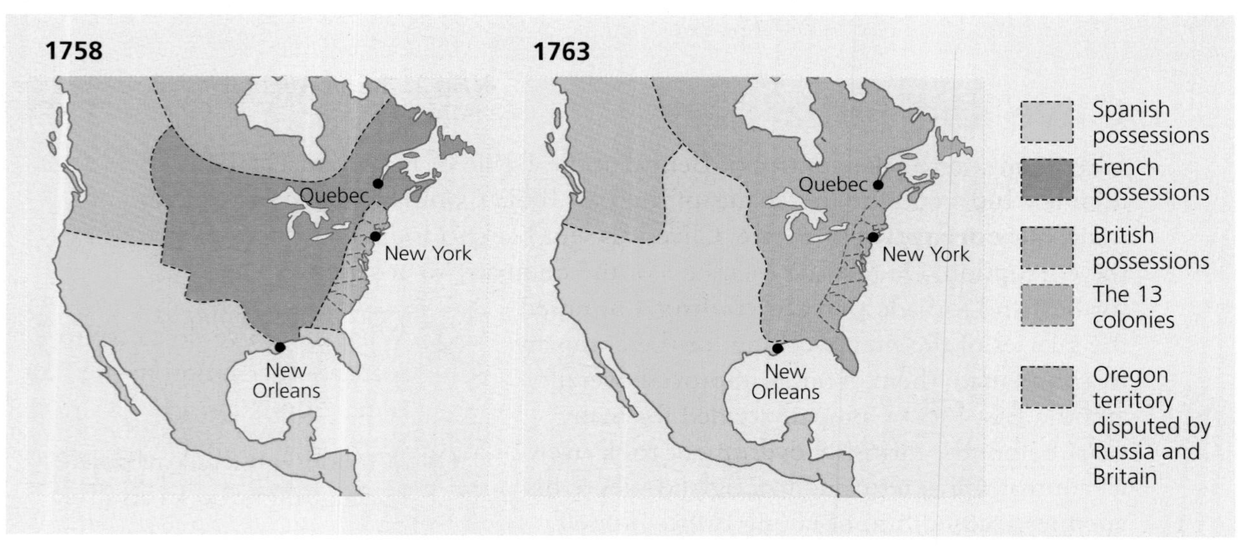

▲ ***Fig 1*** *Changing ownership of North America.*

The Seven Years War 1756–1763

In 1756 Britain and France went to war. Part of the war was fought in Europe, part in India and a very important part in North America. Here the long-running battles between the French and the British settlers erupted into war. The French captured some British forts and looked all set to sweep down on the British colonies. The fighting in Europe diverted the French, however, and the British Navy took the opportunity of stopping supplies getting across the Atlantic to the French in the forts.

Q1 What did the British Navy do?

Q2 What sort of supplies do you think the forts would need?

General Wolfe and Quebec 1759

Then the British were ready to counter-attack; they wanted to take Quebec from the French. A fleet of 170 ships sailed up the St Lawrence River carrying a British army under General James Wolfe. The aim was to take the French forts that guarded Quebec, which were high on the cliffs called the Heights of Abraham. The sailors found a secret path up the cliffs and, during the night, the whole of Wolfe's army climbed to the top. The next morning the French were taken completely by surprise and the British took Quebec. In the next year, 1760, they went on to take Montreal. The war ended in 1763 with Britain gaining more land.

► ***Fig 2*** *The British Army taking Quebec in October 1759: British soldiers climbing the Heights of Abraham.*

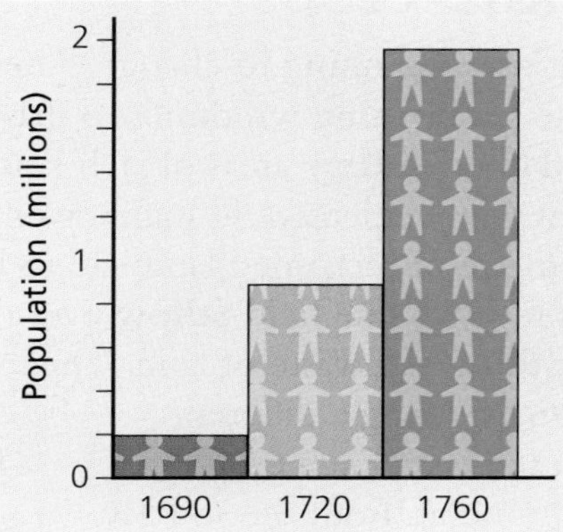

▲ ***Fig 3*** *Growth of population in the 13 British colonies.*

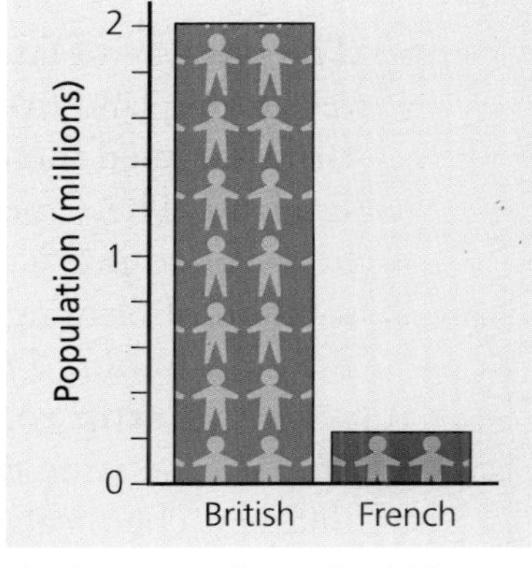

▲ ***Fig 4*** *Numbers of British and French settlers in North America in 1760.*

Q3 What did the British want to take from the French?

Q4 How did the British take Quebec?

Key words

colonies – lands taken over, settled in and run by a more powerful country, often far away

SUMMARY

- The 13 British colonies were on the east coast of North America.
- The French settlers were further inland, on the other side of the mountains.
- Both the British and the French built forts to stop each other gaining more land.
- The British gained most from the fighting, partly due to the British Navy.

SUMMARY *activity*

Why were the British the most likely nation to gain land in North America?

62 Agriculture in 1750

In this section of the book you will learn the following things:

- the old way of farming was beginning to change;
- there were improvements in crop growing and animal breeding.

The Norfolk four-course crop rotation (learnt from the Dutch)

These four crops would rotate in four fields for four years.

The clover put nitrogen back into the soil. The turnips were useful for winter food for cattle.

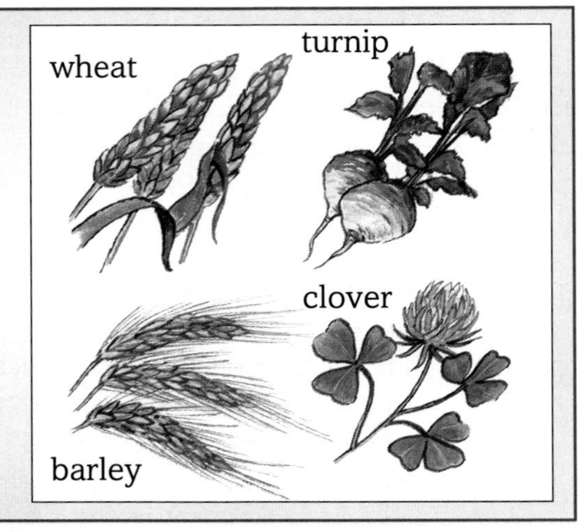

▲ *Fig 1*

More land, more crops

The old way of farming was beginning to change. The Dutch had been reclaiming land from the sea by using windmills to drive pumps. The British copied them and drained large areas of rich land in eastern England. These methods were expensive in manpower and money, however, so every centimetre of reclaimed land had to be used. The old method of farming was to leave one field **fallow** every third year. To the land-hungry Dutch this was a waste of land. They worked out a system of **crop rotation**, growing a different crop on the same field each year. Each crop took different chemicals and minerals from the soil. By the mid-eighteenth century, wealthy British farmers were taking up the idea of crop rotation with enthusiasm.

Q1 What was the old way of farming?

Q2 What was crop rotation?

The seed drill and the horse hoe

Seed had always been sown by throwing handfuls of grain from a basket. Up to three-quarters was blown away or eaten by birds. Jethro Tull invented a seed drill which did three things: it dug a hole, allowed the seed to be trickled in and the hole covered with earth. Once seeds were sown in rows it was also easier to weed between them. Another new machine was a horse hoe: a horse pulled several hoes, so several rows of seeds could be weeded at once. By the middle of the eighteenth century both the seed drill and the horse hoe were growing in popularity.

Selective animal breeding and feeding

Another great improvement was in animal breeding. Robert Bakewell was one of many pioneers of new methods of animal breeding. Before then sheep and pigs were about as big as medium-sized dogs, and cows were less than half the size they are now. The improvements came about by **selective breeding** from the largest, healthiest animals. Another improvement was the growing of root crops like turnips that could be fed to animals during the winter. Before this time, when the grass stopped growing in winter, cows, pigs and sheep had nothing to live on and most had to be slaughtered. Only a few were kept to breed from the next year.

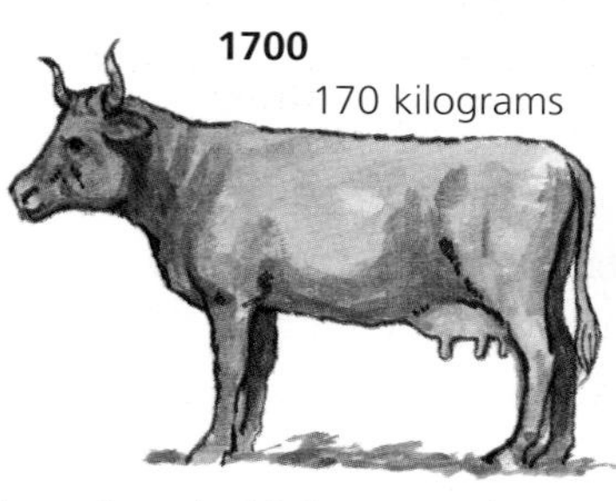

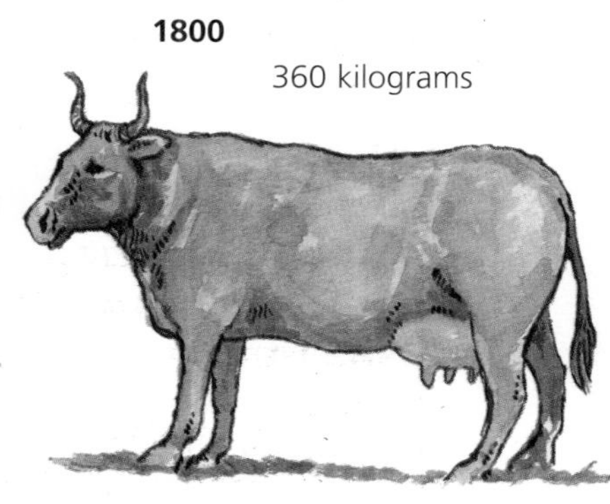

▲ ***Fig 2*** *Breeding improvements.*

Q3 Who was a pioneer of selective animal breeding?

Q4 How were the improvements made?

New farming magazines appeared. Arthur Young was a popular journalist. He wrote in 1768:

'One farmer sowed turnips and was at great pains to hoe them well; the neighbours ridiculed him but were surprised to see what good crops he gained.'

▲ ***Fig 3***

▲ ***Fig 4*** *Sheep shearing went on all over the country in summer. Sometimes wealthy farmers held sheep-shearing competitions. Through meeting at such gatherings, new ideas spread.*

Key words

crop rotation – growing a different crop on the same field each year

fallow – land resting, with no crops growing on it

selective breeding – choosing animals to breed together

SUMMARY

- Improvements in farming were: draining land, crop rotation, seed drills, horse hoes, selective animal breeding and growing root crops.

SUMMARY *activity*

Write about the farming improvements that took place in the eighteenth century. Include the ways in which farmers learnt about the improvements.

63 Changes in agriculture

In this section of the book you will learn the following things:

- **there were arguments for and against enclosure.**

Why follow the new methods of farming?

All the new methods of farming fired the enthusiasm of keen and, usually, wealthy farmers as they sat and talked together at sheep shearing events and other gatherings, or read the latest ideas on manuring in the new farming magazines. What about the ordinary farmer trudging between his strips in the old open fields, however? How could he breed animals selectively when all the villagers' animals roamed together? With unfenced strips, why weed when the weeds from a lazy neighbour's strip blew on to his land? Why manure when he had to carry the **manure** to each scattered strip? How could he afford a seed drill or a horse hoe?

▲ ***Fig 1*** *Jethro Tull.*

A major change

It might look as though there was no point in changing anything. There was one huge possibility looming, however, that would change the face of farming in Britain and the lives of its people within a short time. This possibility was enclosure. Look at the diagram of a medieval open field village on page 29. In many parts of Britain, particularly the Midlands, this was how farming was carried on until the eighteenth century. Then people began to say it was wasteful.

Q1 Why did the ordinary farmer not bother with the new ways of farming? Write down all the reasons you can.

Key dates for agricultural developments

end 1600s	Four-course crop rotation started in Norfolk. Drainage of land in East Anglia
1730s	Jethro Tull invented the seed drill and horse hoe
1760–1820	Peak time of Enclosure Acts
1770–1790	First machines for chopping turnips, **winnowing** and **threshing**
1783	First factory making ploughs

Enclosure

The owners of four-fifths of the land in a village had to agree to enclosure. Then an **Act** could be put through Parliament putting all the land in the village together and sharing it out according to how many strips each person owned. Everyone had to pay the cost of putting the Act through Parliament and of fencing their land. Often a poor farmer found the land he had been given was far from his cottage and was poor land. Many sold up and either worked for a richer farmer or went to the towns. The very poorest were those who had no legal right to strips or grazing land; they got nothing.

◄ ***Fig 2***

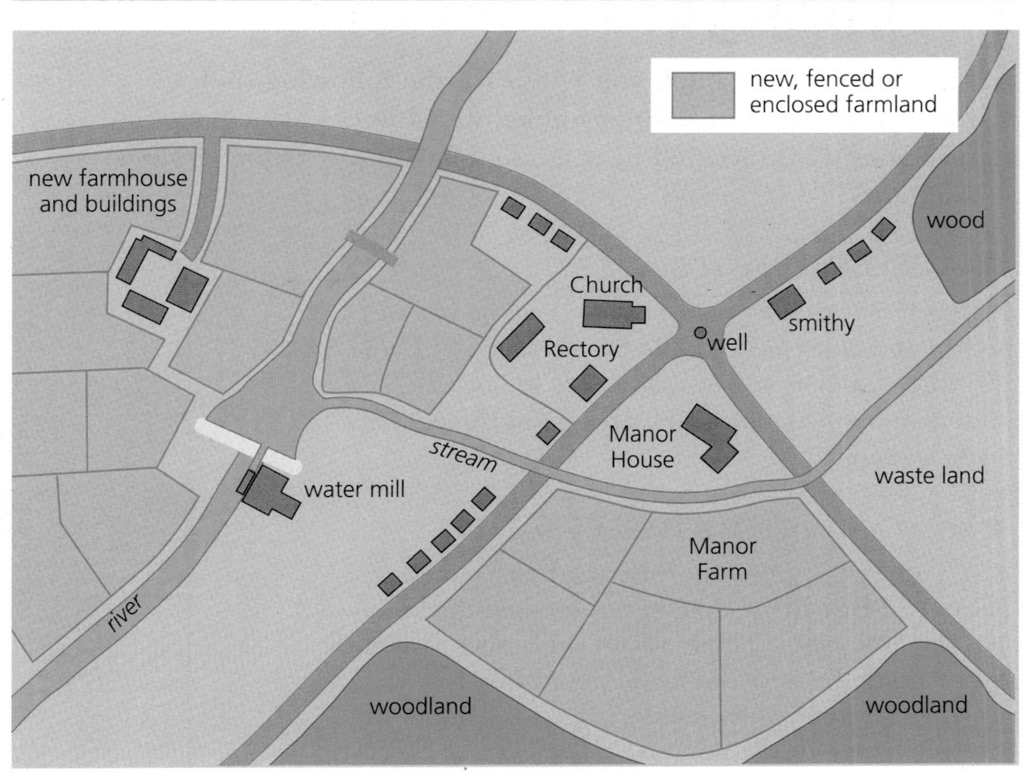

▲ *Fig 3 Part of the medieval open-field village.*

The picture was not all black, however. There was often plenty of work on the large new farms. Some small farmers turned to producing vegetables and eggs for the growing towns. Some moved to, and found a good living in the towns, or in transport, which was also a growing area of work.

Q2 Look at the diagram and compare it to the diagram on page 29. What parts of the medieval village has the new farm been given to fence in?

Q3 What other machines were introduced apart from the seed drill?

Q4 How might these machines affect farmworkers?

Key words

Act – a law

manure – animal dung spread on the land to make it produce better crops

threshing – beating the wheat to make the grain separate from the stalks

winnowing – tossing the grain to make the husks (outer covering) blow away from the solid grains

SUMMARY

- Wealthy farmers were keen to enclose so they could practise the new farming methods.
- The owners of four-fifths of the land had to agree to enclosure.
- Small farmers often found it too expensive to stay on their land.
- The poorest often found they had no legal right to land their animals had grazed on.

SUMMARY *activity*

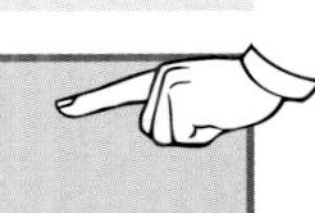

Why do you think enclosed farming was better for all the new methods of farming? Could any of these have gone on under the old open-field system? If they could, why were wealthy farmers so keen on enclosure?

64 Changes in industry: cotton

In this section of the book you will learn the following things:

- **most things were made by hand before 1750;**
- **machines were invented to make spinning and weaving cheaper and faster.**

Industry before 1750

Before 1750, woollen cloth was made in people's homes, and collected and sold by merchants at home and abroad. Other goods, such as bricks, soap and pottery, were made in small works. Most things were made by hand.

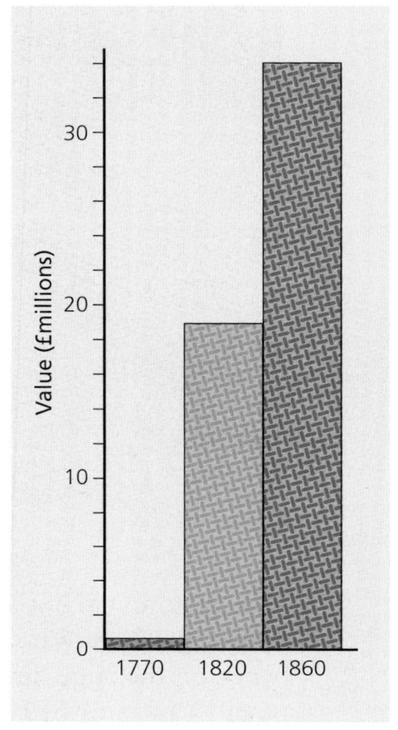

▲ ***Fig 1*** *Value of cotton cloth sold.*

The cotton industry

Raw cotton was grown in America, India and Egypt. Because of Britain's trading, it was brought to Britain to be made into cloth. There was an expanding market for cotton goods because the world population was growing. Cotton is very comfortable to wear and easy to wash. However, the raw cotton had to be spun and woven. It was slow work and made the cloth expensive. How could it be done more quickly and cheaply?

Price of a length of cotton cloth

Year	Price
1770	£2.00
1815	60p
1860	25p

▲ ***Fig 2***

Inventions and factories

Inventions of machines through the eighteenth century meant far more cotton cloth could be made. These machines got larger and larger as they were driven first by water and then by steam. The only place for them was in factories, called **mills**. So people went from working in their homes to working in factories.

► ***Fig 3*** *The spinning jenny was invented by James Hargreaves.*

Changes in the cotton industry

inventor					
	1700			=	1 roll of cloth
John Kay	1733	4 ×	*+ flying shuttle*	=	4 rolls of cloth
James Hargreaves	1764	*+ spinning jenny*	8 ×	=	20 rolls of cloth
Richard Arkwright	1769	*+ water frame*	12 ×	=	30 rolls of cloth
Samuel Crompton	1779	*+ mule*	14 ×	=	50 rolls of cloth
Edmund Cartwright	1785	*+ mule*	*+ power loom*	=	60 rolls of cloth

Key:
= spinner – mostly women because no strength required
= weaver – mostly men because looms could be heavy to work

name of invention (i.e. flying **shuttle**, spinning jenny, water frame, mule, power **loom**)

◀ *Fig 4*

By 1850 there were more than 2,000 cotton factories in Britain. Many of these were in the north-west of England, not far from the port of Liverpool, where the cotton arrived from America and other places abroad. The climate in the north-west was damp, so the cotton threads did not snap when they were spun. Machines meant that cotton goods could be made more cheaply, so more cotton was sold, most of it abroad.

Q1 Who invented the flying shuttle? Was this a spinning or a weaving invention?

Q2 What were the next three inventions – for spinning or weaving?

Q3 How many more rolls of cloth could one spinner and one weaver produce in 1785 than they had in 1700?

Key words

loom – the frame that holds the threads
mills – the factories where cotton cloth was made
shuttle – giant needle for weaving cotton thread in and out of upright threads to make cloth

SUMMARY

- Industries were mostly based at home or in small works before 1750.
- Raw cotton was shipped to Britain to be made into cloth.
- Five men made inventions in the eighteenth century that speeded up spinning and weaving.

SUMMARY *activity*

Who do you think benefited from the new inventions in the cotton industry and who lost out?

65 Changes in industry: steam

In this section of the book you will learn the following things:

- **water wheels drove machines;**
- **steam engines could produce more power than water power.**

A new form of power

The new mills needed power to drive the spinning and weaving machines. Water power was cheap but it meant that mills had to be built by streams and the water flow was unreliable. However, in the eighteenth century, there was a new form of power – steam power.

▲ ***Fig 1*** *James Watt.*

Steam power

Thomas Newcomen had invented a steam-driven pump in 1712 that was used to pump water out of coal mines, but it was very inefficient. Four-fifths of its power was used just to heat up the cylinder at each **working stroke**; it cooled down, then had to be heated up again, and it used enormous amounts of coal. Moreover, no one could make the iron cylinders accurately enough in those days, so they leaked clouds of steam, and the pump could only provide an up-and-down motion. All this was not much use outside a coal mining area.

Q1 What did Newcomen invent in 1712?

Q2 Why did Newcomen's pump use so much coal?

Q3 What were two other disadvantages of the pump?

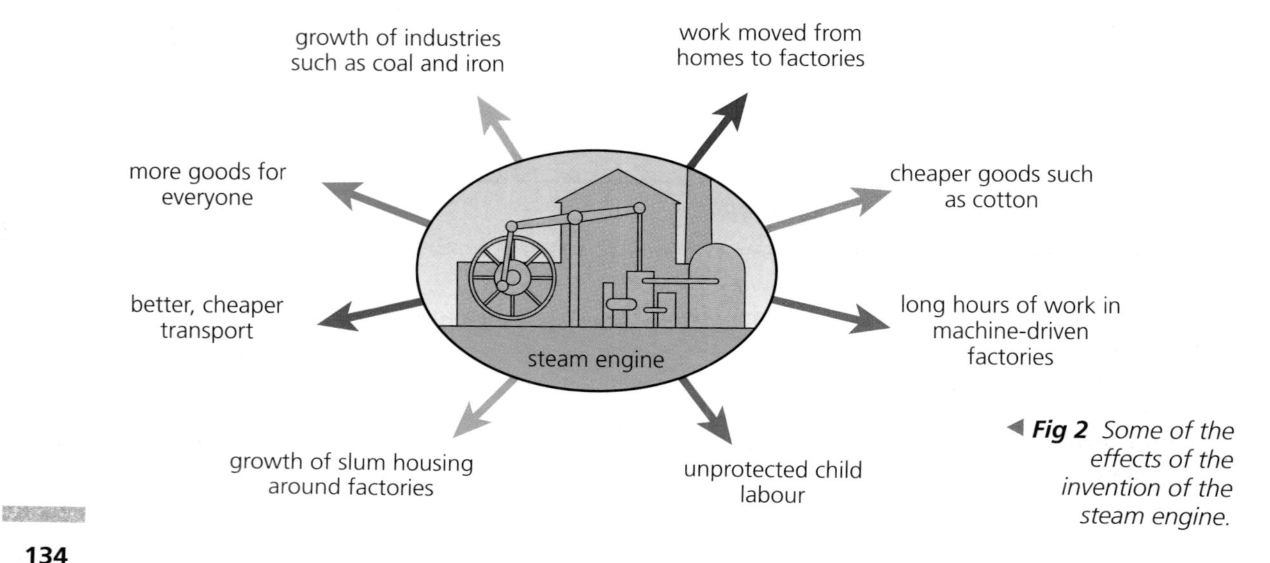

◀ ***Fig 2*** *Some of the effects of the invention of the steam engine.*

James Watt

One of these pumps was sent to Glasgow University to be mended. The man who set to work to repair it was a young Scot called James Watt. He thought of a way to improve it. He saw that if the steam could be drawn off in a separate cylinder, or **condenser**, and cooled, the main cylinder would stay hot and the condenser would stay cool. Watt had no money to develop his idea, so he went into partnership with John Roebuck of the Carron Ironworks, not far from Glasgow. However, Roebuck could not make the cylinders accurately enough.

◀ ***Fig 3*** *Steam power meant engines running large machines. A cotton lace factory near Nottingham 1884.*

Boulton and Watt in partnership

Then a successful engineer and businessman called Matthew Boulton heard of Watt's work, and the two went into partnership. Boulton knew an **ironmaster** called John Wilkinson, who had succeeded in boring accurate holes to make cannons. Here, at last, was the man who could make accurate cylinders, so Boulton and Watt began making steam engines in 1775. Watt went on to make a steam engine that could convert an up-and-down motion to a round-and-round motion. Now steam engines could be used to drive machines in the new cotton mills. The first steam cotton mill was opened in 1785 but it took until the 1840s for steam to overtake water power for mills.

Use of steam-powered machines in cotton mills

1851 seven out of eight cotton mills used steam engines.

▲ ***Fig 4***

Key words

condenser – container where steam cools down and turns back into water

ironmaster – someone who makes iron

working stroke – an up-and-down motion

SUMMARY

- Water power was used to drive machines in the eighteenth century.
- Thomas Newcomen invented a steam-driven pump in 1712.
- James Watt improved Newcomen's pump.
- James Watt and Matthew Boulton went into partnership to make steam engines.

SUMMARY *activity*

Why do you think it took so long for steam power to become the main source of power for machines? Think of as many reasons as you can.

66 More changes: coal and iron

In this section of the book you will learn the following things:

- **coal production increased;**
- **new methods of making iron were discovered;**
- **the ironworks moved to the coalfields.**

The growth of coal mining

Coal was used to heat up water to make the steam to drive the steam engines that slowly began to change the face of Britain. Coal had been mined from shallow pits for hundreds of years. Now, however, the demand for coal was so great that coal mines were dug deeper and deeper. The deeper miners went, the more dangerous the job became. Pockets of gas led to explosions underground. Flooding from underground water was kept under control by the new steam-driven pumps, but ventilation, lighting and roof collapse were problems.

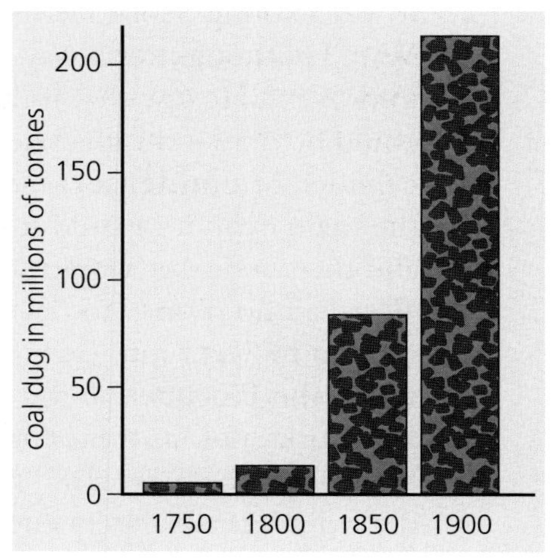

▲ ***Fig 1*** *Coal production 1750–1900.*

Q1 Why were coal mines being dug deeper?

Q2 Write down the five problems or dangers of mining coal in deeper mines.

The iron industry

Iron was also needed to make the new machines that were driven by steam engines, but the growth of the iron industry was held up by one large problem. For centuries **iron ore** had been dug from the ground. The iron was then separated from the rest of the rock by heating up the ore. The iron melted and ran out. The heating up or **smelting** was done by using **charcoal**, which was made from trees. Coal could not be used because its impurities spoiled the iron. By the seventeenth century, therefore, the forests in Britain were in danger of being completely destroyed. In the seventeenth century a young man called Dud Dudley found a way to smelt iron ore using purified coal, but he was hounded out of business by charcoal makers, timber fellers and blacksmiths, and his invention was forgotten.

Q3 Why was coal no use for smelting iron ore?

Q4 Why do you think Dud Dudley was hounded out of business?

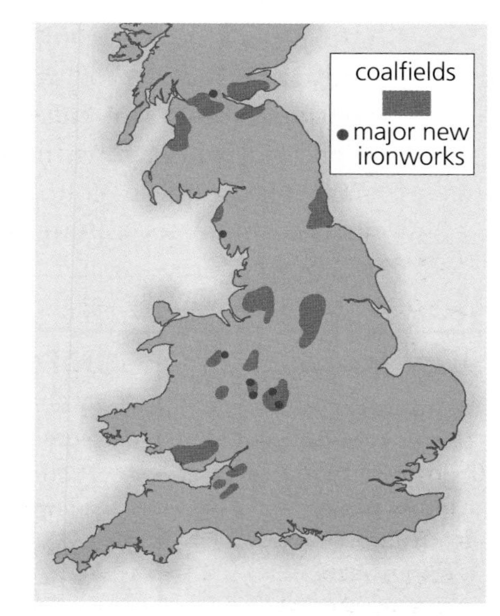

▲ ***Fig 2*** *Expansion in the iron industry 1700–1790.*

Abraham Darby I and Henry Cort

In 1709 Abraham Darby I, like Dudley before him, used purified coal (**coke**) to smelt the iron ore. This discovery opened the way for the widespread use of iron. However, the **cast iron** produced was not as good as **wrought iron**. In 1783, Henry Cort discovered a new method of making wrought iron by stirring the **molten iron**. Soon enormous ironworks were built where iron ore went in at one end and beautifully made iron products rolled out at the other.

▲ ***Fig 3*** *This bridge was built in Coalbrookdale in 1779 by Abraham Darby III, to show people that iron could be used for all sorts of things.*

Steel

Steel is even stronger than wrought iron but it was very expensive to make. In 1856, Henry Bessemer invented a converter, a huge container full of white-hot molten iron. By superheating and the addition of some chemicals, steel was produced. In 1866 the Siemens brothers invented an even cheaper process, and the Gilchrist-Thomas cousins invented a method that could turn any type of iron ore into steel.

Material	Qualities	Good for
cast iron	strong brittle will not bend	weights, girders, rollers, heavy engine parts (e.g. boilers)
wrought iron	strong flexible soft	pipes, rails, sheet metal
steel	very strong flexible very hard	tools, weapons, machines, moving parts of machines, rails

▲ ***Fig 4***

Key words

cast iron – hot, molten iron poured into moulds to set
charcoal – wood that has been charred or partly burnt
coke – coal that has been purified
iron ore – rock that contains pure iron
molten iron – heated until it turns to liquid
smelting – heating up iron ore
wrought iron – cast iron that has been hammered or worked on to make it more flexible

SUMMARY

- Coal production increased enormously between 1750 and 1900.
- Iron production was held up by the need for charcoal (burnt wood) to smelt the iron ore.
- Abraham Darby I was the first ironmaster to succeed in producing iron using coke.
- Henry Bessemer made steel much more cheaply in the 1850s.

SUMMARY *activity*

Why were coal, iron and steel so important for all the changes that led to the growth of modern Britain?

67 Changes in transport: roads

In this section of the book you will learn the following things:

- about the bad state of the roads in the eighteenth century;
- about better ways of building and maintaining roads;
- about faster road transport.

The state of the roads in the 1750s

In the 1750s the roads were in a terrible state. People were supposed to repair the local roads in their area, but they were not interested in the main roads outside the village that they hardly ever used. The quickest way of travelling was on horseback and the speed at which a horse could travel depended on how good the road was. In some places potholes were so deep that travellers had been known to drown in the puddles. Waggons stuck fast in mud and coaches were slow, expensive and often held up by highwaymen. Strings of 30 or 40 packhorses were the best way to carry goods. Something had to be done.

	1750s	1830s
London → Newcastle	6 days	just over 1 day
London → Edinburgh	10 days	2 days
London → Brighton	1 day	$5^1/_2$ hours

▲ ***Fig 1*** *Average time taken to travel by coach in good conditions.*

Q1 What was the best way to carry goods?

Turnpike trusts

Some local businessmen joined together to form **turnpike** trusts. They paid for a length of road to be properly built. They put a gate across the road and charged people a **toll** for travelling on it. The toll depended on how much a vehicle damaged the road. A waggon with wide wheels that acted like a road roller paid less than a heavy cart with narrow wheels that made ruts in the road.

▼ ***Fig 2*** *Royal Mail coach leaving a coaching inn.*

Master road builders

There were three outstanding road builders at this time. One was John Metcalfe (1717–1810) who paid particular attention to the foundations of a road, using heather, stone and gravel. The second was Thomas Telford (1757–1834) who built about 1,600 kilometres of roads, 1,000 bridges and the Caledonian Canal in Scotland. The third road builder was John Macadam (1756–1836). He built cheaper roads than either Telford or Metcalfe. He said that if the subsoil was well drained and the surface of the road slightly raised with a cover of fine, chipped stones tightly packed together, the road would carry traffic all year.

Q2 How did John Metcalfe build roads?

Q3 How did Thomas Telford build roads?

Q4 Why would John Macadam's roads be popular with turnpike trusts?

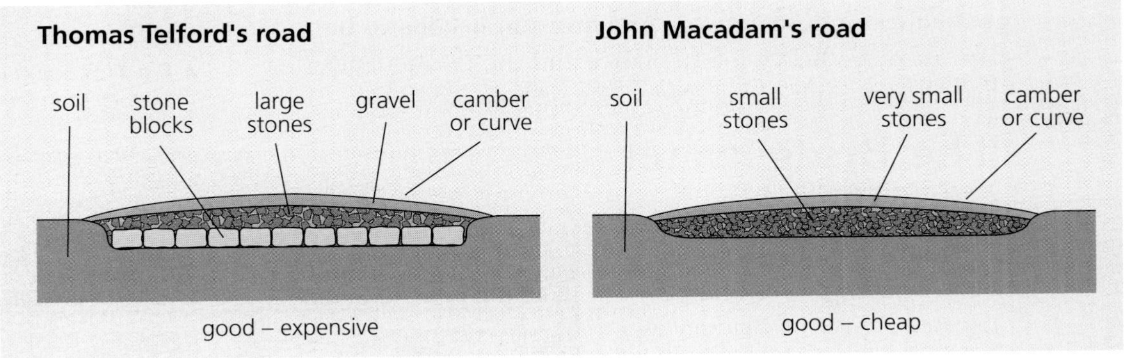

▲ ***Fig 3*** *Road building.*

Faster transport

Between 1790 and 1830 a network of turnpike roads spread all over Britain. Better roads meant that people made better carriages and waggons to travel faster on the smoother roads. Before the 1780s the mail had been carried by postboys on horseback. In 1784, John Palmer was given the Post Office contract to carry the Royal Mail between London and Bristol. Good quality horses, well-paid drivers, a smooth road and an armed guard guaranteed success.

Key words

toll – a charge for using a road or bridge

turnpike – so-called because originally there was just a pole or pike across the road that people pulled or turned to open

SUMMARY

- The roads were in a terrible state in the eighteenth century.
- Turnpike trusts were set up to build and maintain stretches of road.
- Three great road builders were John Metcalfe, Thomas Telford and John Macadam.
- In 1784 the first Royal Mail coach ran between London and Bristol.

SUMMARY *activity*

What improvements were made to roads in the eighteenth century and how did these affect travel by the 1830s?

68 Changes in transport: canals

In this section of the book you will learn the following things:

- **better water routes were needed;**
- **the Bridgewater Canal was the start of serious canal building in 1759.**

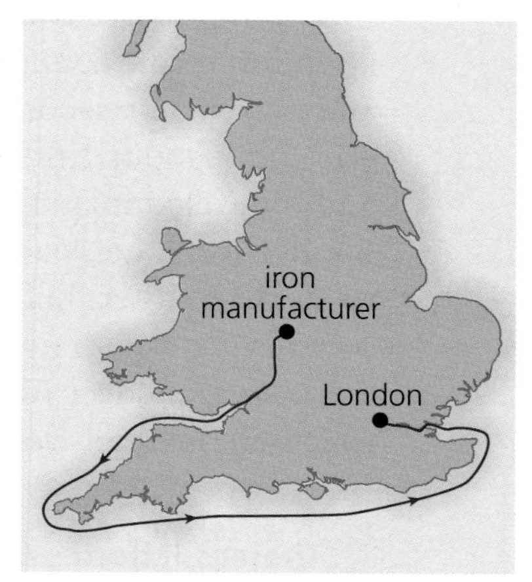

▲ ***Fig 1*** *Sending iron by sea rather than land in 1775.*

The need for better water transport

Even after improvements to the roads it was still costly to send goods by road and **manufacturers** preferred to send them by water. However, sea routes were long and rivers often too shallow for larger boats. By the second half of the eighteenth century the iron, coal and cotton industries were growing and needed to be able to move heavy loads. France and the Netherlands had already built canals. Now Britain followed suit.

The Bridgewater Canal

▲ ***Fig 2*** *James Brindley's aqueduct, on the Bridgewater Canal.*

The most famous names in canal building were Francis Egerton, Duke of Bridgewater (1736–1803), who was rich and well educated, and James Brindley (1716–1772) who did not even learn to read and write properly. The Duke had coal mines on his land around Worsley in Lancashire and in 1759 he wanted to transport the coal cheaply to Manchester, 11 kilometres away. He employed James Brindley to work out how to do it. One of the biggest problems was crossing the River Barton. Brindley decided on an **aqueduct** to carry the canal over the river. People came from all over Europe to see the canal, which by 1764 was carrying coal to Manchester at half the cost of taking it on packhorses. Cheaper coal meant a greater demand for coal.

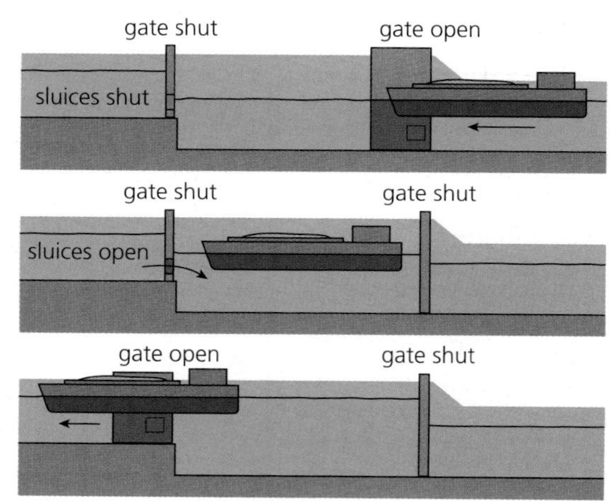

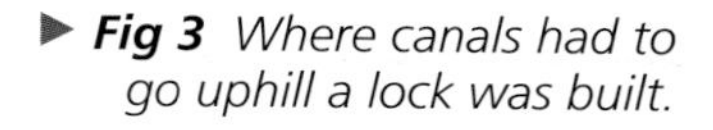

► ***Fig 3*** *Where canals had to go uphill a lock was built.*

More canals: the Grand Trunk Canal System

By 1762 Brindley was already working on an extension to the Bridgewater Canal to meet the Mersey at Runcorn. It was finished in 1776 and the cost of carrying cotton and cotton goods between the port of Liverpool and the city of Manchester was cut by five-sixths. Soon Brindley was working on a canal to join the Trent and the Mersey, which would provide a waterway right across England. One of the main **financiers** of this canal was Josiah Wedgwood, the potter. Wedgwood had to transport china clay from Cornwall to his pottery factory near Stoke. He also needed to distribute his fragile finished goods.

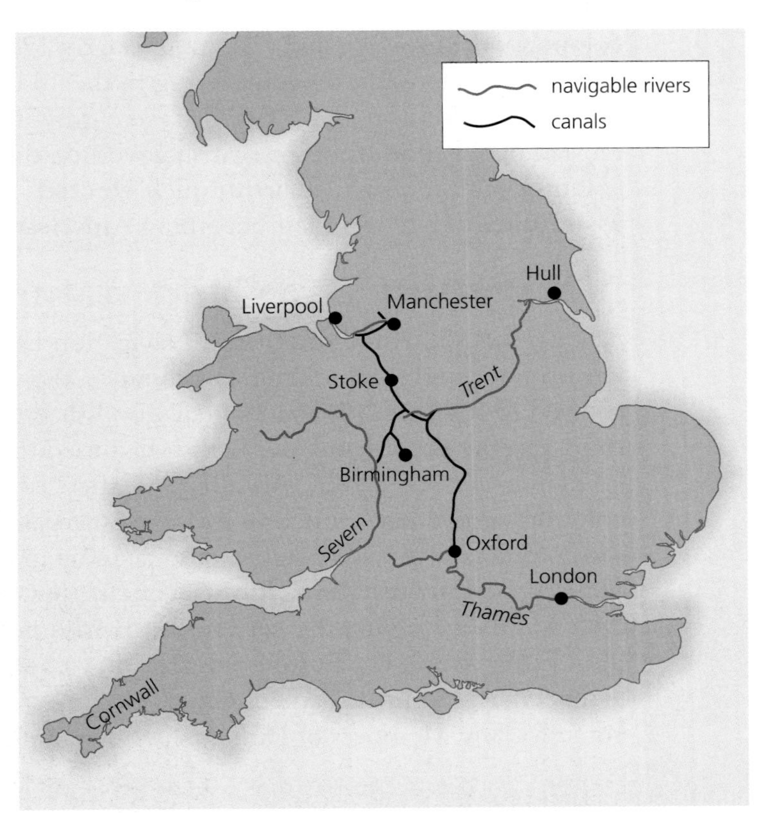

▲ ***Fig 4*** *The Grand Trunk Canal System.*

Q1 How much cheaper was it to carry cotton by canal than by packhorse?

Q2 How would Wedgwood have transported china clay from Cornwall to Stoke before the canals were built?

Q3 Describe the route Wedgwood would have used after the Grand Trunk Canal System was complete.

Key words

aqueduct – a bridge carrying water

financier – someone who invests money in a project

manufacturer – someone who makes something in a factory

SUMMARY

- Sea routes were long and rivers often too shallow for larger boats.
- In 1759 the Duke of Bridgewater and James Brindley started to build the Bridgewater Canal to take coal from the Duke's estate to Manchester as cheaply as possible.
- The Bridgewater Canal was the start of a systematic network of canals.
- The Trent–Mersey Canal provided a waterway right across England and became part of the Grand Trunk Canal System.
- Locks were built so that canals could 'go uphill'.

SUMMARY *activity*

Explain why the Duke of Bridgewater, Josiah Wedgwood, cotton merchants, cotton manufacturers and ironmasters all welcomed the canals.

69 The American Revolution

In this section of the book you will learn the following things:

- the American colonies clashed with the British over taxation and the right to run their own affairs.

The 13 colonies

While changes were occurring in Britain, the American colonies were growing and changing too. By 1770 there were about two million people living in the 13 colonies. Ports such as Boston and New York were growing rich on trading. Despite having a British governor, the colonists ran their own affairs through **elected assemblies**. They were fast becoming Americans.

The American argument against British taxation

No taxation without representation

▲ *Fig 1*

Navigation Laws and stamp duty

The colonists resented the British Navigation Laws, which protected British trade and shipbuilding. For instance, the colonies were only allowed to trade with Britain and all goods had to be carried in British ships. On the other hand, the British had used their army to fight off the French in the Seven Years War. In 1765, they felt it was only fair that the colonists should pay some money in taxes towards the cost of defending the colonies, so they decided to raise taxes by means of a stamp duty, a tax on legal documents. The colonists were furious. They claimed the stamp duty was illegal, saying the very reason British people were freer than most other peoples in Europe was that they could not be taxed unless it had been agreed in Parliament. Since the American colonists had not voted for any Members of Parliament, how could they be taxed?

◄ ***Fig 2*** *The Boston Tea Party. Some of the colonists disguised themselves as Indians and threw the tea overboard in protest against British taxes.*

Q1 What were the Navigation Laws?

Q2 Why do you think the colonists resented the Navigation Laws?

Q3 Why did the British think it was fair to tax the colonists?

The Boston Tea Party 1773

The British repealed the stamp duty but put a duty on tea and sent soldiers to keep order in Boston. Tempers worsened. In 1773, a group of 150 colonists boarded three ships in Boston harbour and threw all the tea overboard. From this time on the colonists and the British moved towards an open conflict.

Declaration of Independence 1776 and war

On 4 July 1776, **delegates** from the 13 colonies agreed to adopt the Declaration of Independence. It explained their complaints about the British King, George III, and went on to describe the sort of Government the Americans wanted and the rights they should have. From then it was war between the Americans and British. It lasted from 1776 to 1783, when the Americans, led by George Washington, finally defeated the British at Yorktown in Virginia.

Leading men of the American Revolution

George Washington	1732–1799
Thomas Jefferson	1743–1826
Alexander Hamilton	1755–1804
John Adams	1735–1826
Benjamin Franklin	1706–1790

▲ *Fig 3*

▲ ***Fig 4*** *The flag of the newly independent 13 states. Each star and red and white stripe represents a state. As more states joined, so more stars were added to the flag, but the number of stripes remained the same to represent the original 13.*

▼ ***Fig 5*** *George Washington.*

Key words

delegate – person voted for or asked to do something by other people

elected assemblies – adults voting for people to represent them, e.g. the British Parliament (House of Commons)

SUMMARY

- The 13 colonies were growing richer in trade.
- The colonists resented British Navigation Laws and taxation.
- This resentment led to the Declaration of Independence in 1776.
- The Americans defeated the British in 1783.

SUMMARY *activity*

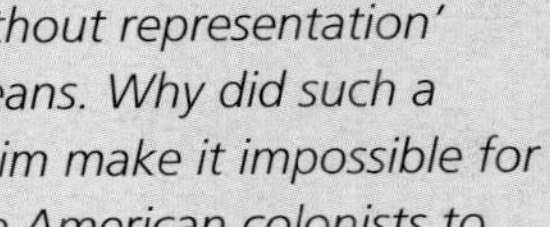

Explain what 'No taxation without representation' means. Why did such a claim make it impossible for the American colonists to remain part of Britain?

70 The French Revolution

In this section of the book you will learn the following things:

- **in the eighteenth century the French King was all-powerful;**
- **the nobles and clergy in France paid no taxes and had all the best jobs;**
- **in 1789 a revolution started in France.**

'People are born free, but are everywhere in chains.'

▲ ***Fig 1*** *Jean-Jacques Rousseau (1712–1778), from his book* The Social Contract.

Growth in trade and population

All over the world the population was growing. Trade between countries was expanding, so there were more merchants, more ports, more towns. The old way of governing countries when kings were all-powerful was becoming **obsolete**. Because of disputes between the King and Parliament in Britain in the seventeenth century, the King was not all powerful. In France it was a different matter.

France in the eighteenth century

In the late eighteenth century, the population of France was about 25 million. Only one million of these were nobles and clergy but, with the King, they owned most of the land. The peasants had to work for the local nobles, pay taxes to the King, and a tithe (one-tenth) of all they earned to the clergy. The middle classes paid taxes, but neither the nobles nor the clergy paid any taxes at all and only they could have the best jobs in the Army, Navy and Government.

Louis XVI and the Estates General 1789

Thinkers such as Jean-Jacques Rousseau (1712–1778) had pointed out the unfairness of the system. In 1789 matters came to a head. The King, Louis XVI, needed money, so he called the Estates General, which consisted of nobles, clergy and 600 **commoners**, mostly merchants, lawyers and bankers. The commoners suggested that in return for paying taxes, they should have a say in the Government. Louis was horrified and locked them out of their meeting hall. They were not to be stopped, however; they met on the tennis court to discuss their complaints.

Q1 Why did Louis XVI call the Estates General in 1789?

Q2 What sort of people were the 600 commoners?

Q3 What did they suggest?

▲ ***Fig 2*** *Louis XVI.*

The storming of the Bastille to the execution of the King

Meanwhile, other people were becoming angry. On 14 July 1789, a mob stormed the Bastille, a royal fortress that stood for the power of the King, nobles and clergy.

Maximilien Robespierre (1758–1794)

He joined the Estates General and believed fervently in the rights of ordinary people. He wanted to get rid of all evil men who were enemies of the people. This led to the 'Terror' as it was called, as Robespierre eventually sent anyone who might oppose him to the guillotine. A total of 17 000 people were guillotined; in the end this included Robespierre himself, as frightened colleagues turned on him.

▲ ***Fig3***

Riots followed all over France. The Estates General renamed itself the National Assembly and called for a limit on the King's power. Since Louis would never agree, he was finally executed in 1793. Until this time, other countries had watched the events in France and many had been sympathetic. The execution of the King, however, followed by more and more executions of nobles, clergy and, in the end, anyone who disagreed with the powerful men now running France, worried countries such as Britain. By 1793, Austria, Prussia, Britain, Spain and the Netherlands were all at war with France.

◀ ***Fig 4*** *The guillotine was named after Joseph Guillotin, who supported the idea of painless, quick execution, no matter what rank a person was.*

Key words

commoners – people who were not nobles or clergy

obsolete – out of date

SUMMARY

- The French King, Louis XVI, was all-powerful in France.
- The King, nobles and clergy owned nearly all the land in France, but only the peasants and middle classes paid taxes.
- By the late eighteenth century there were many middle-class people (merchants, bankers and lawyers) who wanted a say in running the country.
- On 14 July 1789 the mob stormed the Bastille and the French Revolution began.
- Louis XVI was executed (guillotined) in 1793.

SUMMARY *activity*

Why would the countries around France be sympathetic at first and then alarmed by the French Revolution?

71 The French and Napoleonic Wars

In this section of the book you will learn the following things:

- **France was led by Napoleon Bonaparte;**
- **Britain kept control of the sea while Napoleon was supreme on land.**

Napoleon Bonaparte

The violence of the French Revolutionary Governments was followed by the military dictatorship of Napoleon Bonaparte. He was born in Corsica and rose to be a general in the French Army by the age of 26. In 1799, in his thirties, he became Emperor of France. He wanted to have as large an empire as possible and, for over 20 years, wars raged as France fought everywhere, from Spain to Russia.

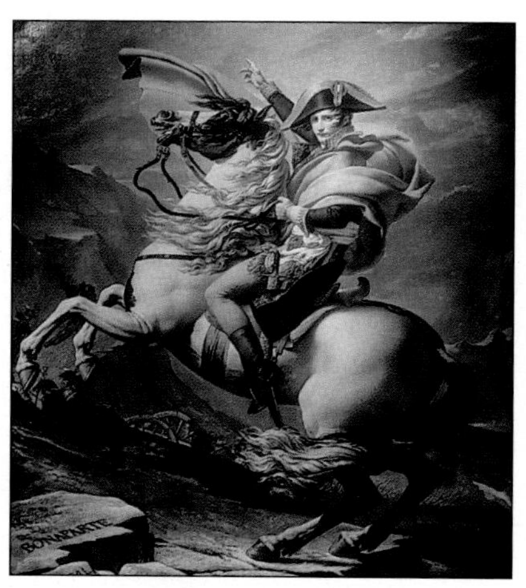

▲ ***Fig 1*** *Napoleon Bonaparte.*

War at sea

In 1802, Napoleon planned to invade Britain and gathered a huge fleet of barges to carry soldiers to England. However, the French Navy could not get control of the Channel to make it safe for the barges to cross, so Napoleon gave up the plan. The British Navy followed up this success by defeating the combined French and Spanish fleets at the Battle of Trafalgar in 1805. Despite the death of the British commander, Admiral Lord Nelson, this was a great victory. It meant that the French could not **blockade** Britain, but the British Navy could blockade France. Although Napoleon ordered countries under his control not to trade with Britain, without a navy he could not enforce this completely, whereas the British could stop supplies reaching France.

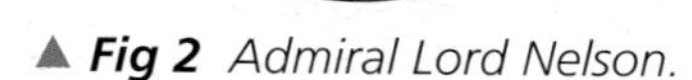

▲ ***Fig 2*** *Admiral Lord Nelson.*

▼ ***Fig 3*** *Battle of Trafalgar 1805.*

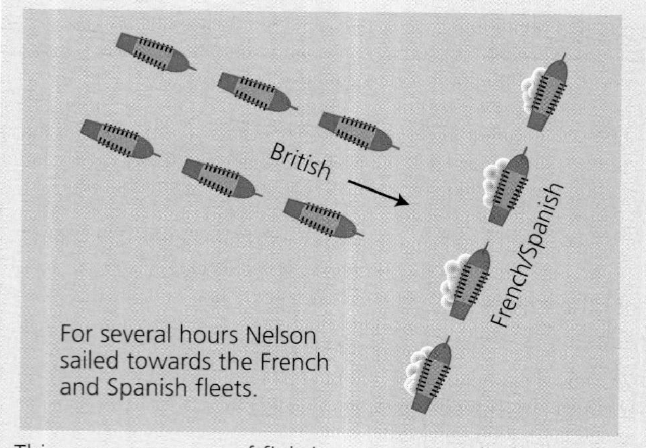

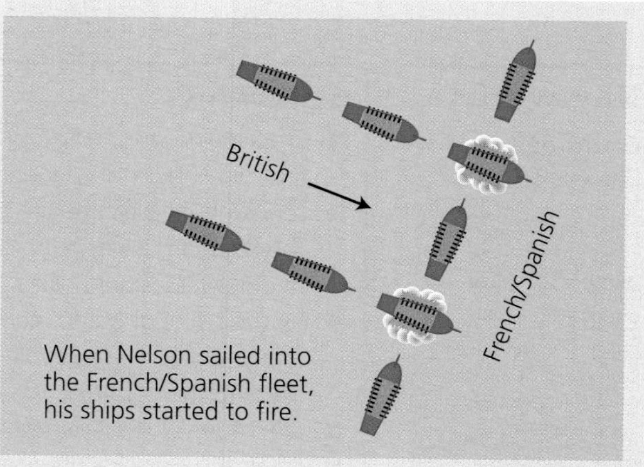

This was a new way of fighting at sea. Usually ships manoeuvred so they were **broadside** on to each other, then fired.

Q1 Why did Napoleon give up his plan to invade Britain?

Q2 Why was the Battle of Trafalgar important to Britain?

War on land

Meanwhile, Napoleon was winning battles on land, culminating in his march to Moscow in 1812. Although he was not defeated by the Russians, he was defeated by the Russian winter and forced to retreat, losing three-quarters of his army. To try to break the deadlock between the British success at sea and the French success on land, Britain had already sent an army to Portugal and Spain under the Duke of Wellington. He fought a number of campaigns and crossed into France in April 1814, only to hear that following the Russian disaster, the French had been forced to surrender.

Battle of Waterloo 1815

Napoleon was banished to the island of Elba in 1814, but escaped and landed in France, where thousands flocked to join him. For 100 days the outcome was in the balance. Then, in June 1815, the **Allies**, under the Duke of Wellington and the Prussian, General Blücher, defeated Napoleon at Waterloo, near Brussels. This time Napoleon was banished to St Helena, where he died in 1821.

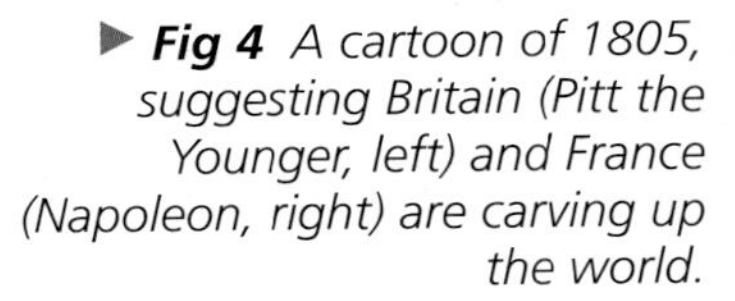
▶ ***Fig 4*** *A cartoon of 1805, suggesting Britain (Pitt the Younger, left) and France (Napoleon, right) are carving up the world.*

Key words

allies – friendly countries
blockade – stop ships bringing food and other supplies to a country
broadside – the side of a ship

SUMMARY

- Napoleon took over as military dictator in France in 1799.
- Admiral Lord Nelson won a decisive victory over the French and Spanish fleets at the Battle of Trafalgar in 1805.
- Napoleon won battles all over Europe, but was defeated for the first time in the Russian campaign in 1812.
- The Duke of Wellington fought successful campaigns against the French in Spain and finally defeated Napoleon at the Battle of Waterloo in 1815.

SUMMARY *activity*

Explain why Nelson's battle plan at Trafalgar was risky and why it paid off.

72 Discontent at home

In this section of the book you will learn the following things:

- about hardship after the war;
- about popular protests and Government fears.

Demobilisation and job losses

The Napoleonic Wars ended in 1815. A quarter of a million soldiers and sailors were rapidly **demobilised** and looking for work. All the contracts for providing guns, ships and clothing for the Army and Navy stopped, so many workers lost their jobs.

The Corn Laws 1815 and taxation

British farmers did not want competition from corn coming from other parts of Europe now the war was over. They persuaded Parliament to pass a law in 1815, forbidding the import of corn into Britain until the price of home-grown corn reached £4 a quarter. This meant farmers were guaranteed good prices for their corn, but poor people had no chance to buy cheap bread.

Q1 What did the Corn Laws forbid?

Q2 Why was tax on ordinary goods worse for poor people than income tax?

With taxation the Government also acted for the better off. The war had cost a lot of money and had to be paid for, but the Government stopped income tax (which did not apply to people on low incomes) and put taxes on ordinary goods (which everyone had to pay).

Hard times 1815–1820

Times were hard. In those days if there was no work, there was no money. As factories closed or laid off workers, families could face starvation. It is not surprising, therefore, that there were marches and demonstrations. Ideas about liberty and equality from the French Revolution were still alive; some working people even talked about a revolution.

▼ *Fig 1*

Habeas Corpus *(that you may have the body – Latin)*

The writ of Habeas Corpus was one of the benefits of Magna Carta (1215). The writ is a legal order requiring a person to be brought before a judge to find out whether they have been lawfully deprived of freedom. The Habeas Corpus Act itself was passed in 1679 to make the position clear in law.

Purposes of the writ of Habeas Corpus were:

- to prevent governments from imprisoning, without a trial, people who opposed them;
- to set free people brought to England as slaves.

There were riots against the Corn Laws and meetings calling for reform, such as the Spa Fields meeting in London in 1816, when a mob rioted. The Government retaliated by suspending the Habeas Corpus Act for a year.

Q3 What was the Habeas Corpus Act?

Q4 What was the Government's purpose in suspending the Act in 1816?

The Peterloo Massacre 1819

One of the biggest demonstrations was in August 1819 at St Peter's Fields in Manchester. A famous reform speaker called Henry Hunt was due to speak to the crowd who had assembled, many with their wives and children. The local magistrates were afraid of a riot; there was no police force in those days. They called out the **yeomanry** who got out of hand and charged the crowd, brandishing their swords. Thirteen people were killed and many wounded. The event became known as 'Peterloo', in a sarcastic reference to the Battle of Waterloo.

▶ ***Fig 2*** *The Peterloo Massacre – a cartoon by George Cruikshank.*

The Six Acts or Gag Acts 1819

Panic stricken, the Government brought in the Six Acts or Gag Acts. These laws severely limited people's rights to hold public meetings and to publish newspapers that might stir up unrest.

Key words

demobilisation – releasing soldiers and sailors after a war

yeomanry – a cavalry force (soldiers on horseback), made up of local volunteers

SUMMARY

- The end of the war brought demobilisation and loss of jobs in war work.
- The Government helped the better off by removing income tax and passing the Corn Laws.
- There were protests, culminating in the Peterloo Massacre.
- The Government clamped down on any protests by suspending the Habeas Corpus Act in 1816 and passing the Six Acts in 1819.

SUMMARY *activity*

Why was the Government so worried about public meetings and protests in the years 1815–1820?

73 Reform: the beginnings

In this section of the book you will learn the following things:

- **reform or changes began to happen in the way people were treated.**

Plot failed

▲ ***Fig 1*** *Victorian policemen, named 'Bobbies' or 'Peelers' after Robert Peel.*

George III died in 1820. He had been insane for some years and his son, who had been Regent, now became George IV. In the same year some desperate **radical** reformers planned to blow up the whole Cabinet while they were at dinner. The plot was betrayed and the conspirators executed. Things were changing, however. New men were coming into Government who were less concerned with fears of revolution and more concerned to make Britain a better place so that people would not want to revolt. One of these men was Robert Peel, who became Home Secretary in 1822.

Robert Peel (1788–1850) and the penal code

Peel was appalled by the severity and inefficiency of the **penal code**. Over 200 crimes carried the death penalty, and often juries refused to convict someone who was obviously guilty because they knew the punishment was so severe. This made a mockery of the law. Peel persuaded Parliament to abolish the death penalty for about half the crimes. Reform continued and, by 1861, no one was hanged in Britain for any crime, other than murder or treason.

Some of the crimes that carried the death penalty in 1820

- stealing a sheep;
- stealing a lamb;
- forgery;
- setting fire to a haycart;
- cutting down a tree in Downing Street;
- stealing a horse;
- damaging Westminster Bridge;
- stealing a loaf of bread.

▲ ***Fig 2***

Q1 Write down three things people could be hanged for in 1820.

Q2 Are the things in the list for which people could be hanged, crimes against a person or against property? What does this tell you about the people making the laws?

Q3 What does the saying 'You might as well be hanged for a sheep as a lamb' mean? Why does a penal code like this encourage murder?

Prisons

Peel was influenced by the **Quaker**, Elizabeth Fry, to make some reforms in gaols. From this time gaolers were paid; before this they took fees from the inmates. Gaols had to be inspected and women prisoners had to have women warders. Although Elizabeth Fry campaigned against **transportation**, it was not abolished until 1853. However, from this time, women no longer spent the long voyage to Australia in irons.

Q4 What were the three prison reforms Elizabeth Fry persuaded Peel to introduce?

▲ ***Fig 3*** *Elizabeth Fry.*

Police

However, Peel was more concerned with preventing crime. One of the reasons Governments were so panicky about large public meetings was that the only way to control a crowd was to call out troops. Peel established a regular police force in London in 1829 – the Metropolitan Police Force. This was so successful that by 1856 every part of Britain had to have a police force.

► ***Fig 4***

Other reforms of the 1820s

- repeal of the **Combination Acts** 1824 – it was no longer illegal to form trade unions;
- Catholics were allowed to hold jobs, become Members of Parliament etc on the same terms as Protestants 1829;
- laws were passed to encourage freer trade for British colonies.

Key words

Combination Acts – laws of 1799 and 1800 forbidding men to combine together to ask for higher wages
emancipation – freeing from restrictions
penal code – a range of punishments for law breakers
Quaker – a Christian movement based on peaceful principles. Meetings are informal and there are no clergy; members run their own meetings.
radical – someone who wants to make great changes
transportation – a punishment; people were taken to Australia to work out a prison sentence

SUMMARY

- New men, such as Robert Peel, came into Government in the 1820s.
- Peel reformed the penal code, set up the first police force, and started prison reform.
- Other reforms included repeal of the Combination Acts, better trading laws between Britain and the Empire, and Catholic **emancipation**.

SUMMARY *activity*

Why was Peel remembered as a great Home Secretary?

74 Reform: Parliament

In this section of the book you will learn the following things:

- about demand for Parliamentary reform in the 1820s;
- about the Great Reform Act of 1832.

Middle-class demands for reform

Despite Peterloo and the Gag Acts, demand for changes in Parliament grew in the 1820s. The demands were loudest and most effective from the new middle classes – factory owners, merchants and professional people. They resented a House of Commons made up of landowners who could pass laws like the Corn Laws of 1815 which, by keeping up the price of corn, only benefited landowning farmers like themselves. This had been acceptable when the wealth of the country came solely from land and farming, but the world was changing. Large cities were growing up in the north of England, where wealth was being built on coal mining, iron making, cotton and woollen manufacturing, engineering and pottery making. These industrialists and merchants wanted laws that favoured their businesses.

The House of Commons before 1832

The old system:

- had too many MPs in the landowning-rich south of England;
- only about 400 000 people (including some women) had a right to vote out of a population of about 18 million.

▲ *Fig 1*

Q1 What sort of men sat in the House of Commons before 1832?

Q2 What sort of men wanted change?

Working-class demands for reform

Many working-class people wanted changes too. Some even went so far as to suggest a system of 'one man, one vote'. Large meetings were held and men such as William Cobbett, the political journalist, wrote about extending the **franchise**. By 1830 everyone was talking about reform of Parliament.

◄ ***Fig 2*** *William Cobbett (1763–1835) attacked the Government's savage policies towards reform. He became an MP in 1832, for Oldham, one of the new northern towns.*

The Great Reform Act 1832

In 1830, the old-fashioned **Tory Party** lost its majority in the House of Commons and the **Whig Party** came to power. In March 1831, it introduced a Reform Bill which was eventually passed by the Commons, only to be thrown out by the House of Lords. The country was at fever pitch: there were riots in Bristol and Nottingham; marches and protests. The Prime Minister asked the King, William IV, to make enough pro-reform men into Lords so that the Bill would pass the House of Lords. Under this threat the Lords backed down and the Reform Bill became law in June 1832.

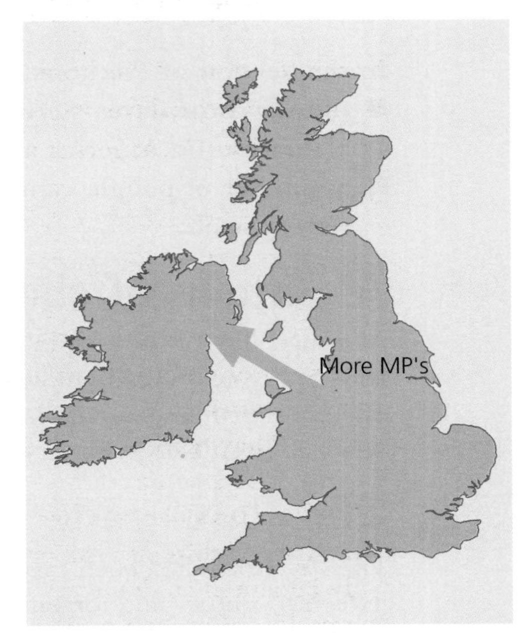

▲ ***Fig 3*** *Thirteen more MPs went to Scotland and Ireland.*

Q3 Where did most of the MPs come from under the old system?

Q4 What proportion of the population had the right to vote in the 1820s?

Working-class disappointment

▶ ***Fig 4***

After all the hopes and excitement, the Reform Act did nothing for the working classes. The property qualification meant that a man had to earn about £150 a year to own enough property to win the vote; most working men earned about £50 a year. Bitterly disappointed, many men turned to **Chartism** (see page 161), the **Co-operative Movement** and trade unions (see pages 166–167).

The House of Commons after 1832

The new system:

- 143 seats for MPs were reallocated; many went to the north.
- The right to vote was given to many middle-class men (women were excluded); it was based on owning property.
- About 300 000 men were **enfranchised**.

Key words

Chartism – movement pressing for Parliamentary and electoral reform
Co-operative Movement – movement which believed that industries should be owned and controlled by the people working in them.
enfranchised – given the right to vote
franchise – the right to vote
Tory Party – very conservative political party
Whig Party – more forward thinking political party

SUMMARY

- The new middle classes in the towns wanted a say in running the country.
- Some working-class people wanted 'one man, one vote'.
- The old system had too few MPs in the northern towns and too few voters overall.
- The Reform Act was passed in 1832, giving the vote to the middle classes.

SUMMARY *activity*

What was the new system after 1832 and why were the working classes so disappointed?

75 Reform: slavery

In this section of the book you will learn the following things:

- thousands of slaves were taken from Africa to work on plantations in America and the West Indies;
- a number of people campaigned to end the slave trade and slavery itself.

A climate of change

Although the sort of men in the House of Commons were much the same as before 1832, there was a different outlook and a far greater interest in bringing about changes to make people's lives better than they had been before. Slavery was just one of the issues tackled.

▼ *Fig 1*

In the British Empire
Number of slaves in 1830 – 800 000

The slave trade and slavery

The slave trade had been carried on since the sixteenth century and fortunes were made by carrying slaves from Africa to America. The conditions under which they were transported were appalling. They were crammed together so they could not move and no one knows how many died on board the ships. By the late eighteenth century, 60 000 slaves a year were carried across the Atlantic, half of them in British ships. In America, they were bought by **plantation** owners and worked in the fields, often tending the cotton that came across to England to be made into cloth. In the West Indies, slaves did all the work on the sugar cane plantations. Their welfare was entirely dependent on their owners.

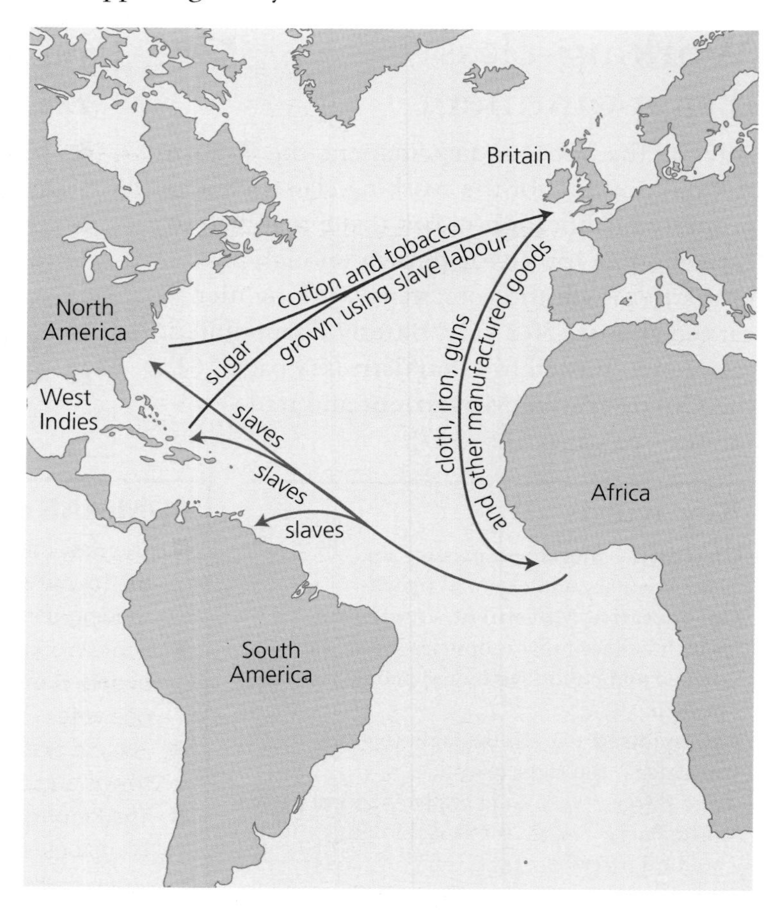

▶ ***Fig 2*** *Britain's triangular trade.*

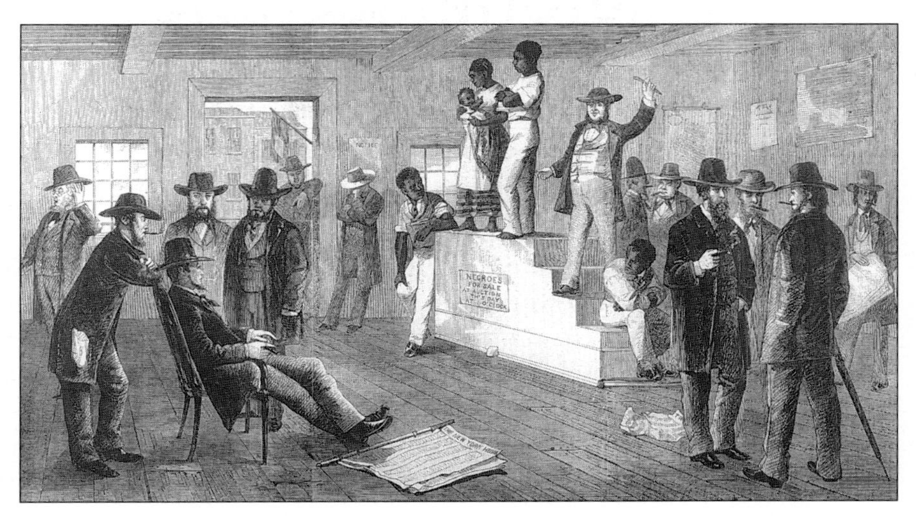

▶ ***Fig 3*** *A slave auction in Virginia, USA.*

The end of the slave trade 1807

After years of campaigning, William Wilberforce (1759–1833) and others persuaded Parliament to outlaw the slave trade in 1807. From that time on, it was illegal for a British subject to take part in the capture or transport of slaves.

▲ ***Fig 4*** *William Wilberforce.*

The end of slavery 1833

The outlawing of the slave trade was a step forward, but Wilberforce was determined to end slavery itself. He and the Rev. Thomas Clarkson founded the Anti-Slavery Society in 1823. On the whole the general public was sympathetic, but plantation owners said they could never run their plantations without slave labour and merchants said the sugar industry would collapse without slaves. Despite ill-health, Wilberforce would not give up and lived just long enough to witness the passing of an Act in 1833 that abolished slavery in the British Empire. Each slave owner was paid compensation of about £35 a slave.

Q1 What was made illegal in 1807?

Q2 What was made illegal in 1833?

Key words

plantation – a large farm growing one crop such as cotton

SUMMARY

- The slave trade had been carried on since the sixteenth century.
- William Wilberforce and others succeeded in getting the slave trade stopped, as far as Britain was concerned, in 1807.
- In 1833 slavery was abolished in the British Empire.

SUMMARY *activity*

Who opposed the ending of slavery and why?

76 Reform: factories

In this section of the book you will learn the following things:

- **factories employed large numbers of children;**
- **reformers wanted to control the number of hours children worked.**

Working children

By 1800 the cotton industry was more important than the woollen industry, but both needed workers in the new factories. From early on children were employed in large numbers. At first many were orphan children sent to the factories by the **parish Poor Law authorities** as **apprentices.** Often, however, families could not earn enough to live on without their children working from the age of four or five. Not that this was anything new; children had always worked – on farms and in home workshops. What was new was the factory discipline, the long hours and strict rules.

Factory Acts 1802 and 1819 and good employers

There had already been two Factory Acts to limit the hours worked by children in factories, but they had been largely ignored. Some employers were excellent, such as Robert Owen in Scotland and Robert Peel (senior), who showed that they could make profits *and* treat their workers well, and Benjamin Gott, who forbade the use of caning or whipping in his Leeds factory. Such employers were rare, however.

Q1 What sort of age might children be when they started to work in factories?

Lord Shaftesbury (1801–1885)

Hard on the heels of the abolition of slavery, reformers turned their attention to children in factories. One of the foremost reformers was Lord Ashley (later Lord Shaftesbury). Although he came from a wealthy background he had spent an unhappy childhood, and devoted much of his life to fighting to protect children. In 1833, the first effective Factory Act was passed.

Q2 What did Robert Owen think were the problems of employing very young children for long hours, even if they were well treated? (See Fig 1.)

Q3 Why do you think the Act of 1833 would be effective when the Acts of 1802 and 1819 had been ignored? (See Fig 4.)

A large factory in Scotland

'The children being well fed, clothed and lodged, looked fresh; yet their limbs were very generally deformed, their growth stunted and they made slow progress in even learning the alphabet.'

▲ ***Fig 1*** *Robert Owen giving evidence in 1816 about a visit to a factory where children under the age of eight were working $11\frac{1}{2}$ hours a day.*

The ten-hour day

The reformers had hoped for more and were eventually aiming at a maximum ten-hour day for all. This was achieved for women and children in 1847 and effectively for men, because the factories could not carry on with only the men working.

Worse than slavery?

'I have thought myself disgraced by being the owner of slaves but never thought it possible to be so cruel as to require a child of nine years old to work twelve and a half hours a day.'

▲ ***Fig 2*** *West Indian plantation owner.*

A small factory in Derbyshire

'Palfry, the smith, had the task of riveting irons upon any of the apprentices, if suspected of running away. The irons were riveted on the ankles and reached by long links to the hips.'

▲ ***Fig 3*** *John Brown in* A Memoir of Robert Blincoe *1828.*

▼ ***Fig 4***

Factory Act 1833 *(only applied to textile factories)*

- children under nine were not allowed to work;
- children under 13, no more than 48 hours a week;
- children 13 to 18, no more than 69 hours a week;
- four full-time inspectors were appointed to see the law was carried out;
- children were to have two hours schooling a day (this was difficult to enforce).

▼ ***Fig 5***

Factory Acts

1844 Act included women in a 69-hour week. Children under 13 limited to $6\frac{1}{2}$ hours a day and dangerous machinery to be fenced.

1847 Act limited hours to 10 a day for women and children (in 1850 it went up to $10\frac{1}{2}$ hours).

1874 Act reduced hours to 56 a week. More inspectors and safety regulations introduced.

All this time Shaftesbury and others campaigned to make the Acts apply to all factories and workshops.

Key words

apprentice – someone signed up to work for a master for a certain length of time and taught the job by him

parish Poor Law authorities – people in every parish appointed to deal with those who could not look after themselves and earn a living

SUMMARY

- Large numbers of children were employed in factories.
- Some employers, such as Robert Owen, Robert Peel and Benjamin Gott, treated their workers well.
- Lord Shaftesbury led the demand for a new Factory Act in 1833 to limit the working hours of children.
- Later Acts included protection for women, shortened working hours more, and raised safety standards.

SUMMARY *activity*

The Factory Act of 1833 did not achieve very much for most workers. Why, then, was it so important?

77 Reform: mines

In this section of the book you will learn the following things:

- more coal was needed so more people worked underground;
- the Mines Act was passed in 1842.

Coal in demand

The development of the steam engine and the increased use of iron meant more coal was needed. In the first half of the eighteenth century very few mineshafts went lower than 100 metres and even big pits employed no more than 40 or 50 miners. However, the demand for coal meant digging deeper for it and this made the coal miners' job more dangerous.

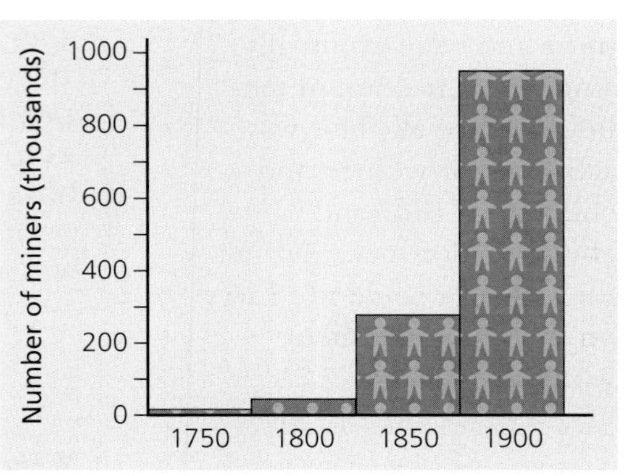

▲ ***Fig 1*** *Numbers of miners, 1750–1900.*

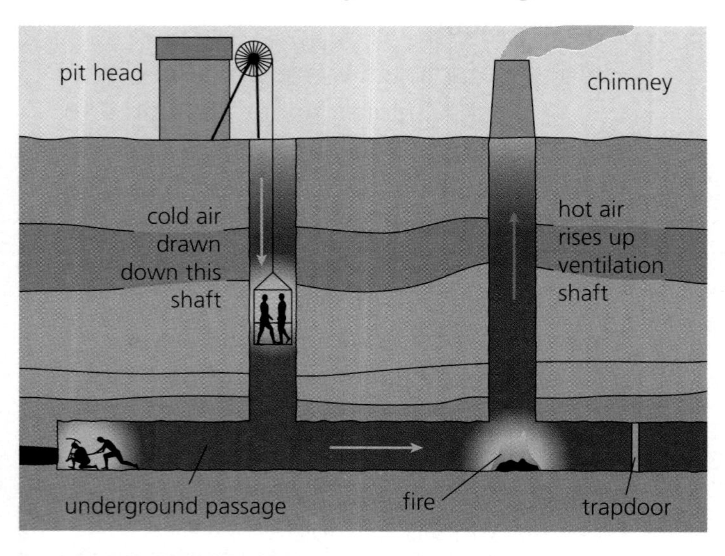

Dangers and what was done about them

The main dangers were from floods, roofs giving way, fire, lack of air and gases. Newcomen's steam engine replaced simple buckets for baling out mines. Wooden pit props were safer roof supports than the old method of leaving a pillar of coal every so often. As pits went deeper, it was important to get fresh air to the miners, so ventilation shafts were dug.

◄ ***Fig 2*** *Ventilating a mine.*

When candles were used for lighting, an explosion could be set off if a miner met a pocket of '**fire damp**'. Sir Humphrey Davy invented a miner's safety lamp in 1815. The flame was shielded by fine metal **gauze** so it was never hot enough to set off an explosion. An added bonus was that the flame turned blue when there was fire damp around.

Each improvement increased safety, but it also meant that mines could go deeper and so dangers increased again. The number of people employed also increased and this included women and children.

◄ ***Fig 3*** *Sir Humphrey Davy testing his safety lamp.*

Q1 Why was Newcomen's steam engine useful in mines?

Q2 What did Sir Humphrey Davy invent and what did it do?

▲ ***Fig 4*** *Arley Pit, at Wigan in Lancashire.*

Jobs underground

Sometimes children started work underground very young. The first job, at six to eight years old, might be as a 'trapper' opening the doors in the underground passages for the pit ponies hauling the coal to come through. Some passages were too low for ponies and often it was women who hauled the tubs of coal along to the shafts. Sometimes the tubs or baskets of coal were winched up, but in many mines they were carried up ladders by women and children.

Mines Act 1842

Although the men's work was hard and dangerous, it was the employment of women and children underground that shocked public opinion when a Government commission reported that girls were carrying baskets of coal weighing up to 150 kilograms, boys of six were sitting for 12 hours alone in the dark operating trapdoors, and women were dragging carts on their hands and knees. The Mines Act was passed in 1842.

Q3 What were the terms of the Mines Act of 1842?

Q4 Why might miners with large families resent the Act?

► ***Fig 5***

The Mines Act 1842

- no women or girls to be employed underground;
- no boys under ten to be employed underground.

Key words

fire damp – explosive gas in a coal mine
gauze – netting

SUMMARY

- More coal was needed for the iron industry and for steam engines.
- More people were employed underground, including women and children.
- Dangers included floods, gases, falling roofs, fire and lack of air.
- Public shock at the conditions in the coal mines helped to pass the Mines Act in 1842.

SUMMARY *activity*

What were the dangers of mining and what was done to try to overcome them?

78 The Poor Law and Chartism

In this section of the book you will learn the following things:

- **the Poor Law Amendment Act replaced the Old Poor Law in 1834;**
- **the working classes wanted to work for a better deal for themselves by having working-class men in Parliament.**

The Old Poor Law

The 'Old Poor Law' started in Tudor times. The old and the ill were given some money and the able-bodied were found some work. This system helped, but by the early nineteenth century the population had grown so much that there was not enough work for all the farmworkers, particularly in the south. In the north there was plenty of factory work when times were good, but if there was a downturn in trade, hundreds of workers were laid off. The Old Poor Law could not cope.

Q1 What was the problem in the south?

Q2 What was the problem in the north?

The Poor Law Amendment Act 1834

Edwin Chadwick set up a new system which became law in 1834. Many people liked its efficiency, some felt it was hard and the poor hated it.

The Poor Law Amendment Act 1834

- workhouses were built to serve a local area;
- conditions in the workhouses were to be more unpleasant than poverty outside;
- men, women and children were to be separated;
- no one was allowed out; uniforms were worn;
- food was basic.

▶ *Fig 1*

Disappointment for the working classes

The working classes were disappointed that the Reform Act of 1832 had not given them the vote. Then, hard on its heels, came the Poor Law Amendment Act, which meant that if people fell on hard times, even through no fault of their own, they had to go to the hated **workhouse**. These two things and the lack of strong trade unions, drove many to **emigrate**. Other men felt that the best hope was to work to get the vote for working-class men who could then speak up for working-class people in Parliament. Only then could they achieve better pay and conditions for working people.

The Charter

A charter of demands was published and three times, in the 1830s and 1840s. The Charter was signed by hundreds of thousands of people and presented to Parliament. When Parliament took no notice, some **Chartists** turned to violence and this split the movement. After 1848 despair set in, as Chartists saw they were not achieving their aims. In the 1850s many of them threw their energy into the new **trade unions** and the co-operative societies. Trade also improved in the 1850s and 1860s.

The Chartist demands 1838–48

- secret ballots;
- vote for all adult males;
- Parliaments elected once a year;
- no property qualification for MPs;
- payment of MPs;
- equal-sized electoral districts.

▲ *Fig 2*

Q3 Which of the Chartist demands would help working-class MPs to be elected into Parliament, and why?

Q4 Which five demands are now part of the voting system?

► ***Fig 3*** *A Chartist meeting on Kennington Common, London, in 1848.*

Key words

amendment – change
Chartists – people working to get the vote for working-class men
emigrate – go to live in another country
trade unions – a number of people in the same sort of job who join together to improve their working conditions
workhouse – an institution which housed and fed people who could not support themselves

SUMMARY

- The Old Poor Law dated from Tudor times.
- A Poor Law Amendment Act was passed in 1834 setting up new workhouses. The law made life inside the workhouses so unpleasant that people only used them as a last resort.
- Many working-class people were disappointed with the Reform Act of 1832 and the Poor Law Amendment Act of 1834.
- Many emigrated; others turned to Chartism, trade unions and the Co-operative Movement.

SUMMARY *activity*

What did the Poor Law Amendment Act say? Why did many working-class people dislike it? Why did some of them think that Chartism might help them?

79 Railways and the post

In this section of the book you will learn the following things:
- **steam engines could be adapted to drive locomotives;**
- **by the 1830s railways were being built all over Britain;**
- **railways changed the way people lived.**

The first steam locomotives

Richard Trevithick was one of the first people to make a **steam locomotive** – in 1804 – and many engineers were interested in his ideas. One of these was George Stephenson, who built the first passenger steam locomotive to run between Stockton and Darlington, in 1825. Then, with his son, Robert, he went on to build the Liverpool to Manchester railway, despite opposition from farmers and canal owners, and difficulties laying the track over marshy areas.

Q1 What did Richard Trevithick do?

Q2 Why do you think the Stephensons met opposition from farmers and canal owners?

The opening of the Liverpool–Manchester railway 1829–30

Not only did the Stephensons build the track, they designed the winning locomotive, the *Rocket,* to pull the carriages. Within weeks of the opening there were 1,000 passengers a day travelling on the trains, as well as **freight**. Soon railways were being built all over Britain.

▲ ***Fig 1*** *George and Robert Stephenson's* Rocket, *the winning locomotive on the Liverpool–Manchester railway.*

Passengers

At first there was very little cheap travel. Then in 1844 an Act was passed compelling railway companies to provide third-class travel at least once a day in each direction at no more than a penny a mile. Suddenly people from poorer backgrounds could travel. This was the beginning of holidays, particularly holidays to the seaside.

Q3 What was important about the 1844 Act?

Other changes

Remote parts of the country were brought into contact with each other. One result was that everywhere in Britain started to use the same time – Greenwich time – rather than local time, which varies by a few minutes across the country. Industry benefited as everything from coal and iron to agricultural machinery and milk could be carried quickly and cheaply. New jobs appeared, **manufacturing** railway engines and track, as well as working on the railways. A whole new industry making and exporting railway stock grew up as other countries laid down railway tracks.

▲ ***Fig 2*** *The Penny Post was brought in by Rowland Hill. Before 1840 letters were charged on the distance carried. Payment was made by the receiver.*

▲ ***Fig 3*** *Isambard Kingdom Brunel, pictured in front of the anchor chain for his ship, the* Great Eastern, *built bridges, railways and steamships. His most famous railway line was the Great Western from London to Bristol.*

The railways quickly took the postal contracts away from the Royal Mail coaches. The speed of travel and the introduction of the Penny Post in 1840 meant a large increase in the number of letters sent and benefited businesses as well as ordinary people. It is estimated that about a quarter of a million workers associated with the running of stage coaches and coaching inns lost their jobs.

Key words

freight – goods
manufacturing – making goods
steam locomotive – a carriage driven by steam power

SUMMARY

- Richard Trevithick used a steam engine to drive a locomotive in 1804.
- George Stephenson built the first successful passenger steam locomotive and ran it between Stockton and Darlington in 1825.
- The Stephensons built the Liverpool–Manchester railway line and the successful steam locomotive, the *Rocket,* in 1829.
- The railways helped industry to grow, created new jobs and enabled people to travel more.

SUMMARY *activity*

How did the railways change the way people lived?

80 Sail to steam

In this section of the book you will learn the following things:

- **people experimented with steam-powered boats;**
- **iron ships were eventually built instead of wooden ones.**

Steam power

Both the French and Americans experimented with steam-powered boats, but the earliest boat in Britain was tried out in 1788 in Scotland by William Symington. His second design, in 1802, was called the *Charlotte Dundas* and pulled barges on the Forth–Clyde Canal. In 1812 Henry Bell started a **steamship** service on the River Clyde. In 1818 steamships were in regular service crossing the Channel, but from crossing the Channel to crossing oceans was a big step.

	Sail	Steam
1850–54	79	21
1855–59	78	22
1860–64	68	32
1865–69	67	33
1870–74	25	75

▲ ***Fig 1*** *British shipbuilding (figures are percentages).*

In 1819 an American steamship crossed the Atlantic, but for most of the time the sails were used instead of the engine (to save on coal). Nearly 20 years later, in 1838, Isambard Kingdom Brunel's steamship, the *Great Western,* crossed from Bristol to New York, and in 1840 Samuel Cunard started a regular transatlantic service.

Paddle versus propeller

All the steamships were driven by a steam engine turning a **paddle**, but paddles were easily damaged so Francis Pettit-Smith built a ship with a **propeller** under the stern, below the water. Brunel's ship, the *Great Britain*, made the first propeller-driven crossing of the Atlantic in 1845.

Wood versus iron

The other new feature of the *Great Britain* was that it was made of iron. Iron was so strong that the hull could be built out of iron plates just over a centimetre thick, instead of wood 30 cm thick. It was, in fact, lighter to build in iron.

▲ ***Fig 2*** *The sails of a clipper would cover 15 tennis courts. The most famous clippers carried tea from India to Britain.*

Q1 Why was a propeller better than a paddle?

Q2 What were the advantages of building a ship with an iron hull?

Sail versus steam

However, it was a long time before steam replaced sail on the long voyages to the Far East. Steamships had to carry so much coal they had little room for cargo. Instead, sailing ships, called **clippers**, were used. These ships had first been built in America in the 1840s. The British copied them and changed the wooden hull for an iron one. These ships were very streamlined and fast and carried an enormous number of sails operated by a small crew using steam **winches**. However, the opening of the Suez Canal in 1869 cut the journey time to India and was a more suitable route for steamships. The days of the clipper were numbered.

The triumph of steamships

1854
- John Elder invented a steam engine which used half the coal normally required;
- coaling stations were set up in places such as Suez;

1869
- the Suez Canal was opened, cutting 5 000 km off the journey to India;
- clippers had to be towed through the Suez Canal.

▲ ***Fig 3***

The *Great Eastern*

One of Brunel's most daring ventures was building the *Great Eastern*. It was five times as large as the largest ship then afloat. With steam engines, paddle wheels and sails, it could sail to India and back without refuelling.

► ***Fig 4*** *Brunel's ship, the* Great Eastern, *was ahead of its time and never made a profit. Here it is seen laying the telegraph cable across the Atlantic in 1866. The electric telegraph had already taken over signalling on the railways.*

Key words

clipper – fast sailing ship used to carry goods
paddle – blades on a wheel
propeller – blades fixed on a shaft, turned by the steam engine to drive a ship through the water
steamship – ship with a steam engine
winch – machine on a ship, to pull in or let out the sails

SUMMARY

- At first ships driven by steam engines were only used on short journeys because they used a great deal of coal.
- Propellers replaced paddles.
- Iron replaced wood for building the hulls.
- Steam eventually replaced sail when there were more efficient engines, coaling stations, and the Suez Canal opened.

SUMMARY *activity*

Make a list of the dates and inventions of steamships from 1788. When did steam overtake sail in the numbers of ships built in Britain?

81 Trade unions: part 1

In this section of the book you will learn the following things:

- **trade unions were in a weak legal position;**
- **friendly societies and co-operative societies helped the better-off working people.**

Trade unions until the 1830s

Trade unions were made illegal by the Combination Acts of 1799 because the Government was panicking that the French Revolution might spread to Britain. Although the Acts were repealed in 1824, the Government was again frightened about **strikes** and they were tightened up again in 1825. During the rest of the 1820s and 1830s trade unions were legal but workers were not allowed to obstruct either their employers or other workers. This made striking almost impossible.

Q1 Why were the Combination Acts passed in 1799?

Q2 What was the situation for trade unions in the 1820s and 1830s?

The Combination Acts of 1799 forbade people to combine together to seek higher wages, i.e. they made trades unions illegal. The Acts were repealed in 1824.

▲ *Fig 1*

The Grand National Consolidated Trades Union 1833

The best-known of the large trade unions that grew up in the 1830s was the GNCTU. It was founded by Robert Owen and aimed to unite all trades under one enormous union of some half a million members. It was distrusted by employers, however, and then suffered a bitter blow over the case of the Tolpuddle Martyrs.

The Tolpuddle Martyrs 1834

Some farmworkers in the Dorset village of Tolpuddle formed a branch of the GNCTU. They were fighting a reduction in their wages from 9 shillings (45p) a week to 8 shillings (40p) a week. The men had taken a secret oath of loyalty to the Union and it was this that gave the magistrates the excuse to have them arrested. They were charged with taking unlawful oaths under an Act of 1797

Robert Owen

In 1800 he was a partner in a cotton mill in New Lanark, Scotland. He cut the working day to 10 $\frac{1}{2}$ hours, stopped child labour, built good homes for workers and paid good wages. He amazed other cotton manufacturers by making a profit.

▲ *Fig 2*

◀ ***Fig 3*** *Four of the Tolpuddle Martyrs, transported to Australia in 1834.*

and six of them were transported. Although the GNCTU fell apart (partly over this threat to trade unions and partly because it was too big to be manageable), the country was swept by protests until the men were pardoned in 1836. However, it was three more years until the last man came home, having seen the news of his pardon, by chance, in an old newspaper. Many working people turned to Chartism to help them improve their lives or joined friendly or co-operative societies.

Friendly societies and co-operative societies

Friendly societies were groups of workers who paid a weekly subscription into a fund. If any of them were sick or out of work they would be paid some money. These were different from trade unions because they did not seek higher wages or better conditions. Co-operative societies were formed when a number of people joined together to buy goods in bulk. They then opened their own shops and sold the goods to fellow workers. Profits were divided among the shoppers.

28 men with £1 each

shop

bought by local people

divided between local shoppers in proportion to the amount they had bought

◀ ***Fig 4*** *Some of the Rochdale Pioneers – 28 men from Rochdale who founded a co-operative society in 1844.*

▶ ***Fig 5*** *How a co-operative society worked.*

Q3 What were friendly societies? How were they different from trade unions?

Key words

consolidated – made solid or joined together

martyr – someone who is punished for their views

strikes – workers withdrawing from work to persuade employers to give them better conditions

SUMMARY

- Trade unions were made legal after 1824 but strikers could not obstruct employers or fellow workers.
- The GNCTU was an attempt to form one big union for everyone.
- The Tolpuddle Martrys highlighted the weakness of trade unions.
- Many working people turned to Chartism, friendly and co-operative societies.

SUMMARY *activity*

What happened to the Tolpuddle Martyrs in 1834 and how did this affect the GNCTU?

82 Towns and public health

In this section of the book you will learn the following things:

- **disease was rife in the growing towns;**
- **Acts were passed to improve public health in the towns.**

Disease and towns

Smallpox was a terrible killer until the early nineteenth century when Edward Jenner's discovery that you could **vaccinate** people against the illness became widespread. However, the killer diseases typhus, typhoid, tuberculosis, diphtheria and cholera remained.

▲ *Fig 1* Edward Jenner.

By 1851 there were more people living in towns than in the country. Towns and cities had grown so fast that there were often no sewers, lighting or paving. There was no refuse collection. Water came from standpipes in the street that were only turned on for a short time each day or from rivers and streams that were easily polluted. Both typhoid and cholera were diseases carried by water.

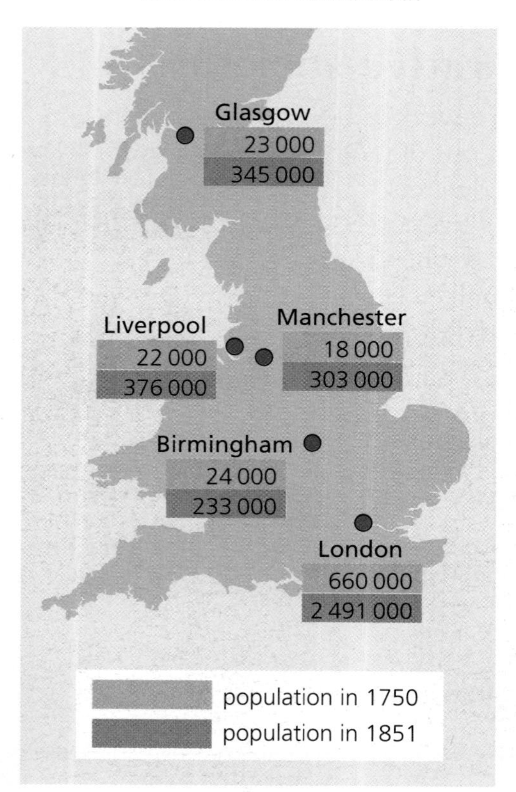

◄ *Fig 2* Growth of towns 1750–1851.

Q1 Why were there often no sewers, lighting, paving, refuse collection or clean water in towns?

Cholera

In 1831 a cholera **epidemic** broke out for the first time in Britain. Spreading from Asia, it began in the port of Sunderland and killed thousands of people all over the country. It was clear that the areas worst affected were the overcrowded slums in the large towns. There were two problems, however: no one knew how disease was carried and no one was responsible for public health.

Q2 What were the two problems of fighting disease in the towns?

The Municipal Corporations Act 1835 and the Public Health Act 1848

The first Act allowed for town councils to be set up, elected by all male ratepayers. This was the beginning of towns organising services such as refuse collection, but it took further outbreaks of cholera for the Public Health Act to be passed in 1848. This allowed local boards of health to be set up to control such things as draining the streets and cleaning. However, it was not compulsory, so unless the death rate was very high, little was done.

Q3 Why was the Public Health Act of 1848 not very successful?

Public Health Act 1875

It took until 1875 for a serious Public Health Act to get through Parliament. A nationwide system was then set up with authorities that were responsible for sewerage, drainage, street cleaning and clean water supply. Medical officers and sanitary inspectors were appointed and, by 1900, British cities were a great deal cleaner than they had been 50 years before, and the death rate had fallen.

► ***Fig 3*** *Jacob's Island, Bermondsey, in London, in the mid-nineteenth century. This open sewer (once a stream) was the only source of free water. In 1875 the Artisans' Dwelling Act allowed councils to clear slums and rebuild.*

Key words

epidemic – widespread outbreak of an illness

vaccinate – inject a small amount of a mild form of a disease into someone to protect them against the severe form

SUMMARY

- Smallpox was controlled by vaccination by the early nineteenth century.
- Other diseases were rife in cities and cholera appeared in 1831.
- Acts were passed to set up town councils and regulate public health.
- By 1900 towns were cleaner and healthier.

SUMMARY *activity*

Why were clean water supplies such a problem in towns in the nineteenth century?

83 Religion

In this section of the book you will learn the following things:

- religion was important to many people;
- John Wesley's Methodist Church grew in the nineteenth century;
- the Church influenced people to help the poor.

The Church of England

Many people went to church at least once every Sunday. As well as catering for the spiritual side of life, churches provided a social life: there were church outings, bands and choirs. The Church of England catered for just over half the population of churchgoers, mostly in the countryside. The squire (the local landowner) and the parson made sure that everyone and everything stayed just as it was. It was different in the towns, however. The Church of England did not appeal to people who had gone to look for better jobs and who were escaping the rigid class structure of the village.

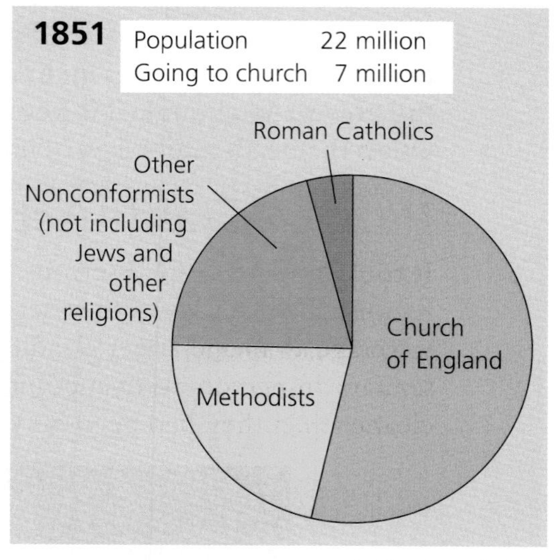

▲ *Fig 1 Religious affiliation in 1851.*

◀ *Fig 2 Going to church in the 1830s.*

Q1 What percentage of the population belonged to the Church of England?

Q2 What percentage were Methodists?

John Wesley (1703–1791) and Methodism

Life was not all good in the large towns. There were long hours of work, overcrowded housing, poverty, drunkenness and disease. Some people looked to religion for help, and found it in John Wesley's Methodism. Methodists built their own chapels and ran their own services, which had rousing hymns and long **sermons**. They were expected to be sober, hardworking people. Many trade unionists learnt the art of public speaking by starting out as Methodist preachers. The Methodists were called Nonconformists, the name given to any Church group outside the Church of England. Other Nonconformists included Congregationalists, Baptists and Quakers.

Q3 What were Methodists expected to be?

Q4 What were Nonconformists?

The Evangelical movement in the Church of England

The Nonconformist example of strict moral behaviour and interest in helping people not only affected the trade union movement but also influenced the Church of England. In the eighteenth century, the Church of England had grown complacent: many parsons spent more time foxhunting and socialising than looking after their **parishioners**. Some serious-minded people within the Church of England started the Evangelical movement. They ran Bible study groups and worked among the poor.

People influenced by the Evangelical movement and Nonconformist religion

Elizabeth Fry (1780–1845) worked to reform prisons.

William Wilberforce (1759–1833) worked to abolish slavery.

Lord Shaftesbury (1801–1885) worked to improve workers' conditions.

Dr Thomas Barnardo (1845–1905) founded Barnardo's homes for street children.

William Booth (1829–1912) founded the Salvation Army in 1878 to help destitute people.

▲ Fig 3

Charles Darwin (1809–1882)

Darwin wrote a book called *The Origin of Species* in 1859. He claimed that all living species had evolved from one original life form. This idea challenged the religious belief that God had created man separately.

▲ Fig 4

Key words

parishioner – someone who lives in the parish or area around a church

sermon – talk by a parson or preacher

SUMMARY

- The Church of England had most followers in the countryside.
- Nonconformist groups, such as Methodists, appealed to people in the towns.
- The Evangelicals in the Church of England, together with Nonconformists, wanted to improve poor people's lives.

SUMMARY *activity*

Why do you think many people were attracted to Methodism and the Evangelical movement in the nineteenth century?

84 Education

In this section of the book you will learn the following things:

- schools and universities were for boys from rich homes;
- religious organisations ran schools;
- the Government started to take an interest in schools for all in 1833.

The state of education 1750

In Scotland by 1750 there was a good school system paid for out of local rates. The same was not true in England and Wales. Very few children had any schooling and rich children had **tutors** or teachers at home. By the nineteenth century there were some expensive boys' public schools such as Eton, Harrow and Rugby. After this a boy might go on to Oxford or Cambridge universities. There were hardly any schools for girls and certainly no university education.

There were some grammar schools for the middle classes but the best schools were probably the ones run by Nonconformists, such as the Quakers. They provided an education that included science and book-keeping as well as the **classics**, which was more or less all that was taught at the public schools. However, by the mid-nineteenth century, the public schools were improving under the leadership of headmasters such as Thomas Arnold at Rugby.

▲ ***Fig 1*** *The first efforts to provide serious education for girls started in 1850, when Frances Buss opened the North London Collegiate School and, in 1858, Dorothea Beale (pictured above) became the principal of Cheltenham Ladies' College.*

Q1 How was the Scottish system of education funded?

Q2 Why were Nonconformist schools giving a better education in the nineteenth century than most other schools?

Beginnings of schooling

As far as the great majority of children were concerned, there was little or nothing in the way of schooling. Robert Raikes founded the first Sunday School in 1783. Poor children might go to a '**dame school**' in the week, but often this was little more than childminding. The Church of England and Nonconformists set up schools in some areas and, in 1833, the Government gave a grant of £20 000 for school buildings.

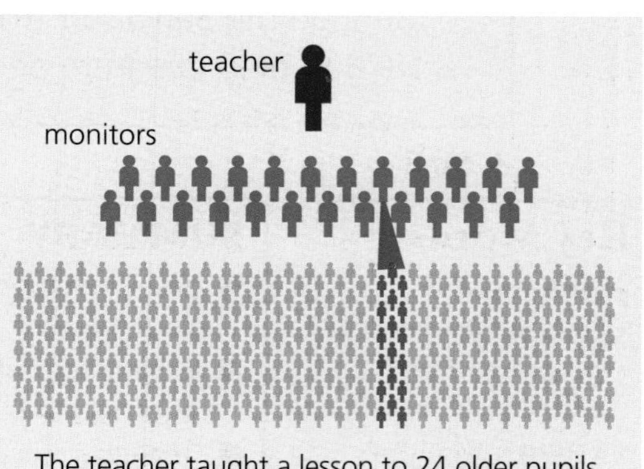

► ***Fig 2*** *The monitorial system.*

◀ ***Fig 3*** *A school run on the monitorial system in the 1830s.*

Q3 What do you think were the advantages and disadvantages of the monitorial system?

Education Act 1870

By 1870 two things had happened. The new industries needed educated people to operate machines and deal with paperwork, and the 1867 Parliamentary Reform Act had just given the vote to all working-class householders in the towns. How could they vote if they could not even read a newspaper to find out what was going on in the world? So, in 1870 the Education Act was passed; it set up schools all over the country. By 1880 all children had to go to school. This brought to light many starving, disease-ridden children from homes that could not afford even the penny a week for school fees. In 1891 all schooling, up to the age of ten, was made free and compulsory.

New universities

1828	University College, London
1832	Durham
1870s	Women's colleges at Oxford and Cambridge
1893	University of Wales
by 1914	Sheffield, Leeds, Manchester, Birmingham and Bristol

▲ ***Fig 4***

Q4 Why was the Education Act of 1870 passed?

Key words

classics – the study of Latin and Greek

dame school – village school usually run by a woman

tutors – a teacher of either one or two people

SUMMARY

- Rich boys were sent to public school and on to university.
- Middle-class boys went to grammar schools.
- The best schools were run by Nonconformists.
- Religious organisations set up schools for poorer children.
- The Government passed the Education Act of 1870, setting up schools all over the country.
- In 1880 schooling became compulsory.
- In 1891 school became free for all up to the age of ten.

SUMMARY *activity*

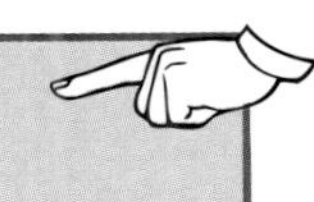

What sort of education did boys have in the eighteenth and nineteenth centuries? What evidence is there that girls were not considered equal to boys? What evidence is there that this was changing in the nineteenth century?

85 Trade unions: part 2

In this section of the book you will learn the following things:

- skilled workers could afford a good subscription to their union;
- unskilled workers could not afford subscriptions, so their unions were weaker;
- laws were passed in the 1870s to protect and control trade unions.

Amalgamated Society of Engineers and skilled unions

In 1851 over 100 different sorts of engineers formed a union. These engineers were well paid and could afford a subscription of 5p a week. The union's great aim was to negotiate with employers to get better pay and conditions. Carpenters and other skilled workers followed suit in the 1850s and 1860s and, because they were well run, these unions were known as 'model unions'.

However, trade unions could still be prosecuted under laws against conspiracy. They were not safe until laws were passed in the 1870s.

Amalgamated Society of Engineers *1 shilling (5p) a week subscription covered:*

- sickness;
- accident;
- loss of tools (by fire etc);
- pensions;
- funeral benefit;
- strike pay.

▲ ***Fig 1***

Q1 What was the aim of the ASE?

Q2 Why were skilled workers' unions known as 'model unions'?

Unskilled unions: the match girls 1888

None of this did much to help unskilled workers, who did not earn enough to pay a subscription to a union. In 1888, Annie Besant, a London journalist, helped the girls who made matches for Bryant and May to strike. When the public learnt that they were only paid one penny an hour for their dangerous work, there was an outcry and money poured in to help their fight. They gained better pay and conditions.

▶ ***Fig 2*** *Match girls.*

Q3 Why was it easier for the engineers to negotiate with their employers than for the match girls to negotiate with theirs?

The dockers 1889

The next year the London dockers, led by Ben Tillett, went on strike. They demanded 6d ($2\frac{1}{2}$p) an hour and a minimum of four hours work at a time. In the long hot summer of 1889 their action closed the port of London and the dockers paraded the streets carrying rotten vegetables and fish heads to show what they and their families had to live on. Again, public sympathy brought in enough money to carry the strike into a sixth week and the dockers' employers granted their demands. Within weeks thousands more dockers joined the Dockers' Union.

Change still needed

It was not all plain sailing, however. When trade was bad, workers could not afford the subscription to their union and employers could easily find other workers to fill their places. Even though **picketing** was allowed after 1875, it was not possible to stop all **blacklegs** from working. The next century was to see even more changes in working and trade union lives.

Q4 What did the London dockers demand?

Q5 Why did the match girls' strike and the dockers' strike succeed?

Q6 Why was picketing an important right for a trade union? (see key words)

▼ *Fig 3*

Government	**Law**
Gladstone and the Liberals	**1871** Trade Union Act – safeguarded union funds. A treasurer who ran away with subscriptions could be prosecuted. **1871** Criminal Law Amendment Act – outlawed picketing

Many working men now had the vote (1867). Angry with Gladstone and the Liberals, they voted Conservative in the general election of 1874. Disraeli and the Conservatives responded with a new law.

Disraeli and the Conservatives	**1875** Conspiracy and Protection of Property Act – allowed peaceful picketing

Key words

blackleg – a worker who goes to work when his colleagues are on strike (usually a non-union worker)

picketing – persuading non-union workers from going to work during a strike

SUMMARY

- Skilled unions were founded in the 1850s and 1860s to negotiate for better pay and conditions for their members.
- Unskilled workers could not afford high subscriptions or negotiate so well.
- There were three trade union acts in the 1870s, safeguarding and controlling the unions and their activities.

SUMMARY *activity*

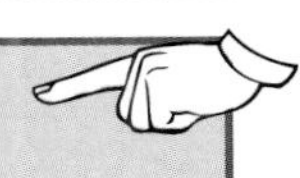

Explain how the trade union Acts of the 1870s helped or hindered trade unions.

86 Women

In this section of the book you will learn the following things:

- **there was a big difference between the lives of rich and poor women;**
- **towards the end of the century women demanded more rights.**

▲ ***Fig 1*** *Two rich women pictured in 1895 driving one of the newly invented motor cars.*

Rich and poor women

There was a big difference between the lives of rich and poor women. Rich women were hemmed in by lack of education, lack of any opportunity to work, lack of exercise and heavy, cumbersome clothes. Poor women were hemmed in by the same lack of education but they had too much work.

Q1 What was the main difference in the lives of rich and poor women?

▲ ***Fig 2*** *Women gathering potatoes.*

Most unmarried working-class women were domestic servants. This was a good job in a large household with plenty of servants, but in smaller households a single girl servant could work from dawn till dusk doing the heavy cleaning work by herself. In the country women worked on farms. In the towns they worked in factories.

▲ ***Fig 3*** *Married women.*

New opportunities

Florence Nightingale came from a wealthy family. She did not marry and carved out a career for herself as a nurse. This unusual case was an example to a growing number of middle-class women. Girls' schools and the coming of a national system of **state education** began to open up opportunities for women. In 1874 the London School of Medicine opened and by 1900 there were 300 women doctors. Even more women trained as nurses. More offices dealing with increasing business from trade and industry meant more opportunities, and the invention of the telephone brought jobs for women. After 1891 compulsory education for children under the age of ten also brought teaching jobs to women.

Q2 What job opportunities were there for women by 1900?

New universities were set up and even Oxford and Cambridge opened women's colleges, although women were not allowed to be awarded degrees!

Married women, property and voting

▶ *Fig 4*

Married Women's Property Acts

1870 married women allowed to keep their own earnings;

1882 married women granted the right to own property.

Henry Fawcett was a keen reformer. One day his wife lost her purse on a train and went to the Lost Property Office to claim it. They would not hand it over because it belonged to her husband; she was a married woman and had no right to own anything. Henry Fawcett was appalled and worked to change the law. The results were two Acts allowing married women to own property.

In 1888 women gained the vote in local county council elections and some began to campaign for the vote in Parliamentary elections.

▼ ***Fig 5*** *A suffragette – a campaigner for votes for women.*

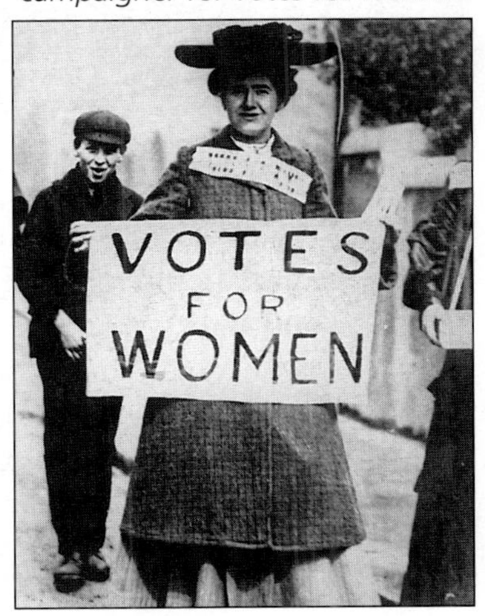

Birth control

There was no widespread, effective method of birth control, so once women were married they often faced years of one pregnancy after another, just as women had for centuries. Towards the end of the century, however, by using methods of birth control middle-class women were beginning to limit their families and gain more control over their lives.

Key words

menial – poorly paid unskilled work

state education – education provided free by the Government for all children

SUMMARY

- Until the 1850s women had few opportunities to do anything except marry or do **menial** jobs.
- Better education led to middle-class women obtaining jobs such as nurses, teachers, office workers and doctors.
- The Married Women's Property Acts gave married women rights over their earnings and property.
- At the end of the century, middle-class women were beginning to limit the size of their families.

SUMMARY *activity*

In the nineteenth century, for the first time in history, women began to gain some freedom and opportunities. Why did it happen then and not in 1066?

87 Britain and the world

In this section of the book you will learn the following things:

- Britain imported raw materials and turned them into manufactured goods;
- the British Empire was important to Britain for both imports and exports.

▲ *Fig 1* *Queen Victoria with her husband Albert, in 1861.*

Workshop of the world

In 1897 Queen Victoria had been Queen for 60 years. She was Queen of the largest empire the world had ever seen. Since 1750 Britain had thrived on importing raw materials, making goods out of them and exporting those to other countries. One of the best examples was cotton. Britain imported raw cotton, some from Egypt and India which were part of the British Empire, but most from the USA. The raw cotton arrived in bales, was unloaded at Liverpool docks and taken to one of the hundreds of cotton mills in Lancashire, where it was spun into cotton thread and woven into cotton cloth. About one-third of the cloth was sold in Britain, but the rest was packed on board ships and exported to other countries. Although Britain sold to the USA, South America and Europe, the easiest markets were the countries in the British Empire. They had ties with Britain and favourable trade agreements. Other exports included railway engines and tracks, machines of all kinds, metalwork (knives, cutlery, nails, tools, screws, needles), china, guns, household goods and furniture. For many years Britain was known as the 'workshop of the world'.

Q1 From which countries did Britain import raw cotton?

Q2 What happened to the raw cotton when it reached Liverpool?

Q3 To which countries did Britain sell the cotton goods?

Q4 List other British exports.

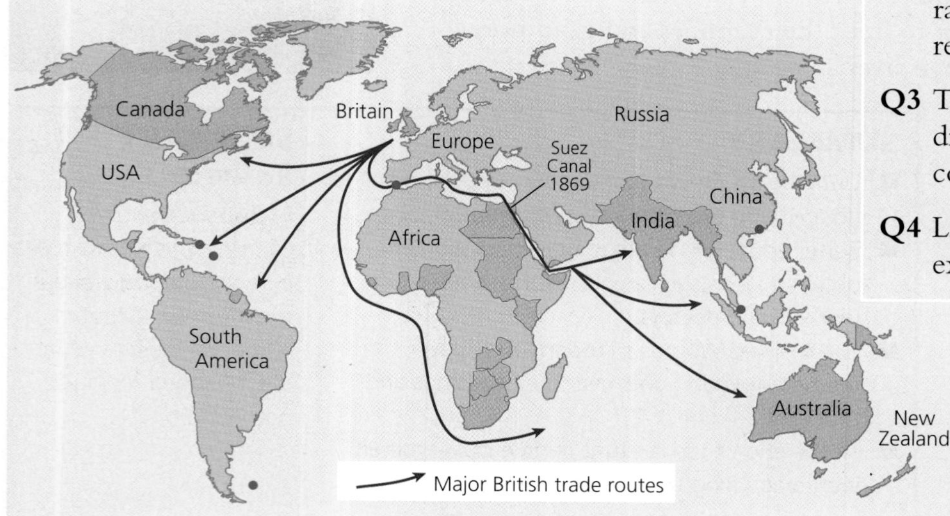

◄ *Fig 2* *The British Empire in 1900.*

Importing food

Britain imported a great deal of food. Some, such as sugar, wheat and cocoa, was refined and some, such as tea, coffee, fruit and meat, sold straight to the customer in Britain. Much of this food came from the countries in the empire. Cheap raw materials from the colonies, which were also a ready market for buying British goods, suited Britain very well.

Q5 Why did Britain like having an empire?

The USA and Germany catch up

By 1900, however, the world scene was changing. Both the USA and Germany had overtaken Britain as producers of coal and steel. This was a measure of the way in which they were catching up on the lead Britain had taken because it was the first country to have an industrial revolution. Soon they would be producing their own manufactured goods and, as ties within the British Empire loosened, the twentieth century would be a very different place for Britain.

Q6 Which countries had overtaken Britain in coal and steel production by 1900?

Changes

However, in 1900, most people in Britain were better off than they had been in 1750 or even when Victoria had come to the throne in 1837. There was education for all and reforms and trade unions had made some improvements in working conditions. From 1850 more people lived in towns than in the country. Working-class men could vote, and their own political party – the Labour Party – was growing. Women had more chance of an education and a better job. Medical advances included **anaesthetics** and **antiseptics.** Local councils were responsible for cleaning up towns and even rebuilding some slum areas. The country was covered with a network of railway lines. There were 20,000 motor cars on the roads and somewhere, someone was thinking of building a machine that could fly.

Key words

anaesthetic – a drug to make a person unconscious

antiseptic – a solution to kill bacteria

SUMMARY

- Britain imported raw materials such as cotton, made it into cloth and exported the cloth.
- Britain exported many manufactured goods.
- Britain imported food cheaply from countries in the Empire.
- By 1900 the USA and Germany had overtaken Britain in the production of coal and steel.
- People's lives had changed a great deal since 1750, in transport, education, work and where they lived.

SUMMARY *activity*

Write about the social and economic changes between 1750 and 1900.

Kings and Queens 1727–1901

	born	reigned	died
George II	1683	1727–1760	1760
George III	1738	1760–1820	1820
		Regency 1811–1820	
George IV	1762	*Regent* 1811–1820 *King* 1820–1830	1830
William IV	1765	1830–1837	1837
Victoria	1819	1837–1901	1901

Note: See the key to the crowns on page 250.

Expansion, trade and industry: Timeline 1760–1897

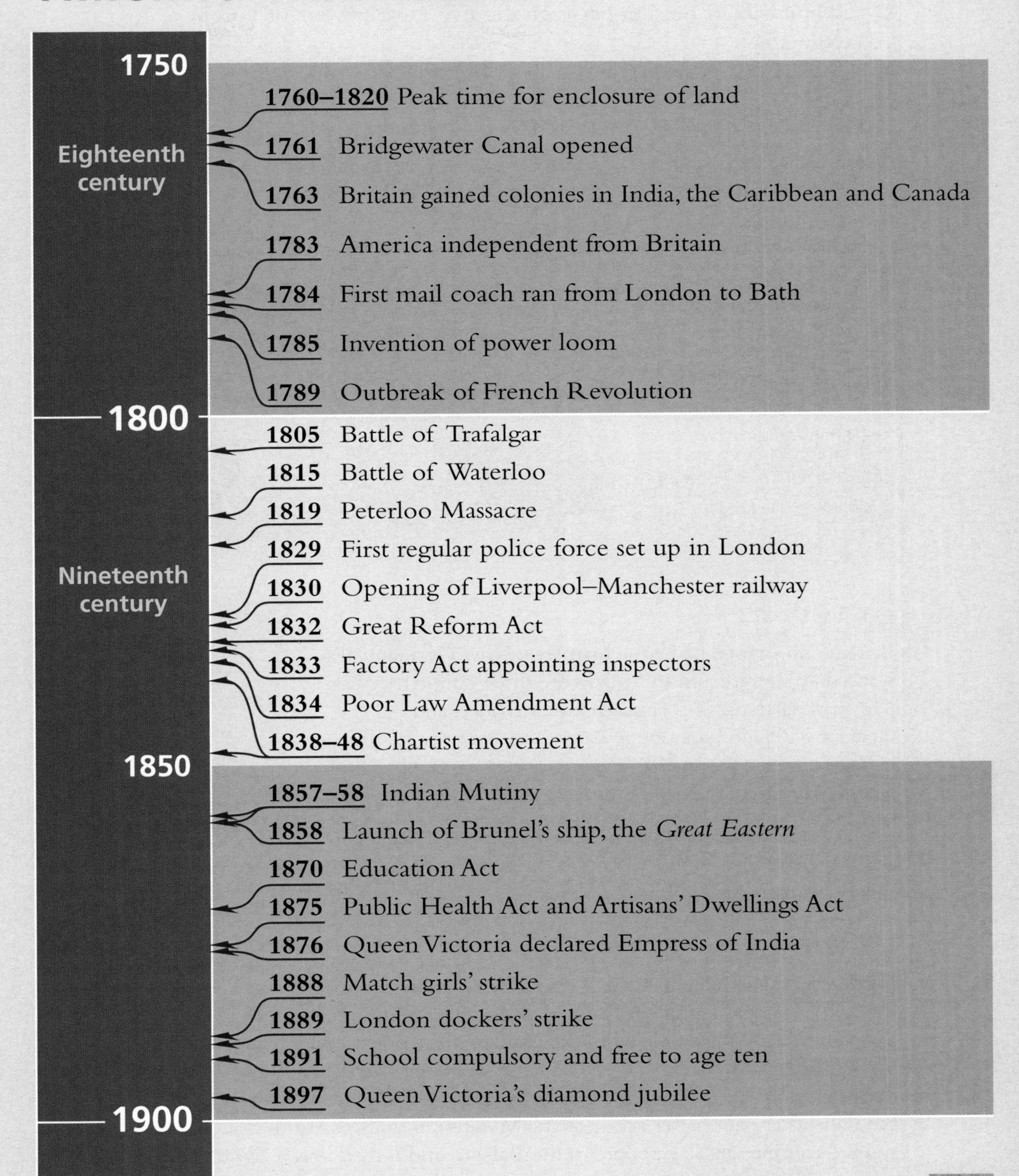

88 Causes of the First World War

In this section of the book you will learn the following things:

- the build-up of tension between the five great powers of Europe before 1914;
- the spark that started the war in 1914.

The five great powers

There were five powerful countries in Europe at the beginning of the twentieth century: Britain, France, Germany, Russia and **Austria-Hungary**.

▼ ***Fig 1*** *Europe and the First World War.*

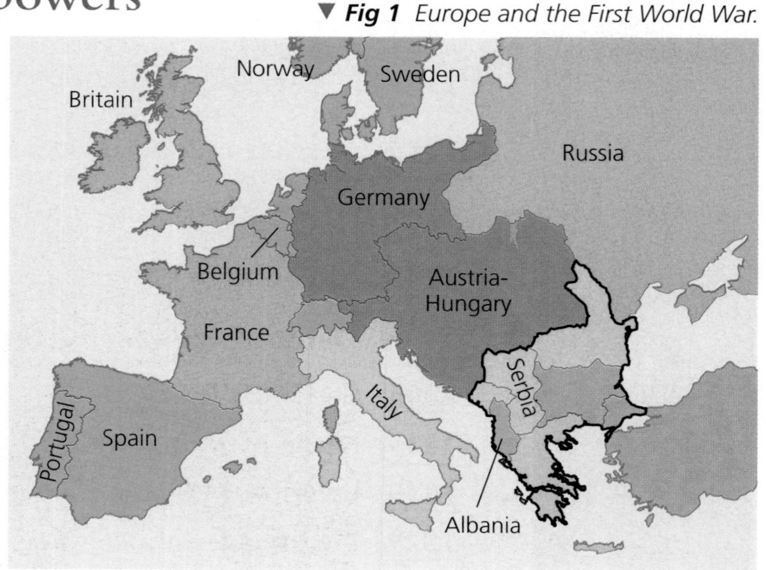

In the west

Britain and France had large **empires**. Now Germany also wanted an empire and this made the three countries rivals. This was particularly so in the case of Britain and Germany. Britain had a huge navy to protect the British Empire all over the world. When Germany started to build a large navy, Britain became nervous.

Q1 Why was Britain worried about Germany?

Q2 Why did France have reason to dislike as well as fear Germany?

France had other reasons to be worried. In 1871 Germany had taken **Alsace-Lorraine**, land that lay on the borders between the two countries. France wanted the land back and feared Germany's ambitions.

In the east

Further east, Russia and Austria-Hungary were bitter rivals. To the south of the two countries lay the Balkans, a collection of states including Serbia. People of different races lived in the Balkans. One of the chief groups was the Slavs. Since many Slavs lived in Russia as well as in the Balkans, it was logical that Russia would support the Slav people. Russia was also keen to control the Balkans to gain better access to the Mediterranean Sea. At this time, Serbia wanted to unite all Slav people in the Balkans and Russia was ready to help.

Like the Balkans, many different races, including Slavs, lived within the Austro-Hungarian borders. A united Slav Serbia could be all they needed to start demanding independence from Austria-Hungary and looking to Russia for help.

Q3 Explain why Austria-Hungary was uneasy about her neighbour Russia.

Assassination at Sarajevo

Tensions were building up. It took only one spark to set them alight. On 28 June 1914, Archduke Franz Ferdinand, the heir to the Austro-Hungarian throne, was visiting Sarajevo. He was shot dead by a Serbian student called Gavrilo Princip. Austria-Hungary declared war on Serbia. Russia came in on the side of Serbia and declared war on Austria-Hungary. The other major countries of the alliances were drawn in. The last one was Britain, when Germany marched through Belgium to attack France (Britain had a treaty to protect Belgium).

Q4 Look at the map of Europe. Why do you think Britain was interested in protecting Belgium?

▶ ***Fig 2*** *Archduke Ferdinand and his wife in Sarajevo shortly before his assassination.*

Key words

Alsace-Lorraine – two provinces of France, on the borders of Germany, to which Germany felt it had some claim

Austria-Hungary – an empire in central Europe, made up of a number of different groups of people

empire – group of countries controlled by another, more powerful state

expansionist – country wanting to expand or increase the lands it controls

SUMMARY

- Britain and France feared German designs on their empires and land.
- Russia and Austria-Hungary were rivals for control of the Balkans.
- The spark that started the war was the assassination of the heir to the throne of Austria-Hungary by a Serbian on 28 June 1914.

SUMMARY *activity*

*Which of the five great powers was the most **expansionist** at this time? Give reasons for your answer.*

89 The Front Lines 1914–1918

In this section of the book you will learn the following things:

- the First World War started in August 1914;
- there was fighting on the Western and Eastern Fronts;
- Germany was defeated in November 1918.

The Western Front

When the German Army marched into Belgium on 3 August 1914, Britain declared war and sent the British Expeditionary Force (BEF) over to France. The French and British troops frustrated the German plan to force France out of the war quickly – the Schlieffen Plan – at the Battle of the Marne. The Germans then planned to move round the north of the British and French. This resulted in both sides rushing soldiers north, where they clashed near the town of Ypres. The month-long battle prevented the Germans from moving forward but it did not push them back out of France and Belgium. Both sides dug trenches to maintain their positions and, by early 1915, the war had become a **stalemate**.

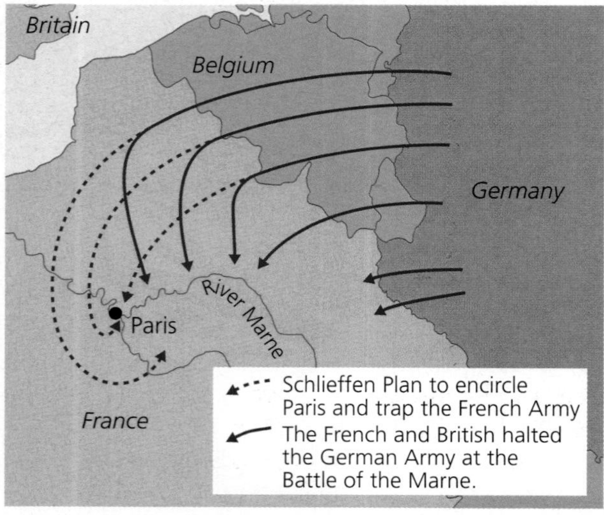

▲ ***Fig 1*** *The German attack in 1914.*

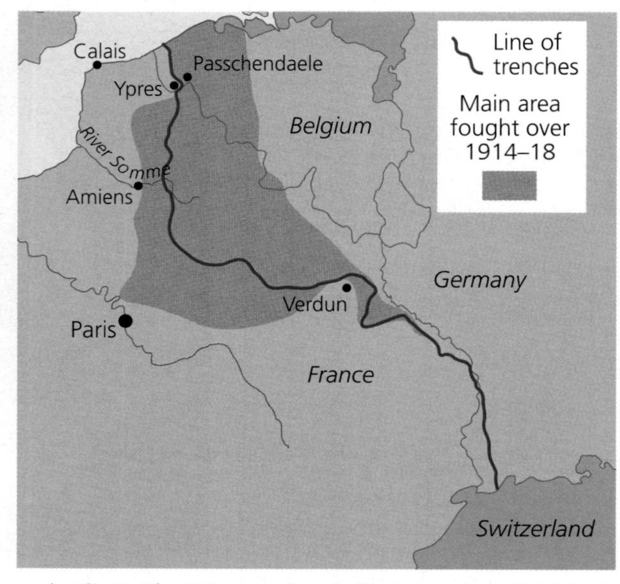

▲ ***Fig 2*** *The Western Front. By December 1914 both sides had dug trenches that stretched from the Channel to the borders of Switzerland.*

Q1 How was the Schlieffen Plan frustrated?

Trench warfare

For four years, the French and British faced the Germans in deep trenches. Sometimes the trenches were far apart, but in some places they were so close the soldiers could hear the voices of their enemy when the guns were not firing. The trenches were protected by thick fences of barbed wire and by machine guns which could fire 600 bullets a minute. This made attacking an enemy trench very difficult. Both sides tried attacking at different times, but against strongly defended trenches casualties were very high.

▲ *Fig 3* British 'Tommies' in the trenches.

The Eastern Front

Meanwhile the Germans, with the Austrians, were fighting the Russians on the Eastern Front. After two years of fierce fighting, the Germans were in a stronger position than the Russians and, by the winter of 1916–17, Russian resistance was collapsing. The Germans could now transfer half a million soldiers from the Eastern Front to the Western Front.

Q2 Why was the collapse of Russia serious for the British and French?

Verdun and the Somme

The Germans attacked the French at Verdun and the French Army fought them to a standstill. Both sides lost thousands of men, but the French held Verdun. Meanwhile, to take some of the pressure off the French, the British had agreed to attack the Germans further north, on the River Somme. The Battle of the Somme started on 1 July 1916. The British had 60,000 casualties on the first day and the fighting went on until November, when both sides were exhausted. The British had taken only 15 kilometres of land.

▲ *Fig 4* British Army Indian machine gun crew.

Q3 What was gained from the British attacks on the Somme?

1917 and 1918

The USA entered the war in 1917 and just as the Russians withdrew from the war. Germany was keen to defeat Britain and France on the Western Front before American soldiers began to arrive in France. German forces attacked in March 1918, but by July, after early success, they were driven back, short of supplies because of the British **naval blockade**. The guns stopped firing at 11 o'clock on the morning of 11 November 1918. The war was over.

Key words

naval blockade – using ships to stop the enemy's ships taking supplies to their own country

stalemate – when neither side can win

SUMMARY

- The British and French frustrated the German Schlieffen Plan by holding the Germans on the River Marne.
- After this the Western Front was a more or less static line of trenches for four years.
- The Germans defeated the Russians on the Eastern Front.
- Germany was defeated in 1918 partly due to the arrival of the first USA soldiers and partly to the British naval blockade of German ports.

SUMMARY *activity*

Why did fighting on the Western Front become a stalemate?

90 War at sea

In this section of the book you will learn the following things:

- **the British Navy protected supplies and troopships and blockaded Germany;**
- **the Germans used submarine warfare to disrupt supplies to Britain.**

Protection by the British Navy

Britain used its navy to take control of German colonies around the world and there were raids on shipping. The two main clashes were at Coronel near Chile and the Falkland Islands, but for most of the war the value of the British Navy lay in what did not happen. The Navy protected all the troopships crossing from Britain to France (not one was sunk) and the troopships from the colonies. Supplies to Britain also mostly arrived safely.

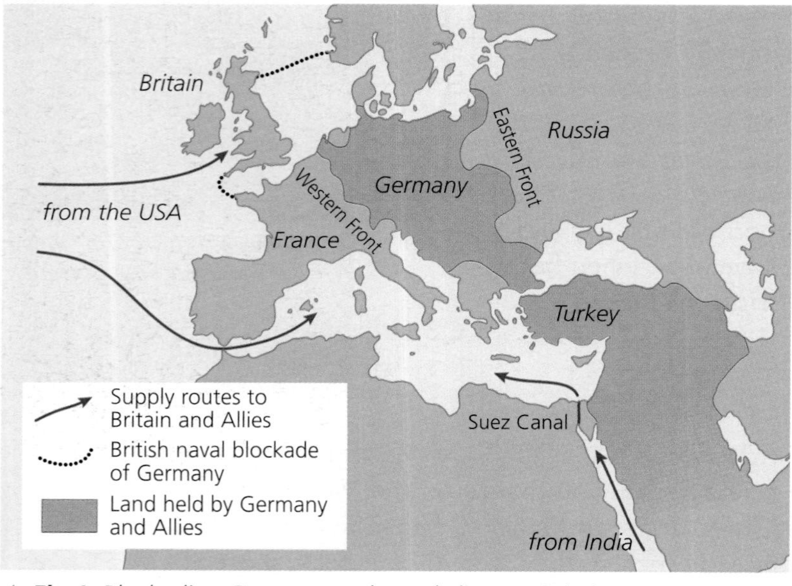

▲ ***Fig 1*** *Blockading Germany and supply lines to Britain.*

British blockade of Germany

Most important of all, the fleet kept supplies from reaching Germany by blockading the North Sea and the Channel. This blockade starved Germany of supplies and helped towards its surrender in 1918.

Q1 What four things was the British Navy used for?

Q2 Why was the blockade of Germany important for Britain?

▶ ***Fig 2*** *Battleships in action at the battle of Jutland.*

German submarine warfare

▲ *Fig 3 The poster reads: 'U-boat attack!'*

Moreover, knowing that it could not go on fighting without supplies coming by sea, Germany was led to **retaliate**. To do this, it started a counter blockade using submarines (**U-boats**). However, submarines cannot stop ships and destroy cargoes; they can only sink them. This meant that to be effective Germany had to sink **neutral ships**. The most dangerous power to do this to was the USA. In 1915 a German submarine sank the *Lusitania* with over 100 American passengers on board. The uproar was so great that Germany feared the USA might enter the war, so it stopped sinking neutral ships. This meant that all sorts of goods reached Britain in neutral ships and helped to keep it fighting.

By 1917 the Germans wanted to bring more decisive action to the war and started all-out submarine warfare in an effort to destroy Britain before the USA could join the war. It did not succeed, although Britain ran dangerously low on food and other supplies, and within a short time the USA joined the war on the side of Britain and France.

Q3 What event nearly brought the USA into the war in 1915?

The Battle of Jutland 1916

The only large battle between the surface fleets of Britain and Germany took place in the North Sea. Both sides were nervous of meeting, yet the Germans were desperate to break the blockade of their ports and the British wanted the excellent German fleet kept safely out of the way of shipping routes to Britain. The battle was indecisive. The British lost more ships and men, but the overall result was that the German fleet went back to port and did not dare venture out for the rest of the war. The Germans decided to rely on submarine warfare.

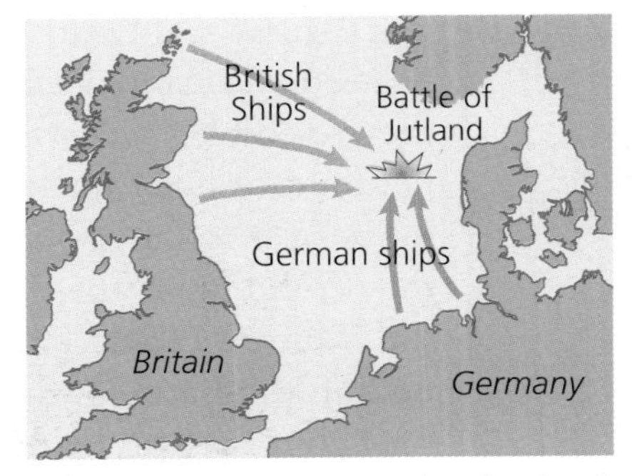

▲ *Fig 4 The Battle of Jutland.*

Q4 Why did the German and British fleets want to meet?

Key words

neutral ships – ships belonging to countries which are not at war

retaliate – to take action in return

U-boats – German submarines

SUMMARY

- The British Navy protected ships coming and going from Britain.
- The British Navy prevented ships going to and from Germany.
- The Germans resorted to submarine warfare against both British and neutral ships.
- This action brought the USA into the war on the side of Britain and France.
- The Battle of Jutland in 1916 was the only major surface battle of the war and resulted in the German fleet staying in port.

SUMMARY *activity*

Why did Germany resort to all-out submarine warfare in 1917?

91 Breaking the deadlock

In this section of the book you will learn the following things:

- **there was deadlock in the fighting on the Western Front;**
- **several things were tried to break the deadlock.**

The deadlock

Each infantry division in the Army (18,000 men) needed 5,500 horses and each cavalry division 11,000 horses. Horses carried men; they pulled carts carrying water and food; they carried ammunition in packs on their backs; they pulled field guns; they charged into battle. This was the last war where horses were used in any number. Newly invented barbed wire, machine guns and high explosives ripped both soldiers and horses apart. How could any army move forward and break the deadlock on the Western Front? What was needed was a way of carrying soldiers across open country and barbed-wire fences in the face of enemy fire – a metal box with guns. In this way the idea of the tank was born.

Q1 What new inventions made men and horses so vulnerable in battle?

Tanks

The British tried out several metal boxes (code-named 'tanks' because they resembled water tanks). They ran on caterpillar tracks and could move over rough ground. Maybe they could break the deadlock on the Western Front. They were first used in the Battle of the Somme in 1916, but they broke down easily and got bogged down in the mud. However, they did break through the German trenches and this was a sign of hope for the future.

▲ ***Fig 1*** *British tanks going into action in 1918.*

When they were used on the hard chalk soil at the Battle of Cambrai they were more successful, and were ten kilometres behind German lines by lunchtime. Unfortunately the Germans counter-attacked the next day and won back the land, but the tanks had proved they could cross barbed wire and trenches and be impervious to machine guns. By the battles of 1918, tanks were used by both sides and helped to break the stalemate on the Western Front.

Q2 What was a tank?

Q3 What were the weaknesses of tanks at the Battle of the Somme?

Q4 What did the tanks prove at the Battle of Cambrai?

Gas

One way to break the **deadlock** on the Western Front was to kill all the enemy soldiers in the opposite trench, walk across and take it. Poisonous gas was first tried in 1915, but it was unpredictable and if the wind changed it blew back on to the side that had used it.

The attack on the Dardanelles 1915

Another scheme to break the deadlock was to attack in a different place. In 1915 Winston Churchill, who was First Lord of the Admiralty, suggested attacking Germany's ally, Turkey, to divert German forces and open up the possibility of advancing north to Germany itself. However, the British, Australian and New Zealand forces were soon pinned down at Gallipoli by the Turkish Army. Both sides dug trenches here, too, so the war moved no further forward.

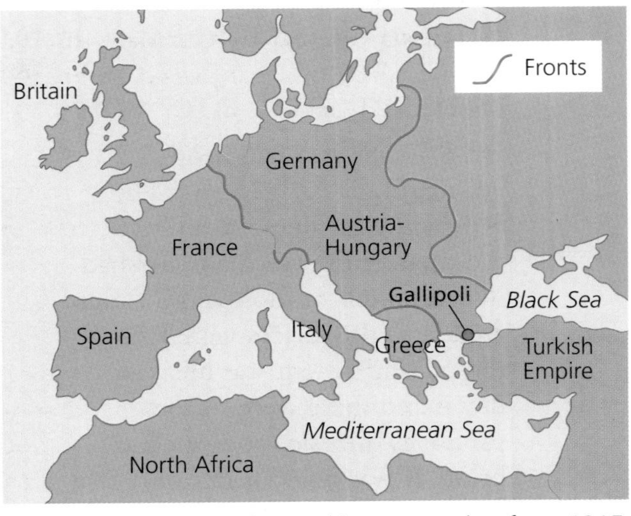

▲ ***Fig 2*** *Gallipoli: attacking on another front 1915.*

Aeroplanes

Some people hoped that aeroplanes would help to break the deadlock, but they were most suitable for **reconnaissance** and could do little in the way of bombing. Indeed, some people felt they just opened up another arena to fight in, without having a decisive effect on the war.

► ***Fig 3*** *The battlefield at Passchendaele on the Western Front 1917. Photographs from the air could show damage, troop concentrations, and so on.*

Key words

deadlock – situation in which no progress can be made

reconnaissance – observation to find out information about the enemy

SUMMARY

- Weapons of defence were developed before weapons of attack in the First World War, and this led to a deadlock in the fighting.
- Various means were tried to break the deadlock: tanks, gas, an attack on Turkey (Germany's ally), and aeroplanes.

SUMMARY *activity*

Why was the First World War so deadlocked on the Western Front? What was done to break the deadlock?

92 The Russian Revolution

In this section of the book you will learn the following things:

- Russia's defeat by Germany in 1917 led to a revolution in Russia.

Russia and the war

By 1917 the war had been continuing for three years. The Russians were being steadily defeated by the Germans and had lost hundreds of thousands of men. Added to this, prices were rising, the railway system was breaking down and there were serious shortages of basic foods such as bread. It was obvious not only that Russia was losing the war, but that the **Tsar** of Russia and his Government were incompetent.

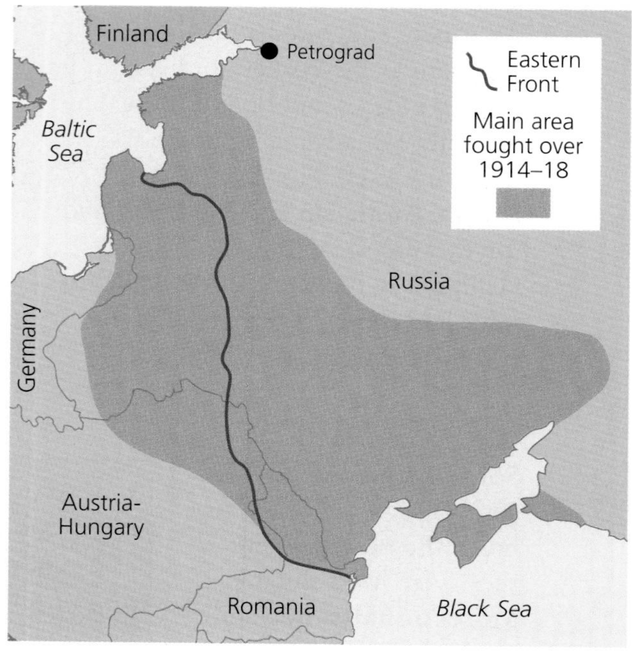

▲ *Fig 1* *The Eastern Front.*

Tsar Nicholas II and most of the Russians believed that it was God's will that he ruled, so Russians did not rebel easily. However, in 1917, the situation was so bad that strikes and food riots broke out in **Petrograd**. Many of the soldiers who were called in to quell the riots sympathised with the rioters and even joined them. In a short time, the all-powerful Tsar abdicated and a Provisional Government was formed under the leadership of Alexander Kerensky. There were others who were thinking of taking power too.

Q1 What sparked off the revolution in Petrograd in 1917?

Karl Marx

Karl Marx was the 'father of communism'. He said that the workers should own the means of production (factories, mines and farms). Lenin adapted many of his ideas.

◀ *Fig 2*

The Soviets

Groups of people in towns, factories and even army regiments began to form committees or **soviets**. They held a meeting in Petrograd of representatives of soviets from all over Russia. This Congress of Soviets claimed to have as much right to speak for Russian people as Kerensky and the Provisional Government.

▶ ***Fig 3*** *Lenin was leader of the Bolsheviks.*

Q2 What was a soviet?

Vladimir Ilyich Lenin and the Bolsheviks

Lenin was the leader of a small party called the Bolsheviks. He told his members to act as leaders in the soviets, wherever possible. In this way a small party could gain power. By November 1917, the Bolsheviks controlled the Petrograd soviet and had an army of 20 000 soldiers, called the Red Guard. On 6 November, Lenin sent the Red Guard to arrest the members of the Provisional Government. The next day he announced that the soviets were the Government of Russia. Seeing how hopeless the war was, Lenin signed the Treaty of Brest-Litovsk with Germany, which gave vast areas of Russian land to Germany. Lenin was not worried, however; he was buying time to make Russia strong again. After Lenin came to power, Tsar Nicholas II and his family were put to death.

It took a long time for Russia to recover because civil war broke out between the anti-Bolsheviks (Whites) and the Bolsheviks (Reds) and continued until 1921. Once the Bolsheviks were firmly in power they changed their name to the Communist Party. Russia became known as the Union of Soviet Socialist Republics (USSR) in 1922.

Key words

Petrograd – the capital of Russia (other names for the city are St Petersburg and Leningrad)
soviet – committee
Tsar – emperor

SUMMARY

- Russia was being defeated by Germany in 1917.
- This defeat and shortages caused by the war led to revolution in Petrograd and the fall of the Tsar.
- A Provisional Government was set up under Alexander Kerensky.
- Soviets were set up all over the country.
- The Bolshevik Party led by Lenin seized power in November 1917.
- Lenin made peace with Germany in 1917.
- The Bolsheviks finally won the civil war in 1921 and Russia became the USSR in 1922.

SUMMARY *activity*

How did Lenin gain power in Russia?

93 Peace: the Treaty of Versailles

In this section of the book you will learn the following things:

- **it was difficult to make a fair peace treaty in 1918;**
- **France, Britain and the USA made many of the decisions about the peace treaty.**

The war ends

At 11 o'clock on the morning of 11 November 1918 a ceasefire or **armistice** was agreed; the war was over. It took several months for the delegates of different countries to meet to talk about a peace treaty. The main meeting was at Versailles and the main peace treaty was called the Treaty of Versailles.

Wilson, the Fourteen Points and self-determination

Woodrow Wilson was the President of the USA. He was an idealistic man and wanted a better, fairer Europe. He made a list of Fourteen Points or rules. One of the things Wilson believed in was **self-determination**: he wanted the frontiers of Europe redrawn so that all races ruled themselves. This was difficult in practice. First, it was hard to say exactly what indicated a separate race or nation. The only possible guide was the language they spoke, yet many subject people spoke their conqueror's language. Second, in some places, such as the Balkans, races were so mixed up that they could only have been divided by moving large groups of the population.

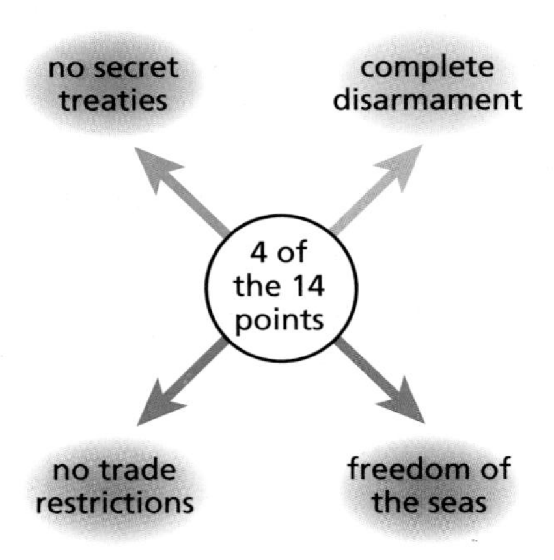

▲ ***Fig 1*** *The other points dealt with particular countries.*

Q1 Who was Woodrow Wilson?

Q2 Write down four of the Fourteen Points.

Q3 What were the two problems of self-determination?

Map of Europe redrawn

However, the post-war map of Europe was redrawn in 1918, but it was a patchwork superimposed on many minorities. For instance, Yugoslavia contained Slovenes, Bosnian Muslims, Magyars, Germans, Albanians, Romanians and Macedonians.

◄ ***Fig 2*** *From the left, Clemenceau, the French leader, Woodrow Wilson the US President, and Lloyd George, the British Prime Minister.*

Land taken from Germany

The other problem was what to do about Germany. Most European countries, and particularly France, wanted to make sure that Germany could never be strong enough again to threaten the peace of Europe. Most of the land that Germany had gained since the eighteenth century was taken away and Germany was partially disarmed.

Reparations

Many, especially in France and Belgium, believed that Germany must pay for the damage its armies had caused. However, it was difficult to work out the cost and it was even more difficult to know whether Germany could afford to pay such compensation.

Q4 What four things were done to Germany after the war?

Q5 Which of the four were done to keep Germany weak? Which might have been done more for revenge?

▼ *Fig 3*

Germany after the war

War guilt

Germany was blamed for the war.

Land loss

Alsace-Lorraine	→	France
Malmédy and Eupen	→	Belgium
Schleswig-Holstein	→	Denmark
East and West Prussia and Silesia	→	Poland
German colonies	→	South Africa, Australia, New Zealand, Japan, Britain, France

Armed forces reduced

Army reduced to 100 000

Air force destroyed

Navy reduced to six light battleships

Reparations – Germany to pay for war damage

League of Nations

The fourteenth point in Wilson's list was to set up a League of Nations. Each nation would send representatives to a permanent world assembly which could settle disputes between countries. The idea was welcomed and a headquarters was set up in Geneva, Switzerland.

Key words

armistice – an agreement by opposing sides to stop fighting

reparations – money paid for repairing damage done

self-determination – the right of every country to choose the way it is governed

SUMMARY

- Woodrow Wilson put forward Fourteen Points or rules, which included his idea that all nations should choose their own Government (self-determination).
- The leaders of France, Britain and the USA made most of the decisions in the peace treaties.
- Germany was to be kept weak and to pay for war damage.
- The League of Nations was set up.

SUMMARY *activity*

How might the peace treaty cause problems in Europe later on?

94 The League of Nations

In this section of the book you will learn the following things:

- Woodrow Wilson worked to bring about the League of Nations;
- the League had several problems.

The League of Nations 1920

Woodrow Wilson had worked hard to bring about the League of Nations so that all the countries of the world could settle their disputes peacefully. The League was set up in 1920 with a headquarters in Geneva, Switzerland. Over 50 countries joined the League.

The biggest problem with the League of Nations

Although Wilson was enthusiastic about the League, America was not. The American people were tired of Europe's problems and would not vote to join the League. Wilson travelled over 13,000 kilometres in the USA and made speech after speech telling people how important the League of Nations was for world peace. It was to no avail, however, and exhausted, Wilson had a stroke and remained paralysed until he died.

None of the decisions taken at the Peace Conference were likely to last long without the backing of the USA and Britain. Without the USA, Britain lost interest in Europe and started to disarm. Germany was now surrounded by a weakened France, Russia (now the Union of Soviet Socialist Republics) torn by civil war, and some small countries. It might only be a matter of time before Germany started to make demands.

▲ *Fig 1* Woodrow Wilson was a passionate supporter of the League of Nations.

▶ *Fig 2*

If the USA did not join the League of Nations

'I can predict with absolute certainty that within another generation there will be another world war.'

Woodrow Wilson

Q1 Why did Wilson think it was so important for the USA to join the League of Nations?

Other problems

Although the League had some successes (slavery was made illegal in many parts of the world) and a few territorial disputes were settled, there were serious problems apart from the failure of the USA to join. The **USSR** did not join for many years and Germany left the League in 1933. This meant that three major countries did not belong to the League. One problem was that the League had no way of enforcing its decisions. For instance, in 1923 Lithuania attacked and took the port of Memel from Germany. The League of Nations said that Lithuania must hand it back to Germany. Lithuania just said 'no' and the League could do nothing. When countries saw that the League was powerless they began to ignore it.

Q2 What successes did the League have?

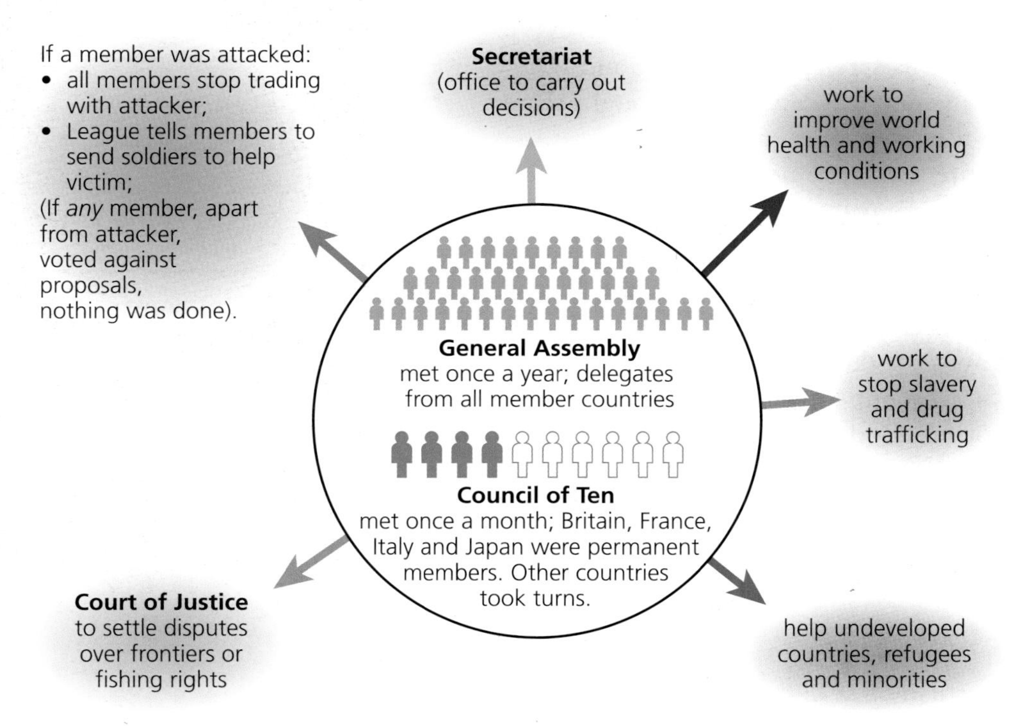

▲ ***Fig 3*** *The League of Nations.*

Key words

USSR – Union of Soviet Socialist Republics, the territory formerly known as Russia under the Tsars, but renamed after the Bolsheviks took power through the soviets or committees all over Russia

SUMMARY

- The biggest problem with the League of Nations was that the USA did not join it.
- The USSR did not join for years and Germany left the League in 1933.
- The League had a few successes but no means of enforcing its decisions, so countries lost faith in it.

SUMMARY *activity*

Describe the structure of the League of Nations and what it could do if a member was attacked.

95 Boom and bust

In this section of the book you will learn the following things:

- **there was a boom in the USA in the 1920s;**
- **Britain and Germany had economic problems.**

The USA

By the 1920s, the USA was a rich, powerful nation. Most people earned much higher wages than Europeans and the country had not been exhausted by four long years of war. Americans were confident that things could only get better. They borrowed money to buy all the new things that were being made, such as motor cars, telephones, radios and refrigerators. Many people bought shares in the companies making the new goods. More and more new goods were made and share prices went up.

▲ ***Fig 1*** *A Ford car 1919.*

Britain

It was different in Britain, which for years had made goods for the rest of the world to buy, and was now facing competition. Japan and India were making cotton goods more cheaply than Britain could; the USA was making cheaper cars. Many countries also put **tariffs** on their **imports** to protect their own manufacturers.

Q1 What were Britain's two problems?

Germany

Germany had different problems. The Treaty of Versailles had laid down that Germany had to pay reparations of £6,600 million to the victorious Allies. Germany said this was not possible and in 1923 stopped paying any reparations. France retaliated by marching into the Ruhr, Germany's main industrial area, and taking coal and steel goods **in lieu of** reparations. The Germans went on strike and very few goods were produced. This meant there was too much money chasing too few goods, which led to **inflation**. Prices went up and up. A person could walk into a café, order a cup of coffee, and by the time

▲ ***Fig 2***

they had drunk it, the price had trebled. Soon paper money was worth nothing. Germany's complete collapse was avoided by agreeing to start paying reparations again and by huge loans from the USA.

Q2 What happened in 1923?

Q3 What did France do?

Q4 What did Germany do?

Q5 What did the USA do?

The Wall Street Crash 1929

Borrowing money from the USA was fine while the USA was booming. However, farms and factories in the USA were producing more food and goods than people needed. From 1925, prices of food started to fall, which meant farmers had less money to spend on tractors, cars, radios and refrigerators. Gradually this had a '**domino effect**'. By 1929 factory sales were falling; then the shares in these factories started to fall. Once the value of shares started to fall, everyone wanted to sell their shares. This drove the price down even further and resulted in the Wall Street Crash of 1929. As the economy fell into depression, the USA asked Germany and other countries to pay back their loans. In this way the economies of many countries also spiralled down into depression.

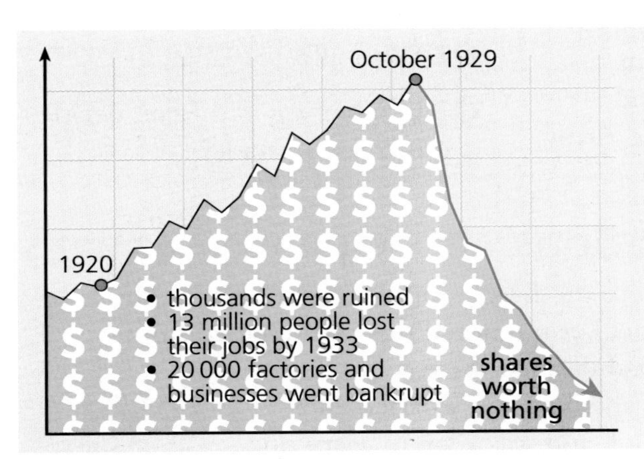

▲ *Fig 3 The Wall Street Crash.*

▲ *Fig 4 Despair as people hear the news of the Wall Street Stock Exchange crash in the USA.*

Key words

domino effect – when one domino falls over it hits others, which then fall; applied to economic and political situations

imports – goods coming into a country

inflation – when the prices of goods rise

in lieu of – instead of

tariffs – taxes or duties on goods

SUMMARY

- The USA economy was booming in the 1920s, as more people bought the new goods available.
- Many people bought shares in the companies making the new goods.
- Economic collapse in Germany was averted by loans from the USA.
- The USA boom ended in 1929 with the Wall Street Crash.

SUMMARY *activity*

Explain how the boom burst in the USA by 1929 and what effect this had on Germany.

96 Would peace last?

In this section of the book you will learn the following things:

- **peace was threatened by countries wanting to expand;**
- **it was also threatened by clashes between communists and fascists.**

Japan and China

Economic problems were not the only problems after the war. In the Far East, Japan was a strong, independent country. In 1929 it was affected by the depression in worldwide trade. Half the country's factories closed down and farmers faced ruin. It was important for Japan's trade to recover and one way to increase trade was to have an empire, as the British had. The Japanese Army was particularly keen on this idea. Japan had already made a start by taking control of Korea, Port Arthur and Taiwan and in 1931 the Japanese Army conquered much of Manchuria.

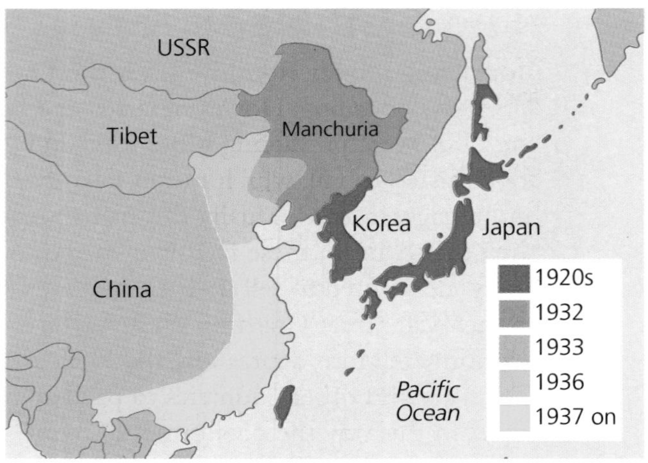

▲ ***Fig 1*** *Japanese expansion in the 1930s in Asia.*

Q1 What affected Japan in 1929?

Q2 In what way did Japan decide to increase its trade?

The League of Nations and Japanese expansion

Both Japan and China belonged to the League of Nations. Although the League condemned Japan's action, Japan ignored this and resigned from the League in 1933. In 1937 Japan invaded the rest of China. Many people in the world were shocked and worried, but the Japanese Army was riding high and was keen to carry on with military conquests to expand Japan's empire.

Q3 What did Japan do in 1933?

► ***Fig 2*** *One of Picasso's most famous paintings (1937) showed the destruction of the city of Guernica in the Spanish Civil War.*

Italy and Abyssinia

Italy felt it had gained very little from the peace settlement after the war. Italy, too, wanted an empire and, led by Mussolini, it attacked Abyssinia (now Ethiopia). Abyssinia was a member of the League of Nations and appealed for help. The League voted for trade **sanctions** against Italy but these did not include oil, steel or copper because France and Britain, in particular, did not want to annoy Italy and push Mussolini into a closer friendship with Germany. Abyssinia was defeated and Mussolini took Italy out of the League of Nations. Despite British and French hopes, Mussolini and the German leader, Adolf Hitler, signed an alliance between Italy and Germany in 1936.

Q4 What was the weakness in the sanctions against Italy?

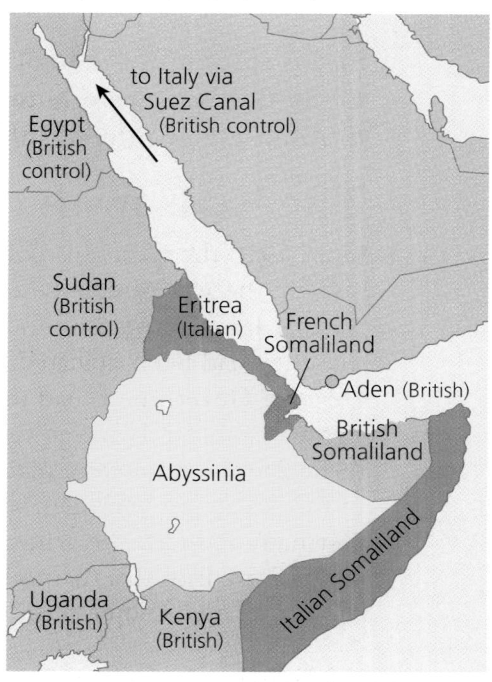

▲ ***Fig 3*** *Abyssinia and its neighbours 1935.*

◀ ***Fig 4*** *Cartoon of Benito Mussolini 1928, showing him as a Roman emperor.*

The Spanish Civil War 1936–1939

Civil war broke out in Spain, where the Government included many communists. General Franco led an Army rebellion against the Government and, with the help of Germany and Italy, won control by 1939. This was a triumph for **fascism** and had given Hitler and Mussolini a good opportunity to try out their new weapons.

Key words

fascism – government by a dictator, characterised by extreme nationalism and restrictions on individual freedom

sanctions – restrictions

SUMMARY

- Japan's desire to expand led to invasion of China and resignation from the League of Nations.
- Italy's desire to expand led to invasion of Abyssinia and resignation from the League of Nations.
- The Spanish Civil War was a triumph for fascism in Europe.

SUMMARY *activity*

What were the weaknesses of the League of Nations in the 1930s?

97 Germany and the rise of Hitler

In this section of the book you will learn the following things:

- **the Germans were bitter after their defeat in 1918;**
- **Adolf Hitler offered solutions to Germany's problems.**

The 'stab in the back'

Until 1918 the German Army had been 'holding its own' in the war. Suddenly it surrendered and made peace. Many Germans found it difficult to believe that they had been defeated. They believed that the German Government had made peace behind the Army's back and betrayed the German people. Such feelings of betrayal were made worse by the terms of the Treaty of Versailles, which took land from Germany, reduced the armed forces and demanded reparations. Into this turmoil of resentment and loss, came a former soldier called Adolf Hitler.

Q1 What did German people believe after the First World War?

Q2 What terms of the Treaty of Versailles did the Germans not like?

The 'stab in the back' theory

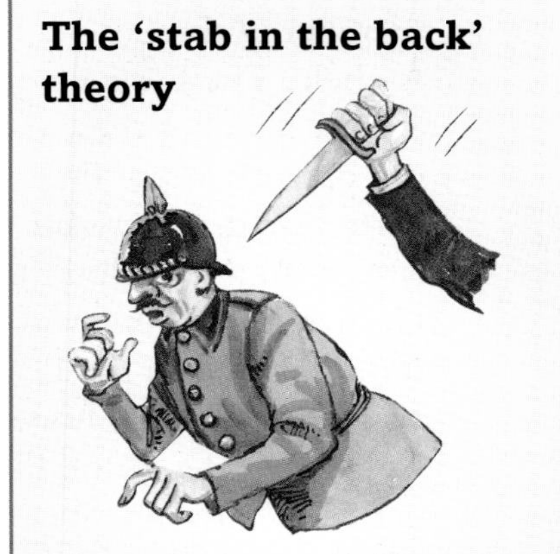

Many Germans believed their Government of 1918 had betrayed Germany by making peace behind the German Army's back.

▲ ***Fig 1***

Adolf Hitler and the Nazi Party

Hitler, too, was bitter about Germany's defeat. He joined the German Workers' Party and soon came to lead it. He changed the name to the National Socialist German Workers' Party (known as the Nazi Party). He made sure the Nazi Party had its own soldiers, called the SA or Stormtroopers. In 1923 he used the SA to try to seize power in the city of Munich in Germany. He failed and was imprisoned for five years, but because there was much sympathy for his ideas, he only served eight months. While he was in prison he wrote his life story, called *Mein Kampf* (My Struggle). It contained his ideas, which centred around the supremacy of Germany.

◀ ***Fig 2*** *The poster say's 'Hitler: our last hope'. Hitler promised to make Germany a rich and powerful nation again, and this appealed to many Germans.*

Once out of prison Hitler continued to build up the SA and the Nazi Party. The Wall Street Crash in the USA and subsequent unemployment made many Germans desperate. They started to listen to Hitler. He was a magnetic speaker: he laid the blame for losing the war and Germany's economic troubles on other people, particularly the Jews and the communists. He promised that he would make Germany rich and great again.

Q3 What was the name of Hitler's book and what was it about?

Q4 Whom did Hitler blame for Germany losing the war?

Hitler and power

After the Nazi Party came to power, Hitler became Chancellor of Germany in 1933. In February the Reichstag (Parliament) caught fire. A Dutch communist confessed to starting the fire and Hitler panicked everyone into giving him more power. He introduced the Enabling Law, which gave him absolute power. Since Hitler's Stormtroopers surrounded the building where the German Parliament was debating the Enabling Law, very few voted against him.

Soon after this Hitler called himself 'the **Führer**' and from then on all members of the Army swore a personal oath of loyalty, not to Germany, but to Adolf Hitler, Führer of the Reich.

Hitler knew that the Army generals did not like the SA and he, too, was worried about the growing power of these Stormtroopers, led by Ernst Rohm. On 30 June 1934, Hitler ordered the SS, his newly formed elite force, to execute Rohm and other SA leaders. This broke the power of the SA and made Hitler popular with the Army.

▲ ***Fig 3*** *A Nazi rally 1935.*

Key words

Führer – German for 'leader'

SUMMARY

- The Germans were bitter about being defeated and about the terms of the Treaty of Versailles.
- Adolf Hitler led the Nazi Party by 1923 and built up a private army, the SA.
- In the Depression, Hitler's ideas of making Germany rich and great again were very appealing to Germans.
- Hitler became Chancellor in 1933 and soon became all-powerful.

SUMMARY *activity*

Write a paragraph tracing Hitler's rise to power.

98 The march to war 1933–1939

In this section of the book you will learn the following things:

- Hitler worked to win back German land in the 1930s;
- Britain and France were not prepared to fight Germany in the 1930s.

The Rhineland 1936

Hitler came to power in 1933 as the Chancellor of Germany. From then on he worked to restore lands taken from Germany after the war and to gain more land. Under the terms of the Treaty of Versailles, Germany was forbidden to have soldiers in the Rhineland, but Hitler defied this part of the peace settlement and sent troops into the Rhineland in 1936. At this stage the German Army was not strong enough to fight France, so Hitler gave orders that if there was any resistance, the German soldiers should withdraw. However, France did nothing and Britain only sent a protest. Neither France nor Britain wanted another war and many British people felt that the Rhineland belonged to Germany, so it had a right to have soldiers there.

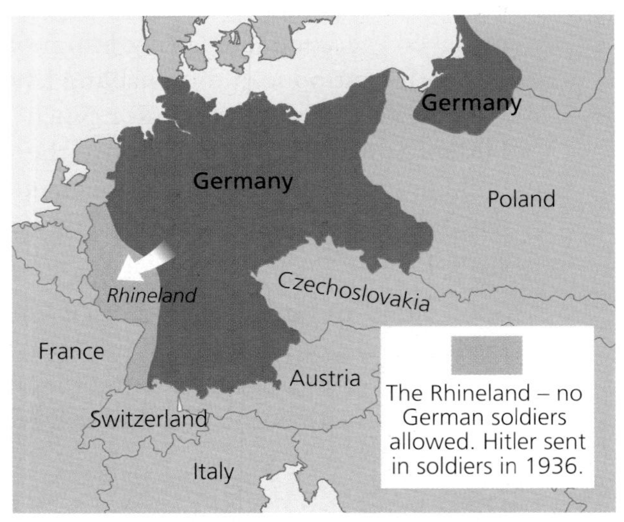

▲ ***Fig 1*** *Germany retook the Rhineland 1936.*

▲ ***Fig 2*** *Crowds cheer as German soldiers enter the Rhineland on 7 March 1936.*

Q1 Why did France allow Germany to send soldiers into the Rhineland?

Q2 Why did Britain only protest to Germany over the reoccupation of the Rhineland? (Give two reasons)

Austria 1938

Then Hitler turned his attention to Austria and Czechoslovakia, both of which had large numbers of German people living within their boundaries. In 1938 he used the Nazi Party in Austria to stir up trouble, then sent in German soldiers and took over the country. Within months he had turned his attention to Czechoslovakia, where three million Germans lived in part of an area called the Sudetenland.

Q3 Why did Hitler feel justified in claiming Austria and part of Czechoslovakia?

Czechoslovakia 1938 and appeasement

Hitler demanded that the Sudetenland be given to Germany. Czechoslovakia protested and looked for help to France and Russia with whom it had signed treaties for help in case of attack. At this point the British Prime Minister, Neville Chamberlain, flew to Munich to talk to Hitler. Hitler promised that this was his last demand and Chamberlain, believing that the peace settlement had not been fair to Germany and also fearing another war, agreed. This policy was called **appeasement**. When Chamberlain flew back to Britain, he was greeted with enthusiasm. He said he had brought back 'peace in our time'. Most people in Britain were delighted.

▲ ***Fig 3*** *1938: Chamberlain promises peace after Munich.*

However, Czechoslovakia's best defences were in the areas lost to Germany and in the spring of 1939 Hitler marched in and took the rest of Czechoslovakia. Other countries could see that his next target would be Poland, particularly the area called the Polish corridor. Hastily, Britain and France promised to help Poland if Germany attacked.

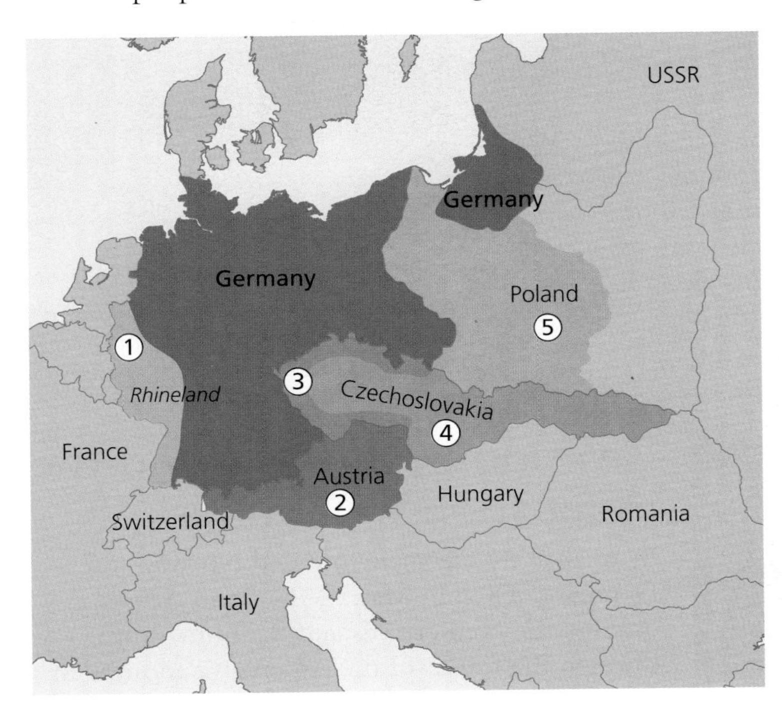

◀ ***Fig 4*** *The five steps to war 1938–39.*

Key words

appeasement – agreeing to do something in order to keep the peace

SUMMARY

- Hitler wanted Germany to have more land.
- In 1936 Germany sent soldiers to reoccupy the Rhineland.
- In 1938 Germany took over Austria.
- In 1938 and 1939 Germany took over Czechoslovakia.
- In 1939, Britain and France agreed to defend Poland.

SUMMARY *activity*

What were the five steps of war?

99 War in the West 1939–1941

In this section of the book you will learn the following things:

- Britain and France declared war on Germany after the invasion of Poland in the east;
- the next year Germany invaded countries to the west.

Invasion of Poland September 1939

On 1 September 1939, Germany invaded Poland and bombed Polish cities. Hitler and Stalin had made an agreement that they would not fight each other and that they would share Poland's land between them. Within a short space of time Stalin sent the soldiers of the USSR to invade Poland from the east. There was little the British or French could do, but they declared war on 3 September 1939. Appeasement was at an end.

Britain and France prepared for war. Both countries evacuated children from the cities and areas likely to be bombed. The French took trainloads of people away from the Maginot Line (the forts along its borders with Germany) and rushed soldiers there. All through the winter of 1939 no bombers or soldiers came.

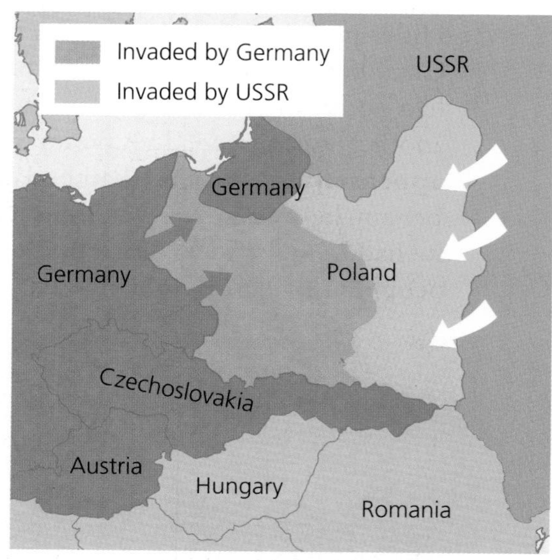

▲ ***Fig 1*** *The fate of Poland, September 1939.*

Q1 Which two countries invaded Poland in September 1939?

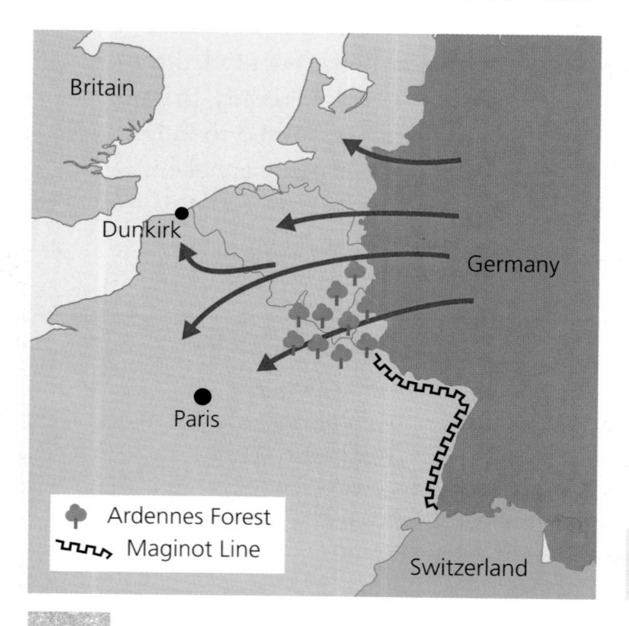

Invasion in the west and the evacuation of Dunkirk

In April 1940 Germany invaded Norway and Denmark. Then in May, the German Army invaded the Netherlands and Belgium, drove through the forests of the Ardennes and invaded France by going around the Maginot Line through hills and forests the French had thought were impassable to an invading army.

◀ ***Fig 2*** *The German invasion of France, May 1940.*

Q2 What was the Maginot Line?

The British sent soldiers – the British Expeditionary Force (BEF) – to help the French. However, very soon both the French and British soldiers were on the run, making for the Channel ports and closely pursued by the Germans. It looked as though they would be surrounded and killed, but the Germans were running low on fuel, and did not think they had to hurry. They could leave the British and French soldiers cooped up in Dunkirk and sweep on towards Paris. In an epic effort, however, the Royal Navy and hundreds of small boats evacuated over 300 000 British and French soldiers from Dunkirk to Britain between 24 May and 4 June.

▲ ***Fig 3*** *A painting done at the time, showing the rescue of British soldiers from the Dunkirk beaches in 1940.*

Q3 How did the British evacuate the soldiers from Dunkirk?

The Battle of Britain and the Blitz

While the Germans were establishing themselves in France, the British were facing the possibility of invasion. Hitler knew he had to destroy the British airforce first so he could sail his invasion ships to Britain without attack from the air. This policy led to the Battle of Britain during the summer months of 1940. The German air force (the Luftwaffe) set out to shoot down British fighter planes and bomb the airfields of the British Royal Air Force (RAF). Britain just managed to keep the Luftwaffe out and Hitler gave up his invasion plans.

Hitler switched to bombing factories and cities, and the winter of 1940–41 saw night after night of bombing in London and other cities. This bombing became known as the **Blitz**.

Q4 What led up to the Battle of Britain?

Key words

Blitz – from the German *blitzkrieg*, meaning 'lightning war', the Blitz was the name given to the German bombing of British cities in 1940–41.

SUMMARY

- Germany and the USSR invaded Poland in September 1939.
- In 1940 Germany invaded Norway, Denmark, the Netherlands, Belgium and France.
- The British evacuated soldiers from Dunkirk.
- The Battle of Britain was fought to stop the Germans invading Britain.
- When Germany did not win the Battle of Britain, it switched to bombing cities and factories.

SUMMARY *activity*

Why was Dunkirk both a triumph and a disaster?

100 The invasion of the USSR

In this section of the book you will learn the following things:

- Hitler and Stalin had signed the Nazi-Soviet Pact agreeing not to attack each other;
- Hitler invaded the USSR in 1941.

The Nazi-Soviet Pact was not meant to last

Although Hitler hated communists, in 1939 he had not hesitated to make an agreement with the communist-run USSR led by Stalin. However, neither side was under any illusions. Hitler always meant to take land from the USSR; he regarded many eastern races such as the Slavs as inferior to the **Aryan** German race, so he thought when Germany needed more living space, it should be taken from these people. Stalin, on his part, needed time. He knew that Hitler intended to attack, but the more time the USSR had, the more weapons it could build. In the end the Nazi-Soviet **Pact** won the USSR about a year and a half of peace.

Living space and raw materials

Apart from living space, Hitler wanted the oil supplies and other raw materials of the USSR. In June 1941 he unleashed the **blitzkrieg** against the USSR, just as he had done in the west a year before. The German Army moved fast and, by November 1941, it was deep inside the USSR, besieging Leningrad and threatening Moscow.

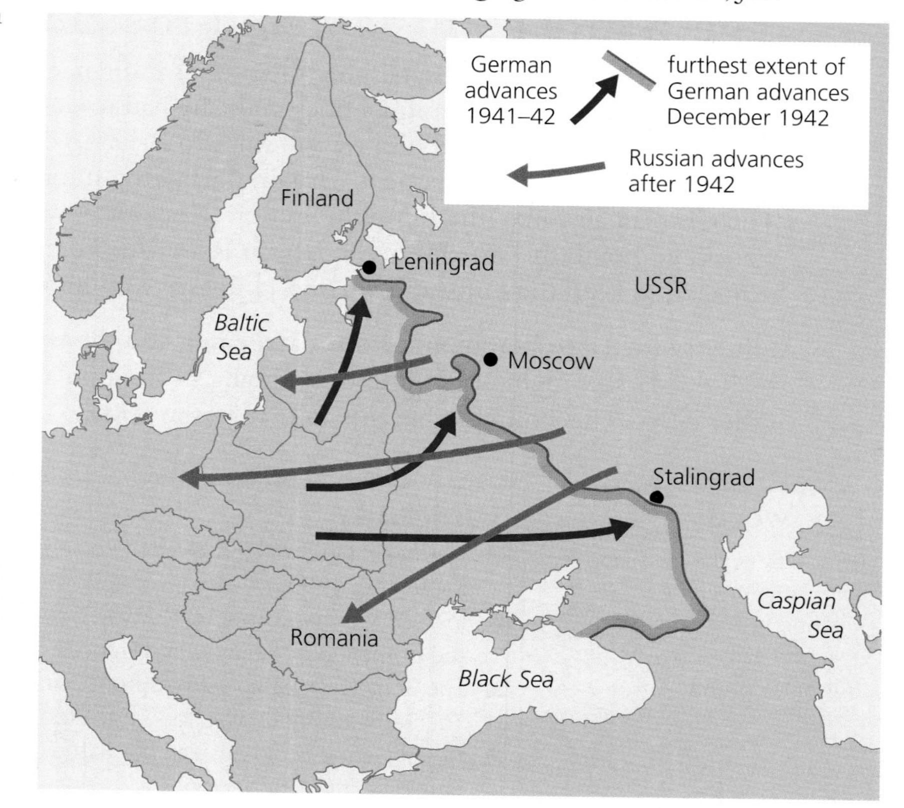

▲ ***Fig 1*** *The Eastern Front.*

Q1 Why did Germany invade the USSR in 1941?

Q2 How many months did it take to reach Leningrad?

The Russian winter bites

The Red Army retreated, burning land and food as it went. Meanwhile, Stalin moved more factories hundreds of miles to the east, beyond the Ural Mountains. These factories poured out guns and tanks as fast as they could and sent them back west by rail for the Red Army to use against the Germans. The Germans were slowing up, however. Winter had come and the German Army was not prepared for the desperately cold temperatures of the Russian winter. They dug in until the next spring.

▼ *Fig 2*

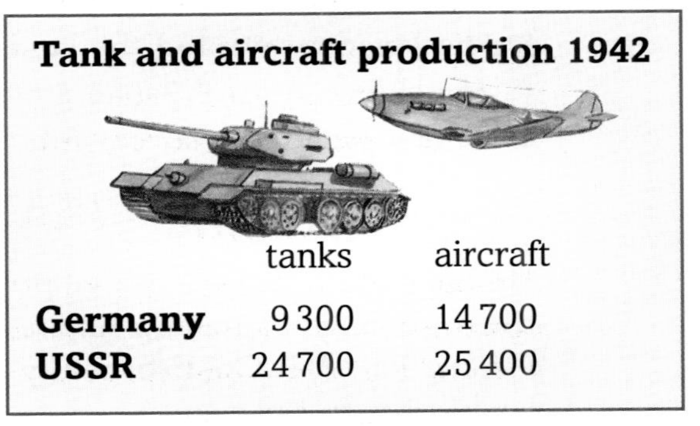

Tank and aircraft production 1942

	tanks	aircraft
Germany	9300	14700
USSR	24700	25400

Q3 How did the USSR deal with the German invasion?

The tide turned

By the spring of 1942, Stalin's efficiency was having an effect: officers were better trained; millions of peasants were recruited; better tanks, such as the T34, arrived at the front in their hundreds. The British and the USA were sending goods to the USSR to help, and the situation changed quickly. Leningrad continued to hold out; Moscow was not taken and Stalingrad was fought for house by house over five months. When the Germans entered this city of rubble, new Soviet Armies attacked and threatened to encircle the 300 000-strong German Army. Hitler would not let his general, von Paulus, surrender and when the Germans were at last forced to, only 97 000 men were still alive.

From this time on the tables were turned, as the Red Army fought its way back across its own territory during 1943 and into Germany by 1945.

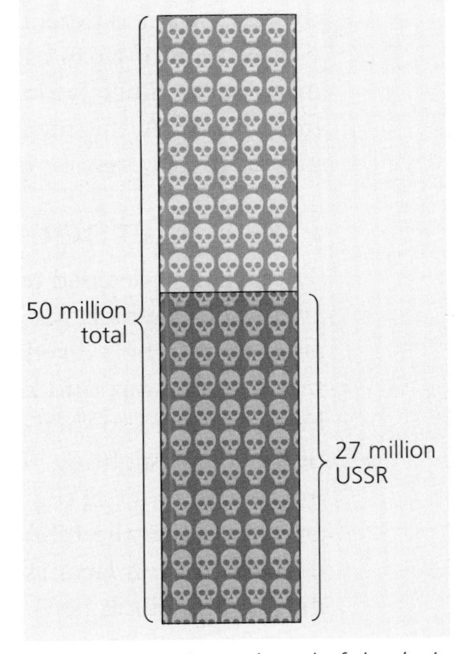

▲ *Fig 3 Estimated total of deaths in the Second World War.*

Key words

Aryan – term used by the Nazis to describe non-Jewish, white, north European people; the 'master race'

blitzkrieg – German word meaning 'lightning war'

pact – agreement

SUMMARY

- The Nazi-Soviet Pact was of short-term use to each country.
- In 1941 Hitler invaded the USSR, wanting land and raw materials.
- The Red Army retreated, but the winter slowed the German advance.
- By 1943 the Red Army was pushing the Germans back.

SUMMARY *activity*

Why did the USSR defeat Germany?

101 War in the Far East

In this section of the book you will learn the following things:

- **the Japanese wanted the lands around Japan under its own control;**
- **to achieve control, Japan attacked the US naval base at Pearl Harbor;**
- **at first Japan was successful.**

Japan and the USA

By 1941 Japan controlled large parts of eastern China. To the Japanese this was the beginning of a trading empire on European lines. They called the plan the Greater East Asia **Co-Prosperity Sphere** and intended to expand it to the lands between Japan and Australia. They were particularly interested in the oil reserves in the area. However, the British, Dutch and the USA already had interests there themselves. The Japanese were prepared to disregard the British and Dutch who were engaged in the war in Europe, but the USA was a different matter. Already the USA was nervous of Japan's ambitions and refusing to sell oil to Japan. Since Japan bought 80 per cent of its oil from the USA, this meant that Japan either had to give in to US pressure or go on and risk war.

Q1 What was the Greater East Asia Co-Prosperity Sphere?

Q2 What pressure did the USA put on Japan to stop expanding in the Far East?

Pearl Harbor December 1941

The Japanese decided to deliver a knockout blow to the USA by destroying the Pacific Fleet which was based at Pearl Harbor in Hawaii. In December 1941 Japanese bombers dived on Pearl Harbor. They destroyed most of the aircraft, many of the ships and killed about 3,000 people. The **aircraft carriers** had been out at sea so they escaped and were to play a vital role in the sea warfare of the Pacific fighting. The immediate result of the attack was that the USA declared war on Japan; so did Britain. Hitler had made an agreement with Japan before Pearl Harbor (the Axis Treaty of 1940), so Germany declared war on the USA.

▼ *Fig 1*

Axis Treaty of 1940

Germany promised to help Japan in the event of attack.

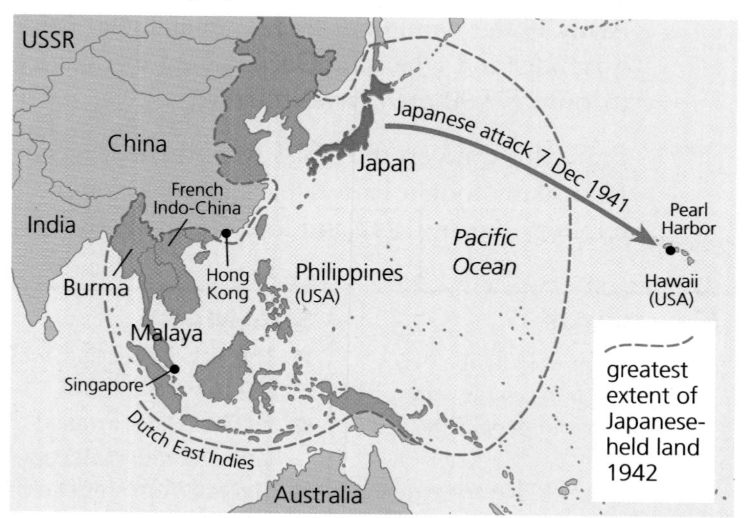

▲ *Fig 2 The Japanese 'empire' to 1942. Singapore, Malaya and Burma were taken from Britain.*

▲ ***Fig 3*** *The USS* Shaw *exploding during the Japanese attack on Pearl Harbor, 7 December 1941.*

Japanese victories

This war in the Far East began with victory after victory for the Japanese. It took the USA six months to build up to strength. The Battle of Midway, in the summer of 1942, was a turning point in the Pacific War, when the Japanese Navy was decisively defeated. Without their powerful Navy they could not continue to hold all their islands in the Pacific. The Americans started a leapfrogging plan: seizing vital island bases, blocking the sea lanes and leaving the island in between to run out of supplies. They fought on, and by 1944 the Americans had island bases near enough to Japan to be able to bomb Tokyo. By June 1945 the Japanese had retreated back to their own islands.

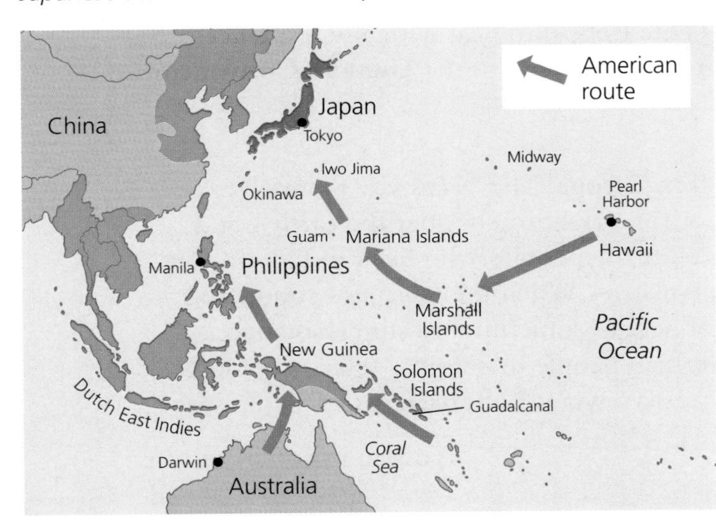

▲ ***Fig 4*** *After the Battle of Midway in 1942, the Americans fought their way across the Pacific to Japan.*

Q3 What was the turning point in the Pacific War?

Q4 What was the American leap-frogging plan?

The Burma Road

The British had been forced out of their Far Eastern possessions in 1942. However, after defeat at Imphal in the summer of 1944, the Japanese began retreating, but it took months of fierce fighting to open the Burma Road and for the Allies to be ready to reconquer Malaya in the summer of 1945.

Key words

aircraft carriers – huge ships used as floating airfields

Co-Prosperity Sphere – trading for everyone's benefit within an area

SUMMARY

- The Japanese clashed with the USA over interests in the Far East.
- The Japanese decided to eliminate US power in the Pacific by destroying the US fleet at Pearl Harbor.
- The attack on Pearl Harbor brought the US into the war against Japan and Germany.
- Although the Japanese were successful for six months, the US fought its way to Japan by mid-1945.
- The British began to win back land lost to the Japanese in 1942.

SUMMARY *activity*

Give reasons for the Japanese attack on Pearl Harbor. Was it a mistake?

102 Europe under the Nazis

In this section of the book you will learn the following things:

- about the treatment of people in Western and Eastern Europe;
- about slave work and resistance to the Nazis.

▼ *Fig 1*

The Geneva Convention was signed by 34 countries in 1929. It laid down rules for the treatment of prisoners of war. These included not using prisoners of war for dangerous or unhealthy work.

Western Europe

By the end of 1942, Germany controlled most of Europe. It had two aims: the first was to make sure that Germany would win the war; the second was to organise the conquered lands for the future benefit of a greater German state.

On the whole, apart from the Jews, the Germans treated the people of Western Europe quite well. In France and Norway the local people ruled as long as they ran the country in the way that Germany wanted. The Nazis used the Gestapo (secret police) and the SS (Hitler's elite troops) to deal with any resistance. Prisoners of war were generally treated according to the **Geneva Convention**.

Q1 What were the Gestapo and the SS used for?

Eastern Europe

The situation was different in Eastern Europe. The Nazis saw themselves as Aryans – part of a master race who had a right to conquer the earth – and other races as inferior. This included many peoples who lived in Eastern Europe, such as the Poles and the Russians. When the Germans conquered such lands, they killed thousands of people, sometimes to stop resistance and sometimes to clear the land for German people to colonise (take over) and farm. This policy of colonisation was known as **Lebensraum** or 'living space'.

▲ ***Fig 2*** *German soldiers shooting Soviet civilians in 1942.*

Russian prisoners of war were harshly treated and although some of this was to do with conditions on the Eastern Front, where food was often scarce for soldiers, let alone prisoners, there are records of many prisoners being deliberately starved and left to die. Three million of the five and a half million Soviet prisoners of war died.

Slave labour

Running German-occupied Europe to win the war, let alone organising the future, was a big task. To win the war required an enormous labour force to work in the munitions and other factories to keep a German Army of several million supplied. Many of the workers in German factories were slave workers. In fact, by 1944 there were seven million slave workers in Germany who lived in labour camps and had barely enough to live on.

Q2 Why were so many slave workers needed in Germany?

Resistance

In many countries underground groups carried on a secret war against the Nazis. They were called the **Resistance**, and did everything from printing secret newspapers and helping Jews to escape, to bombing railway lines to disrupt German supplies. Anyone caught resisting the Germans was killed; this might include their family or even the whole village. Some of these resistance groups, particularly in France, were in contact with Britain, where information from the Resistance about gun emplacements and troop movements helped to plan the Allied invasion of Europe in 1944.

▲ ***Fig 3*** *Members of the French Resistance in 1944.*

Q3 What sort of things did the Resistance groups do?

Key words

Geneva Convention – agreement on how to treat prisoners of war

Lebensraum – German policy of taking over (colonising) land in other countries for Germans to live in

Resistance – underground groups in German-occupied countries working against the Nazis

SUMMARY

- Germany had two aims: to win the war and to organise its conquered lands.
- In Western Europe conquered peoples, apart from the Jews, were treated reasonably on the whole.
- In Eastern Europe the Germans were harsher.
- There was resistance to German rule in many countries.

SUMMARY *activity*

Why did the Nazis treat the peoples of Eastern Europe more harshly than in the West?

103 The sea and air war

In this section of the book you will learn the following things:

- the importance of the USA in supplying Britain and the USSR;
- the Germans attacked supplies coming to Britain;
- bomber and fighter aeroplanes were used.

The importance of supply lines to Britain and the USSR

▲ *Fig 1* *An American Flying Fortress bomber.*

Until 1942 Britain was effectively on its own against Germany. The strain of war and bomb damage to factories meant that Britain could not produce enough weapons to keep fighting. However, by 1942, Britain, the USA and the USSR were allies, but only the USA was free from war damage, so it was the USA that became the **arsenal** for the Allies. Ships, planes, guns and tanks poured out of American factories for shipping to Britain and the USSR. Food and fuel were shipped too and, if at any time these supply lines had been cut, Britain would have had to surrender and the USSR might have found it more difficult to supply its armies.

Q1 Which three countries were allies by 1942?

▲ *Fig 2* *Farmers and ordinary people grew more food in wartime.*

The Battle of the Atlantic

Sometimes it was touch and go whether the supply lines would be cut. The Germans were well aware of the importance of the supplies reaching Britain. They found that surface ships were easily sunk, so they used submarines to intercept the ships and sink them with **torpedoes**. They organised the submarines (U-boats) into '**wolf packs**'. To counteract this, the Allies formed the merchant ships carrying the supplies into convoys, guarded by warships such as destroyers. This cut losses, but even so, at its worst one in four ships sailing to Britain were sunk, and in all 23,351 merchant ships were lost for the cost of 782 U-boats.

Q2 How did the Allies guard against U-boat attacks?

The convoys to the USSR

If the Atlantic convoys were dangerous for the merchant sailors and the Royal Navy, the convoys that went around the north of Scandinavia to the Russian port of Murmansk were not only attacked by German aircraft and ships based in occupied Norway, they also faced freezing Arctic conditions. Nevertheless they kept supplies going to the USSR.

Some answers to the U-boats

Once the British were able to break the naval codes sent out by the Germans, they knew when and where wolf packs would attack. Planes were sent to hunt the wolf packs and to bomb the tankers sailing to refuel the U-boats. Convoy losses began to drop from 1941. In addition to the code breaking and more escorts for the convoys, radar and sound waves could be used to locate the U-boats and by 1943 aircraft had been developed that could fly longer distances and could be sent to drop depth charges to sink the U-boats. Some losses continued up to the time that the advancing Allies destroyed the shipyards where the U-boats were built.

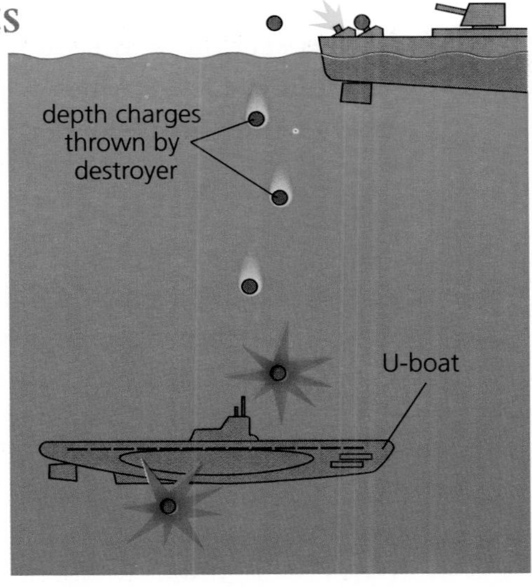

▲ ***Fig 3*** *Depth charges from escort ships could be fired to explode at different depths.*

Aeroplanes

Aeroplanes were only invented in the twentieth century, but their use in the First World War led to further development. By 1939 they had developed along two lines: bombers and fighters. The bombers delivered the bombs to the target (ships, factories, cities, airfields, supply depots); the fighters shot down enemy bombers or protected their own bombers from enemy fighters. As far as the war in the Pacific Ocean was concerned, aircraft carriers were the most important ships.

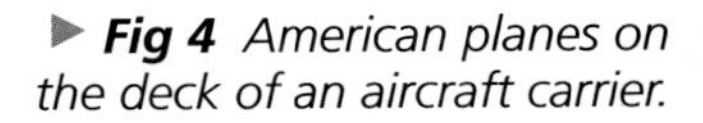

► ***Fig 4*** *American planes on the deck of an aircraft carrier.*

Key words

arsenal – place where weapons are produced
torpedoes – underwater shells
wolf packs – a large number of submarines chasing ships like a pack of wolves

SUMMARY

- By 1942 the USA was making thousands of weapons and shipping them to its allies, Britain and the USSR.
- Britain organised the ships bringing the weapons and other supplies into convoys to combat the German submarine menace.
- Radar, longer-range aircraft and depth charges helped to reduce convoy losses.
- Aeroplanes – bombers and fighters – played a large part in the war.

SUMMARY *activity*

Why was the USA so important to Britain and the USSR after 1941?

104 Victory in Europe

In this section of the book you will learn the following things:

- **after 1943 the Allies were fighting their way towards Germany;**
- **the Allies reached Berlin by May 1945.**

North Africa and Italy

North Africa was important to Britain because of the oil supplies in the Middle East and the Suez Canal, so fighting there between Britain and Germany was fierce. It was not until November 1942 that the British won the Battle of El Alamein, drove westward, invaded Italy, together with US forces, and fought their way north.

Q1 Why was the fighting in North Africa important?

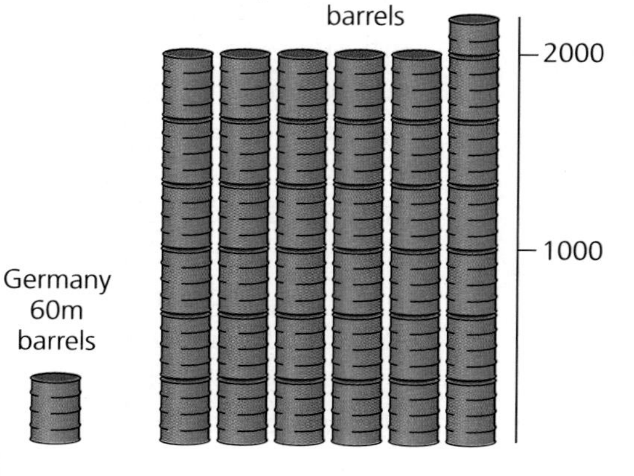

▲ ***Fig 1*** *Oil production during the Second World War in areas controlled by the Allies and by Germany.*

The USSR

Meanwhile, far to the north-east, the USSR had turned the tables on the Germans. During the winter of 1942–43, the Soviet Army had defeated and destroyed the German 6th Army at Stalingrad. There were many battles after this, including the largest tank battle of the Second World War, at Kursk, but the Germans were pushed steadily back. Through 1944 and 1945, the Soviet armies were approaching Germany from the east.

Q2 Why was the USSR vital to the Allied victory over Germany?

Numbers of people in the armed forces in the Second World War	
USSR	12 million
Germany	12 million
USA	11 million
Britain	4.5 million
Japan	4 million

▲ ***Fig 2***

D-Day 6 June 1944

Stalin had asked the USA and Britain many times to open a second front to take the strain off the Soviet armies, and by June 1944 they were ready. Planning had been going on for well over a year for a huge American and British seaborne invasion of German-occupied France. The Royal Navy had to make sure the Channel was free of submarines. The RAF had to make sure it had superiority in the air. On 6 June 1944, 7 000 ships carried 156 000 men from Britain across to the

◀ ***Fig 3*** *Landing supplies on the Normandy beaches after D-Day.*

Normandy beaches. Once the soldiers had established a **beach head** they pushed inland, but it took them until 25 August to take Paris and it was not until March 1945 that they crossed the Rhine into Germany.

▶ ***Fig 4*** *Luxury liners such as the* Queen Elizabeth *were used to bring American troops to Britain for the D-Day invasion. These liners were so fast they could outrun U-boats. They carried 15 000 troops.*

Q3 Why did Stalin want the USA and Britain to invade Europe as soon as possible?

Q4 How many months did it take from D-Day for the Allies to reach Germany?

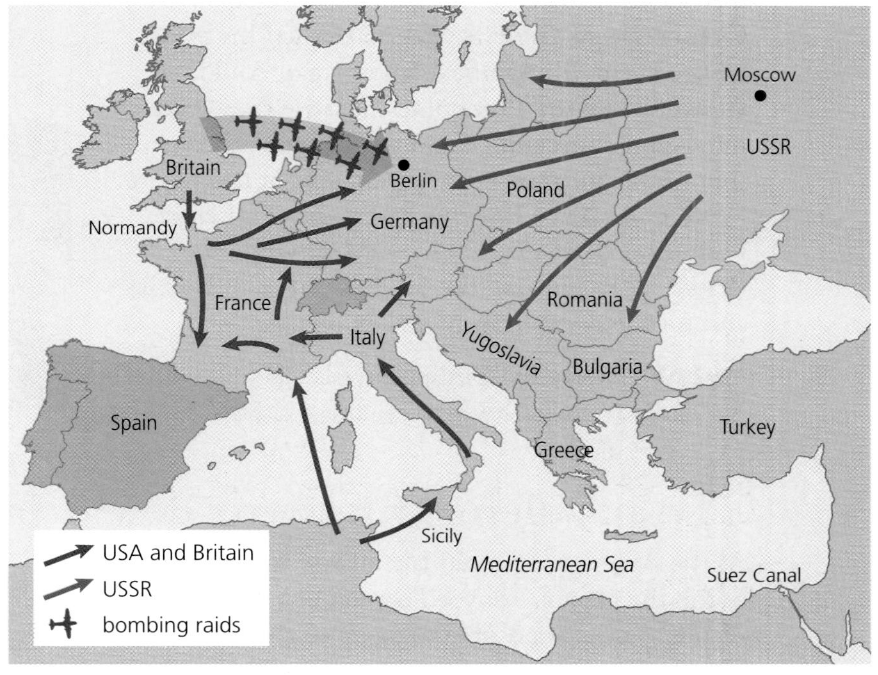

▶ ***Fig 5*** *Victory in Europe 1945.*

The Soviet advance

The Soviet armies reached Poland in July 1944 and forced Bulgaria and Romania to surrender in September. The Germans could not hold back the Soviets any more and by April 1945 the Russians were closing in on Berlin. Hitler committed suicide on 30 April and Germany surrendered at midnight on 8 May 1945. The war in Europe was over.

Key words

beach head – landing place on a beach, held by soldiers

D-Day – D stood for 'deliverance'

Normandy beaches – beaches in the north of France used for the D-Day landings

SUMMARY

- The Americans and British invaded Europe through Italy.
- The USSR invaded Europe from the east.
- The Americans and British invaded Europe from the north.
- The Allies converged on Germany in 1945.

SUMMARY *activity*

Why did the Allies win the war?

105 Victory in the Far East

In this section of the book you will learn the following things:

- **the Americans fought their way across the Pacific towards Japan;**
- **by 1945 they had to decide how they were going to force Japan to surrender.**

The Philippines, Leyte Gulf and Burma

The Americans had been fighting their way across the Pacific, getting closer and closer to Japan. In October 1944 General MacArthur led his troops ashore at the Philippine Islands. Japan could not afford to lose the Philippines because they were an important source of oil. So the Japanese threw themselves into the largest sea battle of the war, at Leyte Gulf. They lost this battle and the islands, with the loss of 170 000 lives. Meanwhile the British were pushing the Japanese back in Burma and took Rangoon in May 1945.

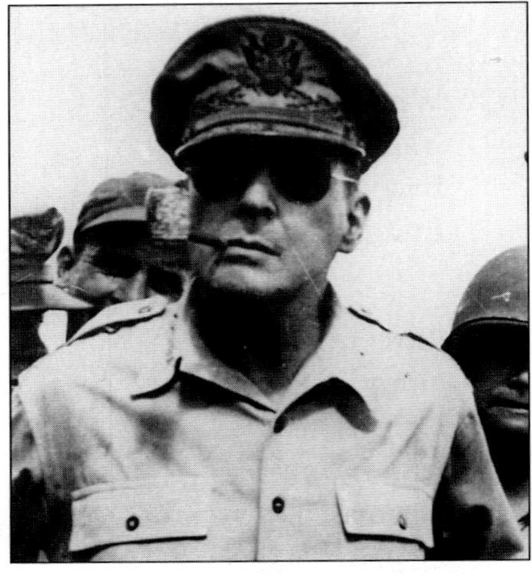

▲ ***Fig 1*** *General MacArthur.*

Q1 Why were the Philippine Islands important to both Japan and the USA?

The problem of how to defeat Japan

As the Americans neared Japan they started to bomb the capital, Tokyo. They set out to capture islands as near as possible to Japan so their bombers had less far to fly. The Japanese resisted fanatically. **Kamikaze pilots** attacked the US ships and the fighting on the islands of Iwo Jima and Okinawa cost the Americans 15 000 lives. It also alarmed the President of the United States and his generals. If the Japanese fought like this over two islands far from Japan, how fiercely would they fight over the homeland of Japan itself? What would the cost be in American, British, Australian, Indian and other Allied soldiers? Some people estimated losses of one or two million. Others said Japan was well on the way to being starved into surrender and another winter of war would force the Japanese Government to sue for peace.

One air raid on Tokyo

14 March 1945
197 000 killed or missing

▲ ***Fig 2***

Q2 Why were the battles at Iwo Jima and Okinawa so important to the Japanese?

Q3 Why do you think the Japanese might have been well on the way to being starved into surrender by 1945?

The decision was very difficult because the United States had an alternative – the atomic bomb, which scientists had been developing during the war. President Truman had to decide, with advisers, whether to use it or not. The decision was to use it.

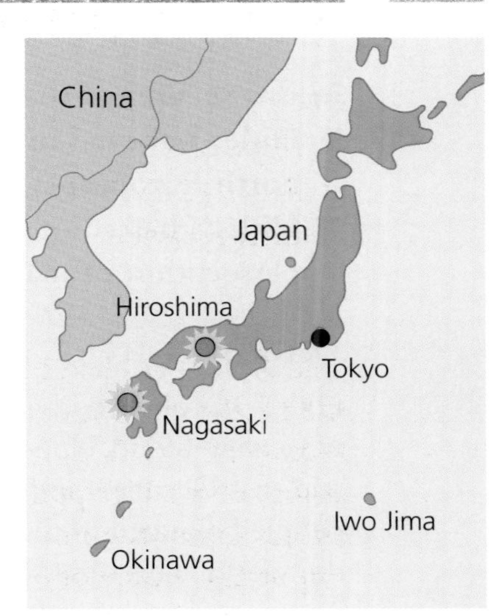

▲ **Fig 3** *Japan 1945.*

Hiroshima 6 August 1945 and Nagasaki 9 August 1945

A B29 bomber, nicknamed the *Enola Gay,* flew over Hiroshima on 6 August 1945 and dropped an atomic bomb on the city. In seconds it was reduced to rubble; 80 000 people died in the most frightening explosion ever. The Japanese Government still would not surrender so another bomb was dropped three days later on Nagasaki. Although some Japanese generals wanted to continue the war, the Emperor Hirohito ordered his people to surrender.

▲ **Fig 4** *The city of Hiroshima after the atomic bomb had been dropped.*

▶ **Fig 5**

1945: would Japan surrender?

12 July Japan asks for peace talks

17–26 July Allies meet at Potsdam. Japan required to surrender completely or be destroyed

28 July–2 August Japan refuses to surrender, but wants more talks

6 August Atomic bomb dropped on Hiroshima

7 August Japanese Army is against surrender

8 August USSR declares war on Japan

9 August Second atomic bomb dropped – on Nagasaki

Key words

kamikaze pilots – suicide pilots, flying planes full of bombs

SUMMARY

- In October 1944 the Americans regained the Philippine Islands.
- The Americans bombed Tokyo from island bases.
- The battles for Iwo Jima and Okinawa cost the Americans 15,000 lives.
- In August 1945 the Americans dropped two atomic bombs – on Hiroshima and Nagasaki.

SUMMARY *activity*

Why did the USA decide to drop the atomic bomb on Hiroshima? What alternatives did it have?

106 The Holocaust

In this section of the book you will learn the following things:

- **Hitler believed in a master race called the Aryans, who were north Europeans;**
- **Hitler's hatred of non-Aryans led to persecution of many people, including Jews.**

▲ ***Fig 1*** *Hitler pictured at a mass rally.*

Aryans and non-Aryans

Hitler was obsessed with a master race of Aryans who were blond, blue-eyed, strong and healthy. He said that Germans and other north European people belonged to the Aryan race and should rule the world. This obsession led to hatred of non-Aryans and people who did not fit into Hitler's world picture. He included Jews, Slavs (from eastern Europe), black people, communists, gypsies, handicapped people, homosexuals and, eventually, anyone who opposed him. Hitler encouraged other people to think the same way by repeating his message in speeches over and over again, and by the use of **propaganda**.

Q1 Who were the non-Aryan people?

Q2 To whom was Hitler's hatred eventually extended?

Q3 How did Hitler encourage other people to hate non-Aryan people?

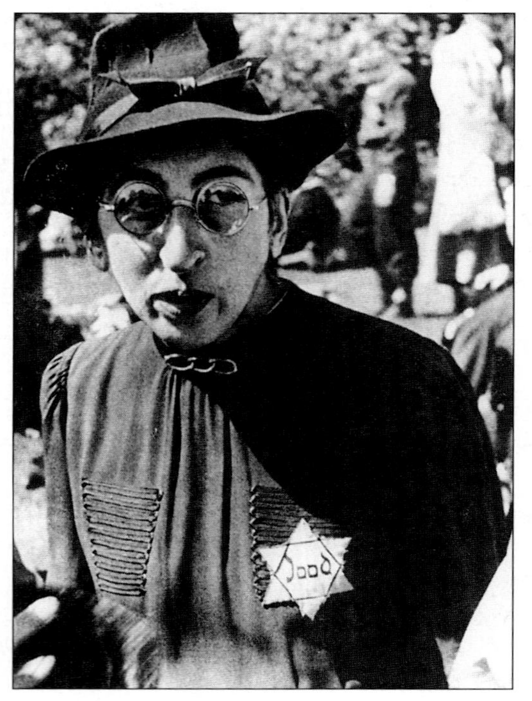

▲ ***Fig 2*** *Jews were forced to wear yellow stars on their clothes.*

Persecution of Jews

His SA troops smashed Jewish shops and attacked Jewish people. Handicapped people were sent to asylums and many were killed or sterilised, as Hitler wanted only a 'perfect' race. Gypsies and communists disappeared to camps or were killed. As the 1930s wore on, the situation for Jews became worse. In 1933 they were banned from working in the Government. In 1935 they were banned from using public places such as parks. Jews and non-Jews were not allowed to marry. Some Jews decided to leave Germany, which had been their home for generations, and seek a new life in Britain or the USA. Those who stayed faced the risk of their homes being attacked, their synagogues smashed and, increasingly, they themselves being sent to **concentration camps**.

Ghettoes and concentration camps

Once the war began in 1939, Germany conquered other countries where Jews lived, such as Poland. Often they herded the Jews into a walled-up part of the city called a **ghetto**, where they had to remain, living, working and, sometimes, starving to death. Other Nazi 'solutions' were concentration camps, where thousands of Jews were sent to work. They lived in terrible conditions, with barely enough food to live.

The 'Final Solution'

Hitler's aim, however, was to destroy the Jewish people. By 1942 he had decided on what was called the 'Final Solution'. The first massacres occurred in Russia and Poland, where young, fit Jews were forced to work as slaves, before being made to dig their own graves. Then they were shot. Later, death factories were established at such camps as Auschwitz, to which Jews were shipped in cattle trucks and marched into gas chambers to be killed. In all, some six million Jews were killed. At some camps Jews were used for medical experiments, which often resulted in death.

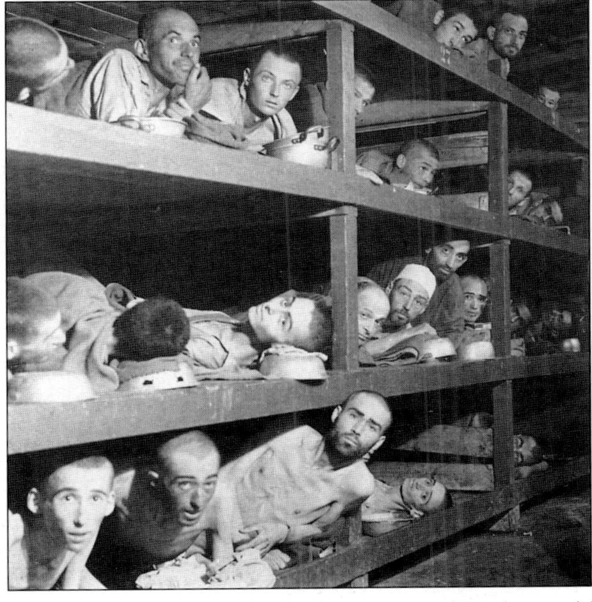

▲ ***Fig 3*** *Inmates of Buchenwald concentration camp, liberated in April 1945.*

As the war was ending in 1945, the Allied soldiers reached the concentration camps and were horrified at what they saw and heard. By October 1946 the full story of this slaughter had been revealed at the Nuremberg Trials, where British, Russian, American and French judges tried the surviving Nazi leaders.

Q4 What was the 'Final Solution'?

Key words

concentration camps – labour camps where thousands of people were concentrated

ghetto – area where a group of people have to live and cannot leave

propaganda – information spread to promote a particular point of view

SUMMARY

- Hitler believed the Germans were part of a master race called Aryans. This led to persecution of non-Aryans, such as Jews.
- In the 1930s Jews were increasingly discriminated against.
- At the beginning of the war Jews were herded into ghettos or sent to concentration camps.
- By 1942 Hitler had arrived at the 'Final Solution' – the killing of all Jews.
- The Allies discovered the concentration camps in 1945 and many Nazi leaders were brought to trial at Nuremberg.

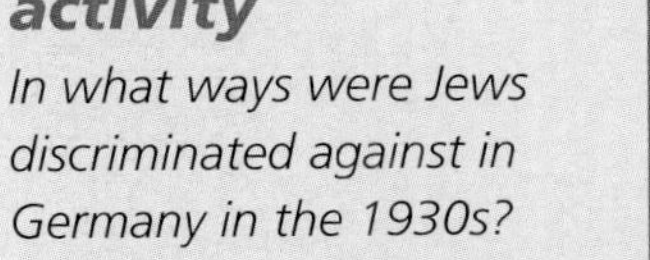

SUMMARY *activity*

In what ways were Jews discriminated against in Germany in the 1930s? How did this become worse when the war began?

107 The United Nations

In this section of the book you will learn the following things:
- **the United Nations was set up in 1945;**
- **how the United Nations differed from the League of Nations;**
- **how the United Nations is organised.**

The United Nations Charter

Once Germany was defeated the representatives of 50 countries met in the United States to work out a system for stopping future wars. They signed the United Nations Charter, which replaced the old agreement of the League of Nations. They agreed to keep the peace, defend human rights and co-operate with each other. How was this going to be any more successful than the League of Nations had been?

> 'We, the people of the United Nations, are determined to save succeeding generations from the scourge of war…'
>
> *from the UN Charter 1945*

▲ ***Fig 1***

The League had failed for two reasons:
- because some of the largest nations had not joined it;
- because it had no armed forces.

The United Nations was different:
- all the major countries (including the USA and the USSR) were members;
- Article 43 of the UN Charter said that the UN could call on its members to provide troops if there was any aggression.

The General Assembly

The General Assembly met every year and was made up of five representatives from every member state. (In 1945 this meant there were 250 meeting together.)

Q1 What was the General Assembly?

Q2 How often did it meet?

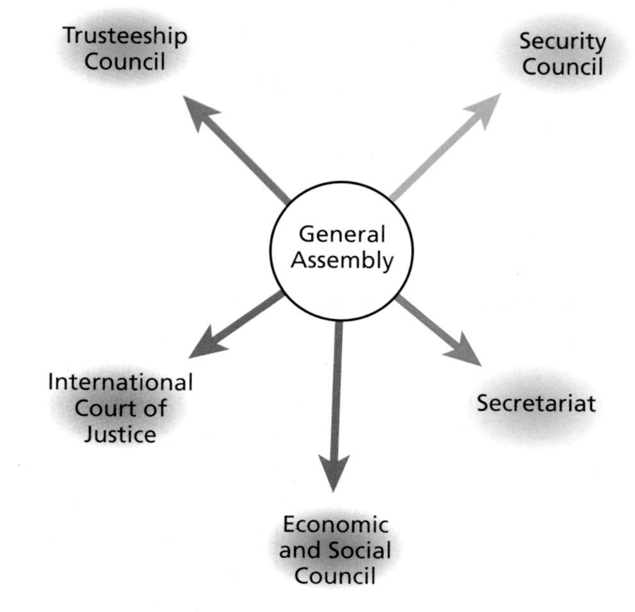

► ***Fig 2*** *The core of the United Nations.*

The Security Council

The Security Council met more often and was made up of 11 representatives: five permanent members of the Council – the USA, Britain, the USSR, France and China – and six other members who served in rotation. Any decision had to be passed by a majority of seven and had to include all five permanent members. Thus the five countries that won the Second World War could, and still can, **veto** any UN decision. For instance, in the early years the USSR used the veto to keep out new members who might be hostile towards it. Japan's membership was vetoed four times.

Q3 Who were the five permanent members of the Security Council?

Q4 Explain what the veto is.

▲ ***Fig 3*** *A special 39-storey building was built in New York to house all the offices and meeting rooms of the United Nations.*

Problems for the UN

The war was hardly over before it was obvious that the two **superpowers**, the USA and the USSR, were becoming bitter enemies. This made co-operation within the UN difficult. In addition, some tensions in the world were very difficult to solve. The quarrels between Arabs and Jews and between India and Pakistan have continued, despite UN attempts to keep the peace.

▼ ***Fig 4***

Well-known UN organisations

IMF	International Monetary Fund
WHO	World Health Organisation
UNICEF	United Nations Children's Fund
FAO	Food and Agricultural Organisation
UNESCO	United Nations Educational Scientific and Cultural Organisation

Other organisations cover: civil aviation, the postal service, meterology, trade, refugees, labour, atomic energy, telecommunications, and so on.

Key words

superpowers – outstandingly powerful countries

veto – say no to a decision

SUMMARY

- The United Nations was set up in 1945 to work out a system for stopping future wars.
- All the major countries were members.
- The UN could call on its members to send troops to keep the peace in troubled areas.
- The General Assembly met every year.
- The Security Council met more often and was made up of five permanent members and six others in rotation.

SUMMARY *activity*

In what ways was the United Nations different from the League of Nations? What difficulties has the UN faced?

108 Europe divided

In this section of the book you will learn the following things:

- **there were divisions among the Allies who had won the war;**
- **these divisions led to the crisis in Berlin in 1948 and the division of Europe.**

Germany divided

The setting-up of the United Nations occurred against a background of bitter divisions between the Allies who had defeated Germany – the USA, the USSR, Britain and France.

Because Germany was completely defeated in May 1945, there was no Government left. The Allies divided Germany into four zones: American, Russian, British and French. Then they divided Berlin itself into four zones. This arrangement would work as long as the four victorious powers remained friendly. The American, British and French had some disagreements, but these were nothing compared with the disagreements with the USSR.

▲ ***Fig 1*** *The division of Germany between the Allies after the war.*

Q1 What was the weakness of dividing Germany and Berlin into four zones?

Q2 Between which powers were the main disagreements?

The Truman Doctrine and the Marshall Plan

The USA was worried about the spread of communism. President Truman said the USA would help any country in the world that was threatened by communists. He went further and gave money and aid to countries in Western Europe to help them recover from the war. This was called the Marshall Plan.

Since it was obvious that the USA was intent on rebuilding Europe as a **bulwark** against the communist Soviet Union, the Russians were annoyed and felt threatened.

Q3 What was the Marshall Plan?

Two different views: the USSR and the West

The USSR had suffered the full force of a German invasion in the First World War and again in 1941 and never wanted this to happen again. Having fought its way to Germany, the Soviet Union wanted, first, to keep a buffer of small countries between itself and Germany and, second, to keep Germany weak. The other three Allies wanted to help Germany recover and take her place in world trade.

Crisis in Berlin 1948

The Western Allies (the USA, Britain and France) had annoyed the USSR by introducing the new Germany currency into West Germany but, in June 1948, they introduced it into West Berlin. The angry Russians retaliated by closing the road and rail links from West Germany to West Berlin. All the power stations supplying electricity to Berlin were in East Berlin; the Russians cut the supply. It looked as though the whole of Berlin would fall to the Soviets. However, the Allies felt that they could not allow the Soviets to advance any further into Europe so they decided to supply West Berlin by air.

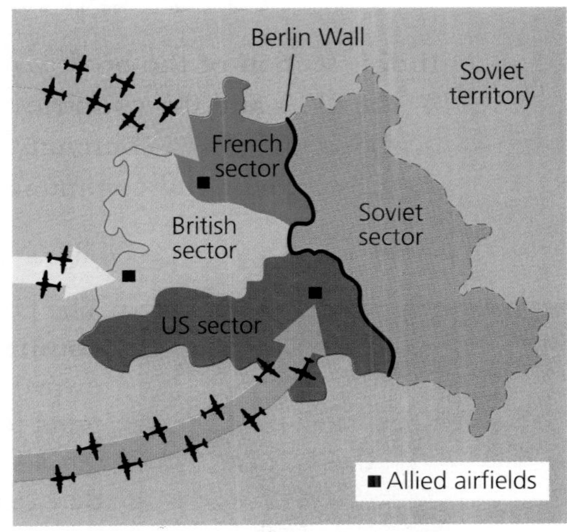

▲ ***Fig 2*** *The division of Berlin between the Allies. Berlin was in the Soviet zone of Germany (see Fig 1). The Berlin Wall was built in 1961.*

Q4 Why was it so difficult to supply West Berlin?

The Berlin Airlift 1948–1949

Supplying two million Berliners was a gigantic task and went on right through the winter. The planes flew along the narrow 'corridors' allowed by the Soviet authorities. By May 1949 the USSR gave up and allowed the road and rail links to re-open. After this crisis the American, British and French amalgamated their zones to form the Federal Republic of Germany (West Germany) and the USSR formed the German Democratic Republic (East Germany). It was obvious that the hopes of a united Germany were lost for many years. Everywhere the USSR strengthened its borders against the West.

▲ ***Fig 3*** *1948: Berliners watch an airlift plane arriving with supplies.*

Key words

airlift – carrying in cargo by air

bulwark – a type of wall, a barrier

SUMMARY

- Germany and Berlin were divided into four zones controlled by the four Allies.
- The Truman Doctrine stated that the USA would help any country threatened by communists.
- Under the Marshall Plan the USA gave aid to help Europe recover after the war.
- The USSR did not want Germany to recover and this led to the crisis over Berlin.

SUMMARY *activity*

Why was the USA so keen for Europe (including Germany) to recover after the war and why was the USSR opposed to German recovery?

109 The Cold War

In this section of the book you will learn the following things:

- the USA and the countries of Western Europe were capitalist countries;
- the USSR was a communist country;
- the capitalist and communist countries were aligned against each other.

The USA and Western Europe and capitalism

▲ *Fig 1 The three major Allies meeting in July 1945. Left to right: Churchill was the Prime Minister of Britain, Truman the President of the USA and Stalin the leader of the USSR. The Cold War was soon to begin.*

The USA and the countries of Western Europe were **capitalist countries**. Capitalism means that businesses are privately owned by individual people who run the business to make a profit for themselves. The business may be as small as one farmer with a small farm or one shopkeeper with one shop, or they can be large companies such as insurance companies, banks or big chain stores. However, the Governments are elected by the people of the country and can be removed by them, so these capitalist countries are also **democratic**.

Q1 What does capitalism mean?

Q2 What is a democratic country?

The USSR and communism

The USSR was a **communist country**. Communism is a system in which the state owns the **means of production**. This means that businesses are owned and run by the Government on behalf of the people. This applies to everything from farms and shops, to railways, banks, coal mines and so on. After the war, this seemed all right in theory. In practice, however, Stalin, who was the head of the Government in the USSR, was a powerful **dictator**. He kept control of everything and did not allow anyone to criticise him or the Government.

So it was not only the tensions over Germany that lay at the root of the antagonism between the USSR and the USA and Western Europe; it was also that both sides had completely different ideas about how to run their countries. After the Berlin Airlift, the two sides distrusted each other even more.

Q3 What does communism mean?

USA and democratic countries of Western Europe	*USSR and communist countries of Eastern Europe*
• fear of attack from the east;	• fear of attack from the west;
• fear of communism;	• fear of capitalism;
• fear of atomic bomb.	• fear of atomic bomb.
NATO 1949	**Warsaw Pact 1955**

◄ *Fig 2*

NATO 1949 and the Warsaw Pact 1955

After the First World War, the USA had wanted nothing to do with the arguments in the rest of the world. This was called **isolationism** and was a factor in the failure of the League of Nations, the failure to keep the peace and the coming of war again in 1939. After the Second World War, however, the USA realised that it was impossible to remain isolated from events elsewhere. In 1949, President Truman invited European countries to join a Western alliance for defence. This was called the North Atlantic Treaty Organisation (NATO). It was an alliance of ten Western European countries, plus the USA and Canada. The aim, certainly as far as the USA was concerned, was to contain any further movement of the USSR into Europe. In 1955, the USSR formed a similar defensive alliance with Eastern European countries, called the Warsaw Pact.

The Iron Curtain speech

'From Stettin in the Baltic to Trieste in the Adriatic, an iron curtain has descended across the continent.'

▲ ***Fig 3*** *Winston Churchill's 'Iron Curtain' speech at Fulton, Missouri, in 1946. The 'Iron Curtain' finally settled along the line shown on the map below.*

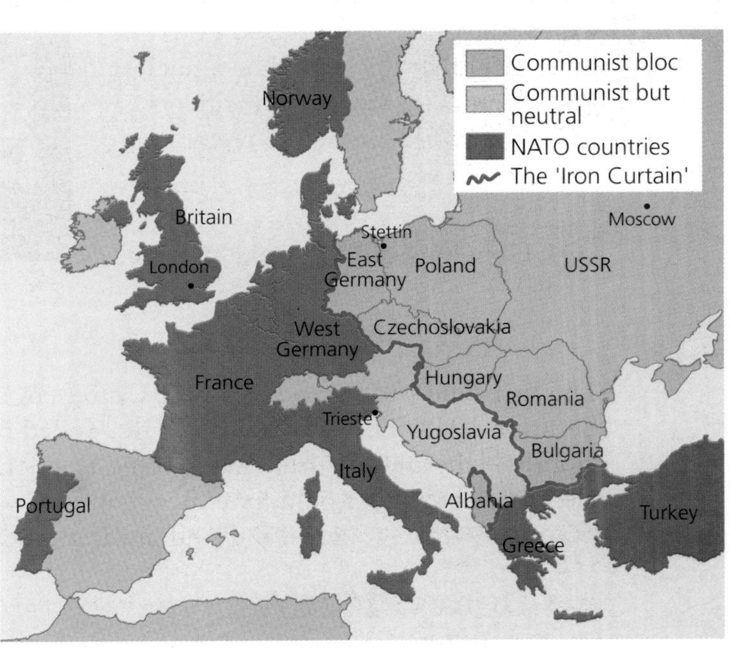

▲ ***Fig 4*** *'Cold War Europe'. Warsaw Pact versus NATO countries.*

Key words

capitalist countries – countries where businesses (large and small) are privately owned and run to make a profit for the owner(s)

communist countries – countries where the state, not individuals, owns businesses, and runs them on behalf of the people

democratic countries – countries where the Government is elected by – and can therefore be removed by – the people

dictator – leader who controls everything and allows no criticism

isolationism – when a country keeps itself apart from events in other countries

means of production – the businesses, such as farms and factories, that make the goods we need

SUMMARY

- The capitalist and democratic countries of Western Europe and North America were aligned against the communist dictatorship of the USSR.
- Ten Western European countries, the USA and Canada formed the North Atlantic Treaty Organisation in 1949.
- The USSR and Eastern European countries formed the Warsaw Pact in 1955.

SUMMARY *activity*

What was each side afraid of?

110 The Cold War onwards

In this section of the book you will learn the following things:

- **the Cold War lasted for nearly 50 years;**
- **there were five main incidents when it could have become all-out world war.**

Fifty years of the Cold War

The Cold War lasted for nearly 50 years. Mostly it was cold to lukewarm, but sometimes the situation deteriorated so much that outright world war was very close and everyone was fearful that this would be a nuclear war. There were five main incidents when the world seemed to teeter on the brink of war.

Q1 How long did the Cold War last?

▲ ***Fig 1*** *Leaders during the Cuban missile crisis:* Left *John F. Kennedy (President of the USA);* Right *Nikita Khrushchev (leader of the USSR).*

Berlin Crisis 1948

The first time was when the Soviet Union cut off road, canal and rail links to West Berlin in 1948. The Western Allies responded by flying supplies into West Berlin for months – the Berlin Airlift (Unit 108). At any time the Soviets could have shot down the planes, but this would have meant all-out war and they pulled back from doing this. Eventually they reopened the land links, and both sides breathed again.

Hungary 1956

In 1956 Hungary announced that it would have free elections and would leave the Warsaw Pact. Its leader, Imre Nagy, ordered the Soviet Army to leave Hungary. The Soviet reply was to send in tanks to control the capital, Budapest. Thousands of Hungarians were killed or fled. Nagy was shot and the Soviets handed power to Soviet-dominated communists in Hungary.

The Berlin Wall 1961

By 1961 West Berlin was booming, with plenty of jobs and plenty of goods in the shops. A steady stream of East Berliners moved to the richer life in West Berlin. The USSR decided to put a stop to this and built the Berlin Wall right across the city, with **checkpoints** to control who went in and out.

▲ ***Fig 2*** *The Berlin Wall going up in 1961.*

Cuba 1962

In 1962 USA spy planes discovered that the USSR was building missile bases on the island of Cuba, which meant that USSR **missiles** could be launched against the USA. The USA sent warships to intercept the missiles that were being delivered to the bases on Cuba. This meant that the warships of the USA and USSR might clash and start a war. In the event, the USSR withdrew.

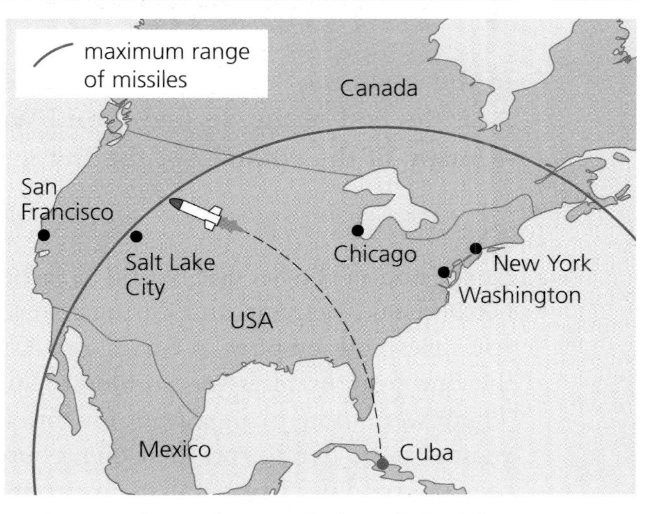

► **Fig 3** *The threat to the USA from Soviet missiles in Cuba.*

▼ **Fig 4**

Dubček's reforms in Czechoslovakia

- control of industry to be shifted to managers and workers;
- press censorship ended;
- political public meetings allowed;
- genuine discussion in Parliament;
- freedom to travel abroad.

Q2 What were Dubcek's reforms?

Q3 Why was the USSR so worried about rebellion against its rule in Hungary and Czechoslovakia?

Czechoslovakia 1968

Czechoslovakia was the only Eastern European country which had been a genuine democracy before the Second World War. Although run by Soviet-type communists after the war, in 1968 Czechoslovakia wanted to return to a more democratic form of Government. The Czech Communist Party chose Alexander Dubček as its leader. He wanted to bring in **reforms** and was enthusiastically supported. However, the USSR saw this as very threatening and, in August 1968, sent half a million troops to seize control of the capital, Prague, and other Czech cities. Dubček was forced to cancel the reforms and resign.

The break-up of the USSR

From the mid-1980s the attitude of the USSR changed under the leadership of Mikhail Gorbachev. This led to greater freedoms, the taking down of the Berlin Wall in 1989, the fall of the Communist Party in 1991 and the breaking up of the USSR into a number of separate countries.

Key words

checkpoints – entrances along the Berlin Wall, manned by armed soldiers; the most famous was 'Checkpoint Charlie'

missiles – weapons fired through the air

reforms – changes

SUMMARY

- There were five main incidents when the Cold War could have led to war between the USA and the USSR. These were: the Berlin airlift 1948, the revolt in Hungary 1956, the building of the Berlin Wall 1961, the Cuban missile crisis 1962 and the reform movement in Czechoslovakia 1968.
- In 1991 the Communist Party fell from power and the USSR broke up.

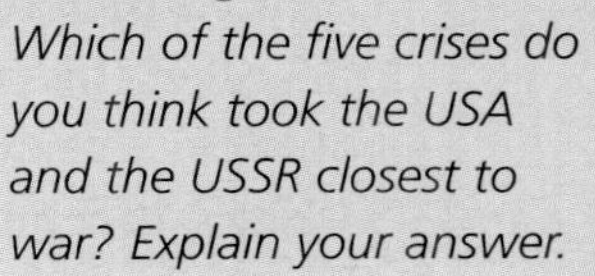

SUMMARY *activity*

Which of the five crises do you think took the USA and the USSR closest to war? Explain your answer.

111 The end of the old empires

In this section of the book you will learn the following things:

- **at the end of the Second World War European countries still had empires;**
- **many of the colonies of the European empires wanted to be independent.**

Reasons for the end of the empires

At the end of the Second World War, Britain, France, the Netherlands, Belgium and Portugal were the main countries with empires in Africa and Asia. The time of the European empires was coming to an end, however. There were three main reasons for this. First, the colonies wanted to be free to run their own countries. Second, they resented the **imperialist countries** taking all the raw materials such as copper, tin, timber and so on. Third, the Second World War had weakened the imperial powers, which had neither the money nor the desire to fight to keep the colonies within their own empires.

Q1 Which European countries had empires at the end of the Second World War?

Q2 What were the three reasons for the ending of the European empires?

▲ ***Fig 1*** *Mahatma Gandhi.*

India

India had wanted to be free of the British Empire for some time. A leader called Mahatma Gandhi emerged. He was a devout Hindu who believed in equal rights for all religions, but more than anything he wanted India to be free of the British. Matters came to a head after the war: India became independent in 1947, becoming two countries – the mainly Hindu India and the mainly Muslim Pakistan. The eastern part of Pakistan broke away in 1971 to become Bangladesh.

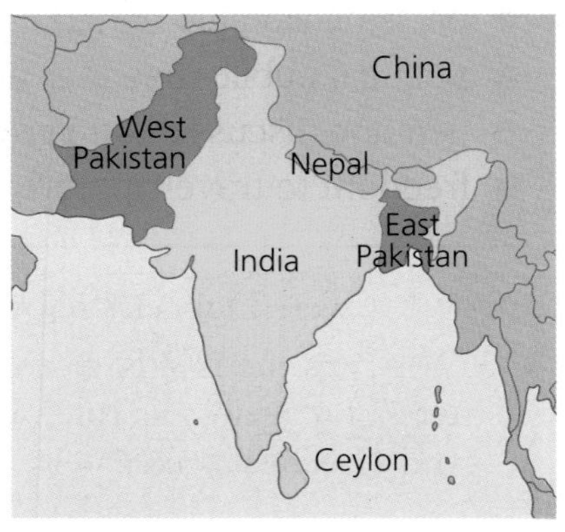

▲ ***Fig 2*** *India after 1947, showing East and West Pakistan.*

Asia

During the Second World War the Japanese had captured the colonies of the European powers, and one effect this had was to show that the Europeans could be defeated. After the war many colonies fought for their independence and gained it. French Indo-China rebelled, for example, and led by the communist Ho Chi Minh, defeated the French in 1954, after a

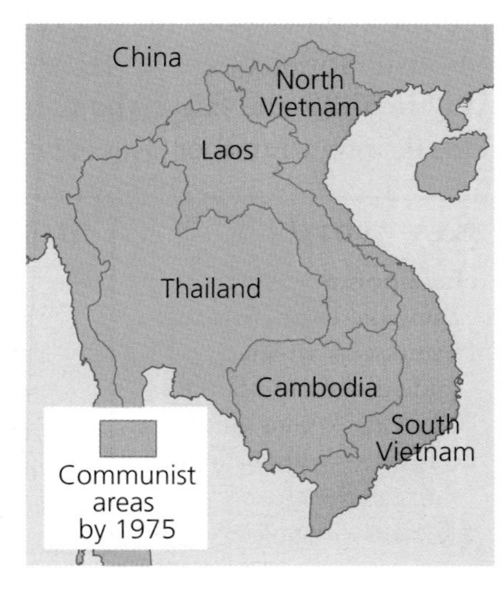

▶ ***Fig 3*** *Vietnam was the scene of a long struggle 1946–75.*

bitter war lasting eight years. Four countries were formed: Laos, Cambodia, South and North Vietnam. During the war, communist China had helped Ho Chi Minh and the USA had helped the French. After the war Ho Chi Minh and the communists ruled North Vietnam while the anti-communists ruled South Vietnam. This was how the USA, in its campaign to stop the spread of communism, became involved in the Vietnam War.

Q3 Who was Ho Chi Minh?

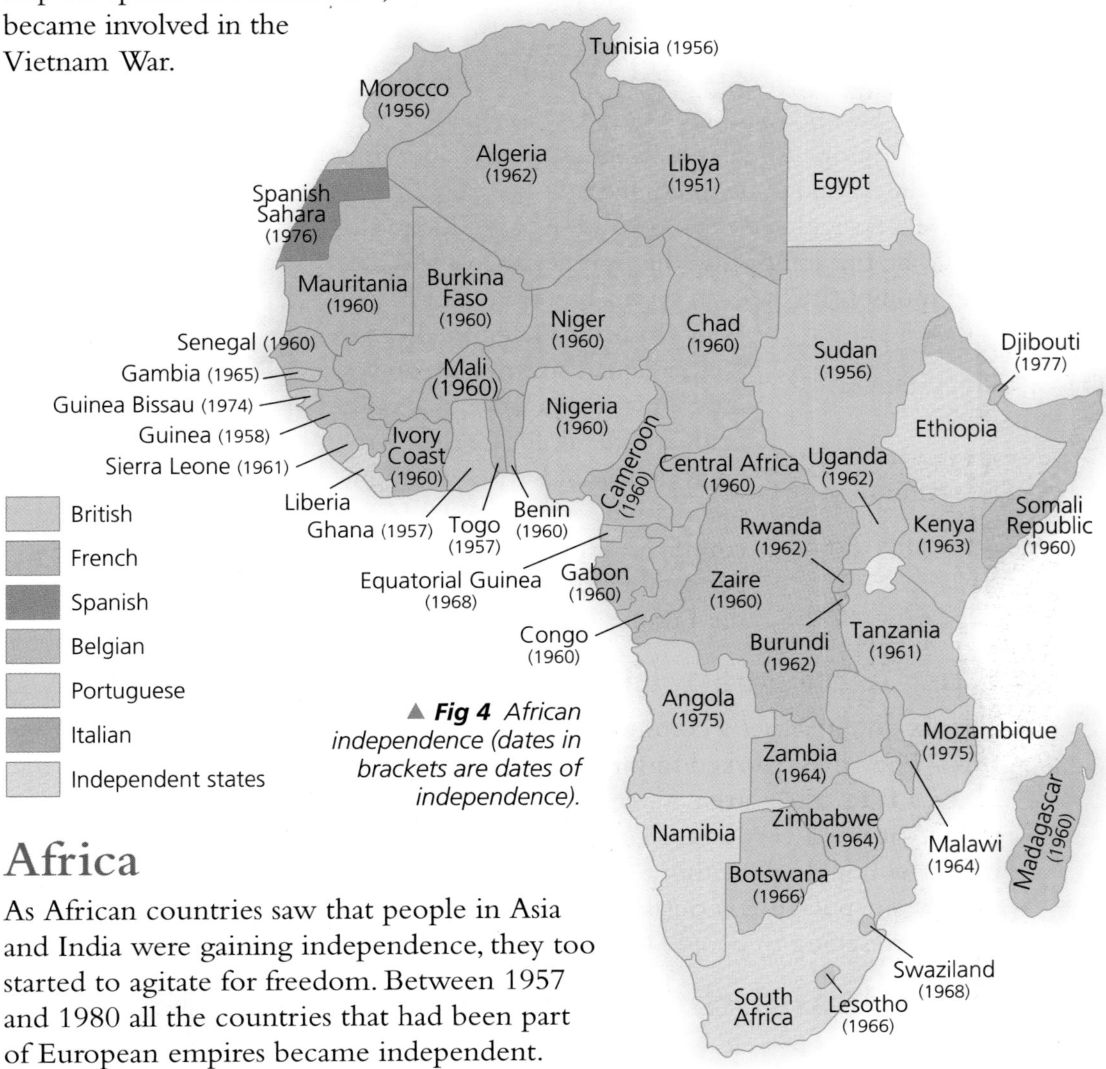

▲ *Fig 4 African independence (dates in brackets are dates of independence).*

Africa

As African countries saw that people in Asia and India were gaining independence, they too started to agitate for freedom. Between 1957 and 1980 all the countries that had been part of European empires became independent.

Key words

imperialist countries – countries which exercise power through their empires

SUMMARY

- Britain, France, the Netherlands, Belgium and Portugal were the main countries with empires at the end of the Second World War.
- Many colonies wished to be independent, including India and many Asian and African countries.

SUMMARY *activity*

Why did the USA become involved in Vietnam?

112 Europe united?

In this section of the book you will learn the following things:

- after the Second World War some European countries decided to trade together on favourable terms;
- in 1957, six countries set up the European Economic Community;
- Britain was not sure whether to join or not.

Trade and industry promoted

After the Second World War the USA helped Western Europe to start up its industry again, but how was industry and trade to continue to prosper? In 1951 the French suggested that coal and steel production should be run jointly and the European Coal and Steel Community (ECSC) was set up. It consisted of France, West Germany, Belgium, the Netherlands, Luxembourg and Italy. This co-operation not only made it difficult for Germany to build up war industries again but also proved very successful in promoting trade and industry within the six countries. Within three years steel production rose by 25 per cent. In 1957 the six decided to go further and set up the European Economic Community.

The six original members of the European Economic Community

- France;
- West Germany:
- The Netherlands;
- Belgium;
- Luxembourg;
- Italy.

▲ *Fig 1*

Q1 Which countries joined the European Coal and Steel Community?

Q2 What benefits did this have?

The European Economic Community (EEC)

The six countries set a common **customs duty** on all goods coming into the EEC. They then worked towards abolishing custom duties between the six to create a **free trade area**. Since the population of the six together was 180 million, it was a very large economic area. Manufacturers living within the six countries could sell, without duties, to 180 million people, whereas manufacturers outside had to pay duty on goods they were selling to people living in the EEC.

Q3 What is a free trade area?

Britain and the Commonwealth or Britain and Europe?

In the 1950s Britain still thought of itself as a world power. Even though colonies in the British Empire were gaining independence, many kept their links with Britain by joining the **Commonwealth**. The countries of the Commonwealth traded together on better terms than with outsiders. Britain felt more connected to the Commonwealth than Europe and refused to join the EEC. However, by 1961 Britain could see that the EEC was doing well and Britain was not. As more and more British colonies became independent and some left the Commonwealth, it became obvious that Britain was no longer a world power.

Britain joined the EEC 1973

Britain applied and was refused membership of the EEC in 1963 and 1967. Some European countries, particularly France, led by General de Gaulle, felt that Britain was too close to the USA and did not have European interests at heart. However, in 1973 Britain did join, together with Ireland and Denmark. There are currently 15 members of the European Union, as it is now called.

▼ ***Fig 2*** *General de Gaulle fought in the First World War and became the leader of French resistance to the Germans in the Second World War. He became leader of France and President in 1958, serving for the next 11 years.*

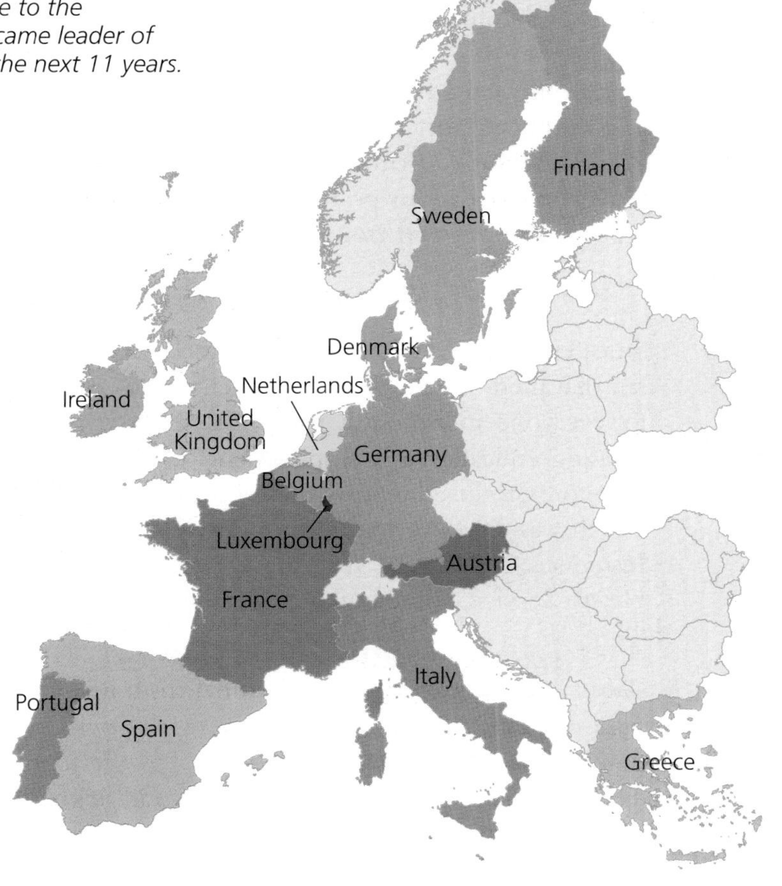

► ***Fig 3*** *The 15 current members of the European Union.*

Q4 Why did France oppose Britain joining the EEC?

Key words

Commonwealth – association made up of Britain and the countries that were previously part of its empire

customs duty – tax on goods coming into an area

free trade area – formed when countries abolish customs duties between themselves

SUMMARY

- The European Coal and Steel Community was formed in 1951.
- The European Economic Community was formed in 1957, consisting of France, West Germany, Belgium, the Netherlands, Luxembourg and Italy.
- Britain joined the EEC in 1973.
- There are now 15 members of the European Union.

SUMMARY *activity*

Why did Britain not join the EEC until 1973?

113 Britain and the welfare state

In this section of the book you will learn the following things:

- a coalition of all parties formed the wartime Government;
- there was an interest in making conditions better for everyone after the war.

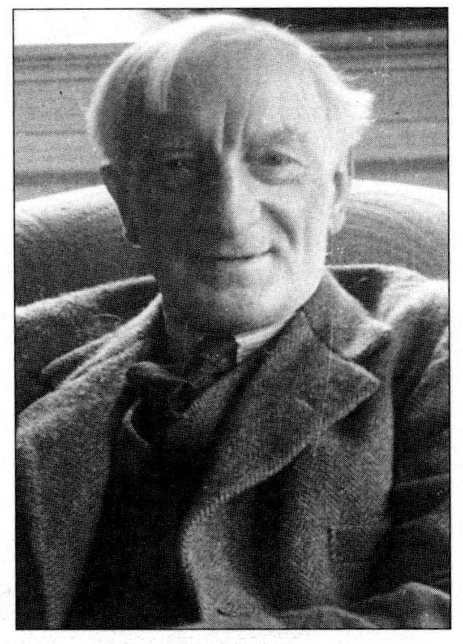

▲ ***Fig 1*** *William Beveridge introduced his report in 1942 by saying there were 'Five Giant Evils'. His report tackled the 'Evil of Want' by introducing National Insurance for all citizens.*

The war effort

In the Second World War, the Government controlled Britain's economic life. Industry was told what it must produce for the war effort and people were directed to join the armed services or to do war work. To gain maximum support for these ideas, Winston Churchill, the Conservative Prime Minister, had brought into his Government Labour politicians, so they all worked in a **coalition government** to win the war.

The ideas for a welfare state

Since everyone had worked to win the war, it seemed fair that there should be an improvement in conditions for everyone after the war, particularly in health, housing, education and employment. The Government therefore produced reports, the most important of which was the Beveridge Report, dealing with National Insurance. Other issues were education, a National Health Service, house building and full employment.

Beveridge and the 'Five Giant Evils'

1. Want (poverty)
2. Ignorance (poor schooling)
3. Squalor (bad housing)
4. Disease (poor health)
5. Idleness (unemployment)

▲ ***Fig 2***

The Evil of Want: getting rid of poverty

'Want' was attacked by the National Insurance Scheme, whereby every working person, except married women, paid in 4s 11d ($24\frac{1}{2}$p) a week to the scheme. They were covered for a pension, funeral, sickness, unemployment, maternity (for a man's wife), and guardian's allowance. Family Allowance was introduced, with 25p a week paid for every child after the first. The National Assistance Board helped people who slipped through the National Insurance net.

The Evil of Ignorance: education for all

Even before the war ended in 1945, the Government had passed the 1944 Education Act. Its theme was free secondary education for all children up to the age of 15. After the war, in 1945, a Labour Government came to power and tackled the remaining four Evils. This was a mammoth task in a Britain made poor by the war. Everything from coal to food was in short supply.

The Evil of Squalor: decent housing for all

During the war half a million houses had been destroyed. Great efforts were made and a million new homes built by 1951. Private building was restricted, to enable councils to build houses for low rents.

The Evil of Disease: health for all

The National Health Service Act was passed in 1946. It aimed to give a free health service to all. When it started on 5 July 1948, it was overwhelmed. Within a year, 187 million prescriptions were written by doctors, eight and a half million people were treated by dentists, and opticians were booked solid for months as people who had done without glasses now queued to get them. Soon some charges were brought in.

The Evil of Idleness: jobs for all

Efforts were made to keep unemployment to about three per cent of the workforce. The upturn in world trade as Europe recovered after the war made this possible.

Q1 What were Beveridge's 'Five Giant Evils'?

Q2 Which 'Evil' did his report tackle?

▲ ***Fig 3*** *After the war people in Britain were keen to have better conditions for all. The Labour Party won the general election of 1945 with a big majority. Members of the Labour Government of 1945–51 are pictured, with Prime Minister Clement Atlee in the middle of the front row.*

Key words

coalition government – a government made up of different political parties; often formed in wartime

welfare state – where the Government provides a national system of education, healthcare, old-age pensions, unemployment pay and other benefits, to ensure the social and economic security of its citizens

SUMMARY

- In 1942 William Beveridge called for an attack on the 'Five Giant Evils'.
- Education, National Insurance, health, housing and employment were all tackled by Governments from 1944 to the early 1950s.

SUMMARY *activity*

Write about what was done to solve each of the 'Five Giant Evils'.

114 First, Second and Third Worlds

In this section of the book you will learn the following things:

- **the world became divided into three sections economically.**

Britain and living standards

Within a few years of the end of the Second World War, Britain no longer had an empire. Although there were still strong links with the Commonwealth countries that had formerly been part of the British Empire, Britain was, in fact, one small country among many. However, by the standards of most people in the world, Britain was a wealthy country.

Q1 What is GNP?

▼ *Fig 1*

GNP (Gross National Product)

A country's GNP is worked out by estimating the total wealth produced by all its people in one year.

If you divide the GNP by the total population of the country you get GNP per head.

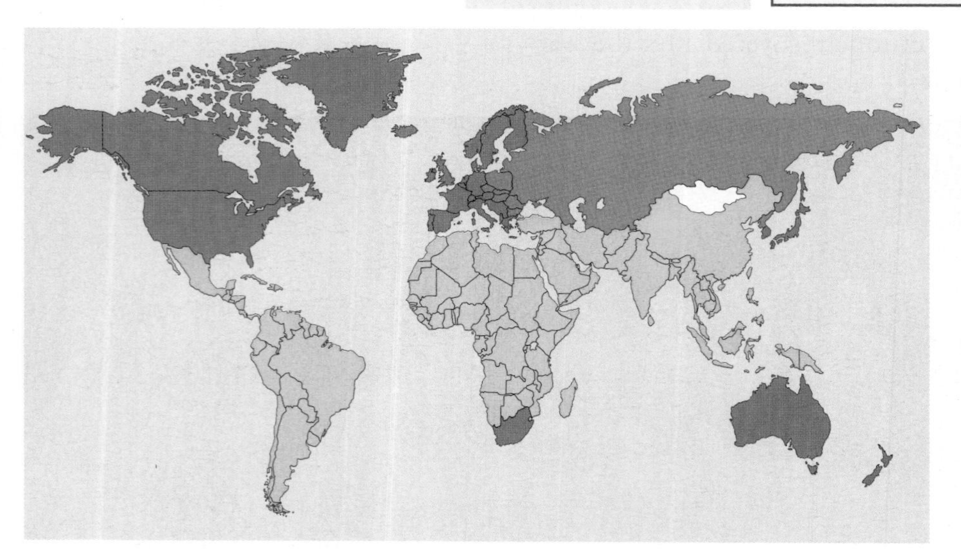

First World

Developed industrial countries with a capitalist economy

Second World

Developed industrial countries with a communist economy

Third World

The 'developing world'

◀ ***Fig 2*** *How the First, Second and Third World countries were named.*

First, Second and Third Worlds
(The developed and the developing world)

The Western capitalist countries were called the First World and the communist USSR was called the Second World. The countries that had recently gained independence from the old empires in places such as Africa, or had gained independence in the nineteenth century, such as the Latin American countries, were called the Third World. Many of these countries complained that although they were free of the old empires, they were controlled by the worldwide trading system that was run by the First World countries. **Business corporations** in the First World countries often owned the mines and plantations in the Third World, and set the prices.

Q2 What were the First, Second and Third World countries?

Q3 What was, and still is, the complaint of many Third World countries?

Giving and lending

The First World countries gave money to help development and raise living standards in the Third World, through the United Nations Organisation, the World Bank or directly. For instance, the World Health Organisation (part of the UN) has worked to eradicate some serious diseases in many parts of the world. However, giving or investing money has not always brought the best results. The First World countries have often lent money with a view both to helping development and to making a profit for themselves. The Third World countries accepted the loans, assuming they would make plenty of money to pay them back. Often this did not happen, and Third World countries could find themselves heavily in debt. They complained that First World countries set the rates of interest for paying back the loans to their own advantage. Moreover, First World countries would not pay good prices for Third World goods. Then, when the **oil crisis** occurred in the 1970s, the price of oil went up ten times. This affected many Third World countries in two ways: first, they needed oil to develop new industries; second, the oil crisis caused unemployment in the First World, so there was less money to buy raw materials and other Third World goods. Both these factors deepened the Third World debt crisis. Third World countries were having to send huge sums of money to First World countries just to pay the interest on their loans. How were their people ever to reach a better standard of living?

First World:	
Japan	$32 380
USA	$29 340
UK	$21 400
Australia	$20 300
Third World:	
Mexico	$3 970
Thailand	$2 200
India	$430
Vietnam	$330
Rwanda	$230
Ethiopia	$100

▲ ***Fig 3*** *GNP per head in 1998 (examples of countries' figures from the World Bank).*

◀ ***Fig 4*** *The population of many Third World countries has increased very fast in the last 50 years.*

Q4 How did the oil crisis of the 1970s cause problems for many Third World countries?

Key words

business corporations – very large businesses, trading worldwide

oil crisis – occurred in the 1970s; the oil producing countries, knowing that developed countries were becoming more and more reliant on oil, put the price up tenfold, causing prices of many other things to rise

SUMMARY

- Many countries in the old British Empire became part of the Commonwealth with Britain.
- Western capitalist countries were called the First World, the communist USSR the Second World and former colonies the Third World.
- First World countries lent money to Third World countries, which has led to problems when Third World countries cannot easily repay the loans.

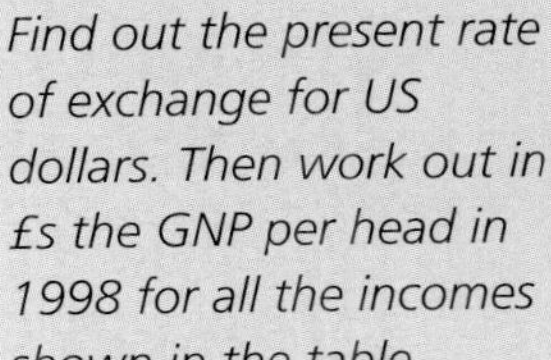

SUMMARY *activity*

Find out the present rate of exchange for US dollars. Then work out in £s the GNP per head in 1998 for all the incomes shown in the table.

115 The changing world

In this section of the book you will learn the following things:

- **in the last hundred years there have been great changes in transport, communications, science and technology.**

Transport

The world has changed more in the last hundred years than at any other time in history. A hundred years ago it took at least five days to go by ship from Britain to the USA. Now it takes a few hours by plane.

Q1 What basic fuel made possible the twentieth-century transport revolution of cars and aeroplanes?

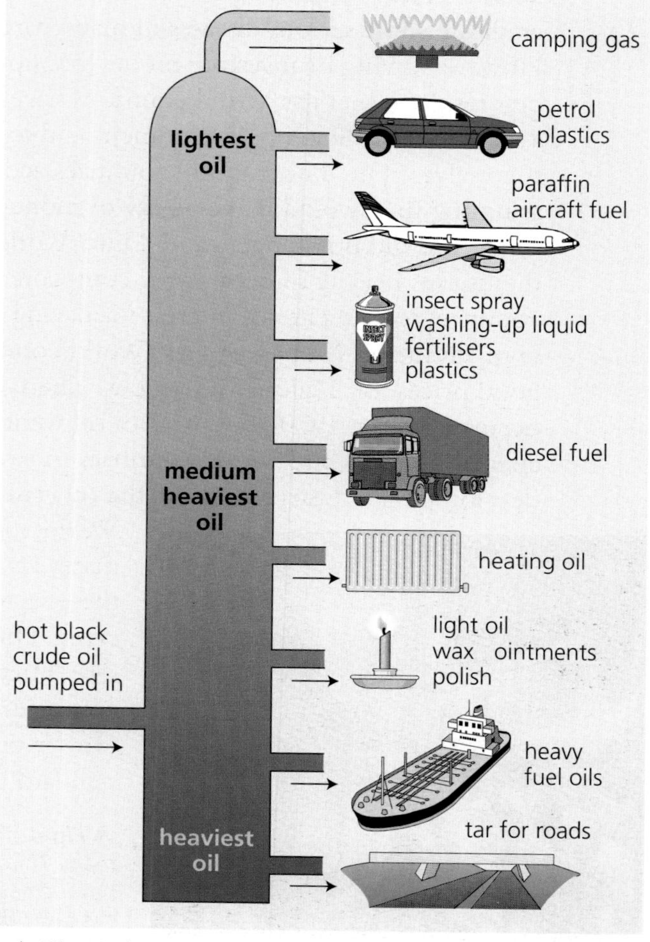

▲ **Fig 1** *The importance of oil. In the first stage of turning crude oil into the many products made from it, it is heated and then pumped through a tall steel tower called a* fractionating column. *Heavy oils pass out at the bottom of the column, lighter oils and gas at the top.*

Communications

Advances in technology have meant that people can communicate with each other all over the world in seconds. A hundred years ago if a person went to Japan, a letter would take weeks to reach home. Now an e-mail is there in seconds and a telephone call is instant. Banks and businesses are linked all around the globe.

Q2 What inventions have made possible the growth of fast communication around the globe?

Science and technology

Great developments in science and technology have become possible by the use of satellites, computers and ever smaller components in computers. Forty years ago the computing power to run a mobile phone could have taken up the space of a whole room; now it is possible to store all the words in the Bible on a pinhead-sized computer chip. An ordinary car has more computing power than was used to send the first manned spacecraft to the moon in 1969.

▲ Fig 2

Medicine has made advances. Major organs can be replaced as well as some joints in the body, and new materials plus advanced electronics have made possible machines to see inside the body and to make artificial limbs. In the Western world people live longer than ever before, with a higher standard of living than ever before. However, a large proportion of the world's children go to bed at night hungry because they do not have enough to eat. Even in the developed world there can be great differences in standards of living.

The environment

More governments are trying to reduce further damage to the environment, but this will mean that people in rich countries such as the USA, France, Germany and Britain will have to lower their standards of living by using less of the world's resources, and reduce the pollution they are putting into the rivers, earth and air. Developing countries will need to curb pollution and their use of non-renewable resources such as fossil fuels and forests.

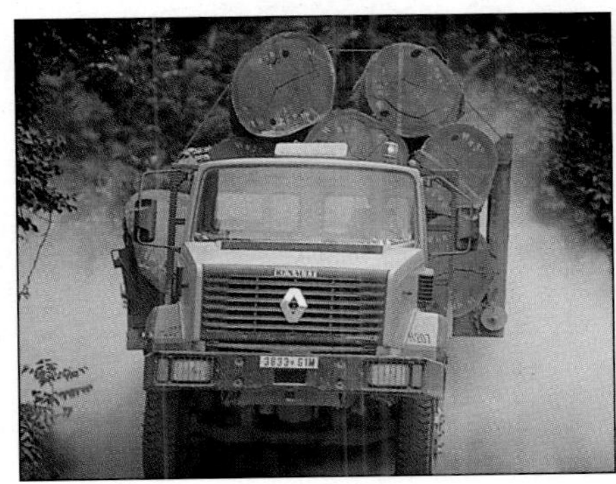

▲ ***Fig 3*** *Logs being transported from a forest.*

Political changes

In 1989 the Berlin Wall was demolished and West and East Germany united, followed by the break-up of the USSR into separate countries. In 1990 **apartheid** came to an end in South Africa; black people were given equal voting rights with white people. There are still many conflicts, all around the world, a large number of which are concerned with the right of people to govern themselves in groups to which they feel they belong. With a rising population and a great mixture of peoples around the world, solutions to the problems are far from easy.

◄ ***Fig 4*** *Nelson Mandela, the first President of South Africa elected after the end of apartheid.*

Key words

apartheid – system adopted by white South African governments, which discriminated against black or coloured people on grounds of race

SUMMARY

- Aeroplanes mean fast travel all over the world.
- Communications have speeded up because of advances in electronics.
- Science has aided the advance of medicine in the Western world.
- There is a need to look after the environment and work for peace.

SUMMARY *activity*

How has life changed in the last hundred years?

Kings and Queens 1837–

	born	reigned	died
Victoria	1819	1837–1901	1901
Edward VII	1841	1901–1910	1910
George V	1865	1910–1936	1936
Edward VIII	1894	1936 (abdicated)	1972
George VI	1895	1936–1952	1952
Elizabeth II	1926	1952–	–

Note: See the key to the crowns on page 250.

The twentieth-century world: Timeline 1903–1991

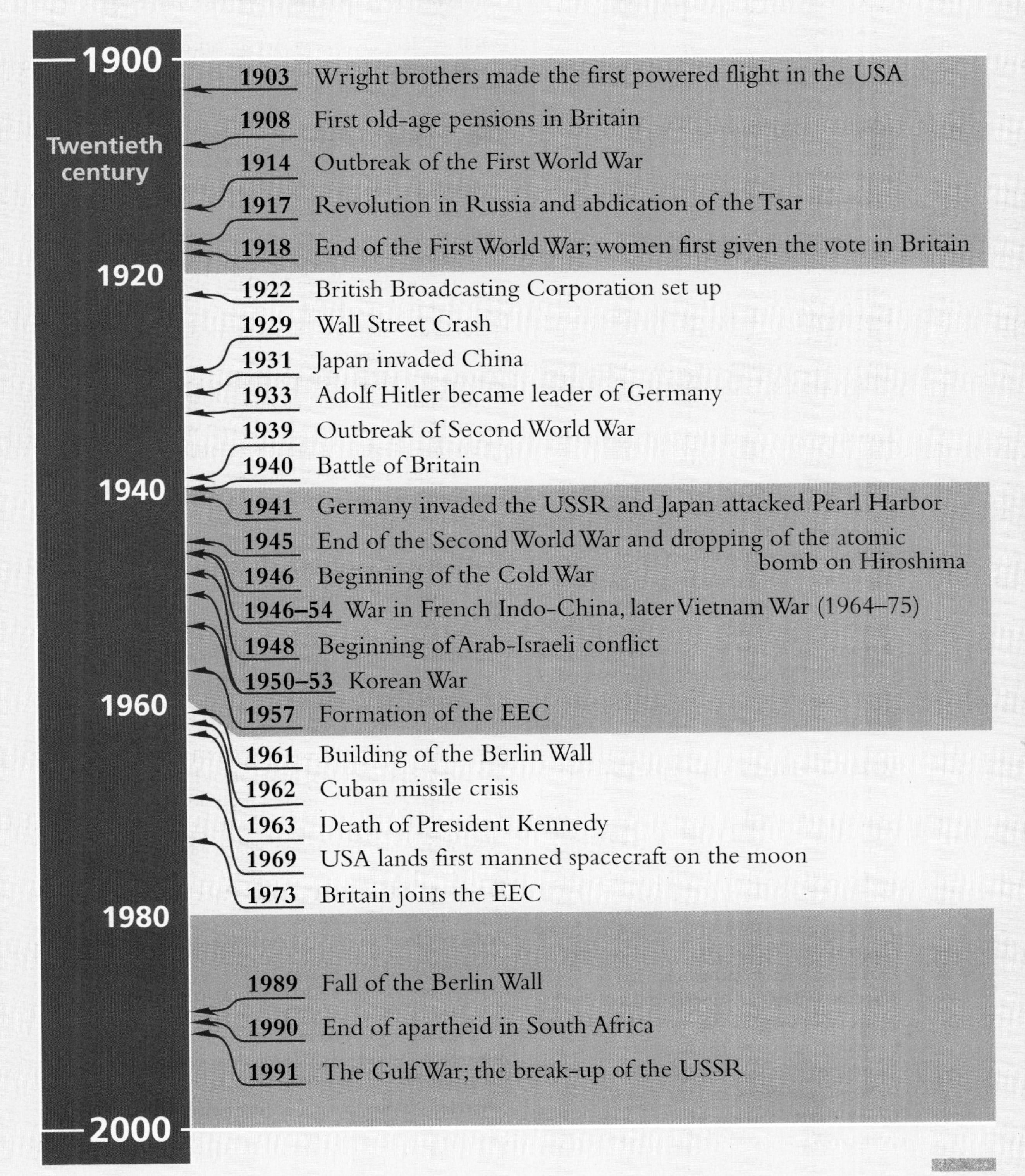

Glossary

A

abbey – a church connected with a monastery
Act of Parliament – a law
aircraft carriers – huge ships used as floating airfields
airlift – carrying in cargo by air
ale – weak beer
ambulatory – a walkway
amendment – change
an Act – a law
anaesthetic – a drug to make a person unconscious
Anglican Church – Church of England
antiseptic – a solution to kill bacteria
apartheid – system adopted by white South African governments, which discriminated against black or coloured people on grounds of race
appeasement – agreeing to do something in order to keep the peace
apprentice – someone learning to do something from a master craftsman
aqueduct – a bridge carrying water
armada – an armed fleet of ships
armistice – an agreement by opposing sides to stop fighting
arsenal – place where weapons are produced
Aryan – term used by the Nazis to describe non-Jewish, white, north European people; the 'master race'
astronomer – a person who studies the stars and planets
Austria-Hungary – an empire in central Europe, made up of a number of different groups of people

B

bailey – a large, level area below the motte, protected by a fence and ditch, used for keeping animals, stores, and as extra living space
baron – a nobleman, often an earl
Bayeux Tapestry – an embroidered cloth about 70 metres long, showing events leading up to the Norman Conquest. It was made for the Bishop of Bayeux in Normandy between 1066 and 1077.
beach head – landing place on a beach, held by soldiers
bear-baiting – a bear put to fight with dogs
besiege – attack a castle for a long period of time
Bill – a draft of a law or Act of Parliament. A Bill has to pass the Commons, the Lords and be signed by the monarch to become law.
Black Death – the bubonic plague which killed many people in 1348–49
blackleg – a worker who goes to work when his colleagues are on strike
Blitz – from the German *blitzkrieg,* meaning 'lightning war', the Blitz was the name given to the German bombing of British cities in 1940–41
blockade – stop ships bringing food and other supplies to a country
Bretons – people from Brittany
broadside – the side of a ship, or when all the guns along the side of a ship were fired
bubonic plague – so-called because the swellings were called buboes
bullion – precious metal, usually gold or silver
bulwark – a type of wall, a barrier
business corporations – very large businesses, trading worldwide

C

Cabinet – called after the small private room in the palace where ministers started to meet
candying – preserving in sugar
capitalist countries – countries where businesses (large and small) are privately owned and run to make a profit for the owner(s)
cast iron – hot, molten iron poured into moulds to set
Catholic Church – Christian Church that everyone belonged to
Chancellor – the King's most important assistant
chantries – chapels where prayers were said for dead people. Rich people often endowed (gave) them their money.
charcoal – wood that has been charred or partly burnt
charter – a document agreeing something

Chartism – movement pressing for Parliamentary and electoral reform
Chartists – people working to get political changes for working-class men
checkpoints – entrances along the Berlin Wall, manned by armed soldiers
choir – where the priests or monks held services praising God
Christendom – all the land in Europe where Christians lived
Christian – follower of Jesus Christ
civil war – a war in which citizens of the same country fight against each other
clan – the extended family or tribal system of the Highlands of Scotland
clergyman – a priest of the Church of England
clipper – fast sailing ship used to carry goods
Co-operative Movement – movement which believed that industries should be owned and controlled by the people working in them
Co-Prosperity Sphere – trading within an area for everyone's benefit
coalition government – a government made up of different political parties; often formed in wartime
coke – coal that has been purified
colonies – lands taken over, settled in and run by a more powerful country, often far away
Combination Acts – laws of 1799 and 1800 forbidding men to combine together to ask for higher wages
commoners – people who were not nobles or clergy
Commonwealth – association made up of Britain and the countries that were previously part of its empire
communist countries – countries where the state, not individuals, owns businesses, and runs them on behalf of the people
concentration camps – labour camps where thousands of people were concentrated
concentric castle – a castle ringed with two walls
condenser – container where steam cools down and turns back into water
Confessor – a religious person
consolidated – made solid or joined together
corruption – not dealing fairly, i.e. taking bribes
crop rotation – growing a different crop on the same field each year
curtain wall – wall surrounding a keep
customs duty – tax on goods coming into an area

D

D-Day – D stood for 'deliverance'; 6 June 1944
damask – heavy, patterned cotton, called after the city of Damascus
delegate – person voted for or asked to do something by other people
demobilisation – releasing soldiers and sailors after a war
democratic countries – countries where the Government is elected by – and can therefore be removed by – the people
deputy – someone who acts in the place of someone else
devout – very religious
dictator – leader who controls everything and allows no criticism
dismiss – to send away
dissolve – to close down or dismiss
domino effect – when one domino falls over it hits others, which then fall; applied to economic and political situations
dowry – money paid by the bride's parents to the bridegroom's family
duke – a nobleman of higher status than an earl

E

earl – a nobleman
elected assemblies – adults voting for people to represent them, e.g. the British Parliament (House of Commons)
emancipation – freeing from restrictions
emblem – a sign
emigrate – go to live in another country
empire – group of countries controlled by another, more powerful state
enclosure – fencing of land
enfranchise – to give the right to vote
epidemic – widespread outbreak of an illness
expansionist – country wanting to expand or increase the lands it controls

F

fallow – land resting, with no crops growing on it

fascism – government by a dictator, characterised by extreme nationalism and restrictions on individual freedom

feudal system – a way of holding land for services instead of money

financier – someone who invests money in a project

fire damp – explosive gas in a coal mine

fireships – unmanned ships that were set on fire and floated towards the enemy

franchise – the right to vote

free trade area – formed when countries abolish customs duties between themselves

freight – goods

Führer – German for 'leader'

G

gauze – netting

Geneva Convention – agreement on how to treat prisoners of war

ghetto – area where a group of people have to live and cannot leave

govern – rule

Great Seal of England – an imprint in sealing wax that only the King could make

guild – group of people belonging to a particular trade in the Middle Ages

H

hackney coach – a seventeenth-century horse-drawn taxi

hawking – hunting small animals using tame hawks

heretic – someone who does not believe the accepted religion

hide – a measurement of land, enough to support a family; usually about 120 acres

Holy Land – the land where Jesus Christ lived

homage – loyalty and devotion

housecarls – Harold's special soldiers

I

imperialist countries – countries which exercise power through their empires

imports – goods coming into a country

indulgence – a piece of paper that a person could buy saying that God forgave them for the bad things they had done

industrialists – people who produce goods to sell

inflation – when the prices of goods rise

insurance – many people pay a small sum of money to insure their house, ship etc. If it is destroyed, the insurance company which collected the money, pays out the value of the house, ship etc

iron ore – rock that contains pure iron

ironmaster – someone who makes iron

isolationism – when a country keeps itself apart from events in other countries

J

Jacobite – from the Latin, *Jacobus*, meaning 'James'

Jesuit – extreme Catholic priest

journeyman – qualified member of a trade who was paid by the day

K

kamikaze pilots – suicide pilots, flying planes full of bombs

keep – strongest, centre part of a castle

King's Council – group of men to advise the King

knights – soldiers on horseback

L

last rites – last blessing before death

Lebensraum – German policy of taking over (colonising) land in other countries for Germans to live in

legitimate – legal

Lent – from about mid-February to Easter

loom – frame that holds threads

M

Magna Carta – Great Charter

manufacturer – someone who makes something in a factory

manure – animal dung spread on the land to make it produce better crops

Marches – land on the borders between England and Wales

martyr – someone who is punished for their views

masons – stoneworkers

masterpiece – article made by a journeyman to show he was good enough to be a master

means of production – the businesses, such as farms and factories, that make the goods we need

merchants – people who buy and sell goods

Methodists – members of a Nonconformist Church founded in the eighteenth century by John and Charles Wesley

mills – factories where cotton cloth is made

missiles – weapons fired through the air

Mogul empire – an empire that controlled most of India for 200 years

molten iron – heated until it turns to liquid

motte – mound

Muslim – a follower of Muhammad

muslin – fine cotton, called after Muslims

mutilation – cutting off a hand, finger etc

N

naval blockade – using ships to stop the enemy's ships taking supplies to their own country

nave – main part of cathedral or church

neutral ships – ships belonging to countries which are not at war

nobles – known as 'barons' in the early Middle Ages

Nonconformists – Protestants who did not conform to (accept the rules of) the Church of England

Normandy beaches – beaches in the north of France used for the D-Day landings

O

observatory – a building from which to look at the stars and planets

obsolete – out of date

oil crisis – occurred in the 1970s; the oil producing countries, knowing that developed countries were becoming more and more reliant on oil, put the price up tenfold, causing prices of many other things to rise

outlawed – put outside the protection of the law so anyone can harm you and you can do nothing about it

P

pact – agreement

parish Poor Law authorities – people in every parish appointed to deal with those who could not look after themselves and earn a living

parishioner – someone who lives in the parish or area around a church

Parliament – from *parler,* meaning 'to speak' in French. It was the place where the government of the country was discussed.

penal code – a range of punishments for law breakers

penance – doing something good to make up for doing something bad

petition – a document asking for something

Petrograd – the capital of Russia (other names for the city are St Petersburg and Leningrad)

picketing – persuading non-union workers from going to work during a strike

pilgrim – someone who journeys to a holy place

placemen – MPs who were given jobs or positions as long as they voted for the Government

plantation – a huge farm in the southern colonies in North America, growing tobacco or cotton

plunder – steal, often by force

poaching – stealing animals from the forests

poll – head

Pope – head or father of the Catholic Church

portholes – small windows in the side of a ship

preserving food – making sure it was fit to eat through the winter by salting, pickling, drying etc

private trading – men employed by the East India Company also traded in their own right to make their own profits

propaganda – information spread to promote a particular point of view

propeller – blades fixed on a shaft, turned by the steam engine to drive a ship through the water

Protestant – name given to the people who protested when they were not allowed to follow Martin Luther's ideas on religion

Puritan – extreme Protestant

Q

Quaker – a Christian movement based on peaceful principles.

R

radical – someone who wants to make great changes
realm – area or country ruled by a king; the kingdom
reconnaissance – observation to find out information about the enemy
reforms – changes
reparations – money paid for repairing damage done
Resistance – underground groups in German-occupied countries working against the Nazis
revolution – a complete change
Royalist – on the King's side

S

sanctions – restrictions
selective breeding – breeding the best animals together
self-determination – the right of every country to choose the way it is governed
sermon – talk by a parson or preacher
shareholder – someone who puts money into an expedition and therefore holds a share of the profits (or losses)
shrine – a holy place
shuttle – giant needle for weaving cotton thread in and out of upright threads to make cloth
smelting – heating up iron ore
smiths – metalworkers
spinners – people who spun wool into thread
stalemate – when neither side can win
state education – education provided free by the Government for all children
statute – a law
steam locomotive – a carriage driven by steam power
steamship – ship with a steam engine
stockbroker – someone who buys and sells shares (sometimes called stocks)
strikes – workers withdrawing from work to persuade employers to give them better conditions
stubble – the cut-off stalks of crops left sticking out of the ground after harvesting
suppress – to keep down

T

tariffs – taxes or duties on goods
theology – the study of religion
theses – a statement that people can debate or argue about
threshing – beating wheat to separate the grain from the stalks
tithe – one-tenth
to be made a saint – declared a holy person by the Pope
toll – a charge for using a road or bridge
torpedoes – underwater shells
Tory Party – very conservative political party
town charter – agreement sold to a town by the King, Church or local lord, allowing the townspeople to run the town themselves
trade unions – a number of people in the same sort of job who join together to improve their working conditions
transportation – a punishment; people were taken to Australia to work out a prison sentence
treason – a crime against the state
treasury – the King's money for running the country
treaty – agreement
Tsar – emperor
turnpike – so-called because originally there was just a pole or pike across the road that people pulled or turned to open

U

U-boats – First and Second World War German submarines
USSR – Union of Soviet Socialist Republics, the territory formerly known as Russia under the Tsars, but renamed after the Bolsheviks took power through the soviets (committees) all over Russia

V

vaccinate – inject a small amount of a mild form of a disease into someone, which gives them immunity (protection) in the future

veto – say no to a decision

villein – a peasant who had to work for a lord in return for his land

W

weavers – people who wove thread into cloth

welfare state – where the Government provides a national system of education, healthcare, old-age pensions, unemployment pay and other benefits, to ensure the social and economic security of its citizens

Whig Party – political party of the eighteenth and nineteenth centuries; more forward thinking than the Tory Party

wild boar – wild pig

winch – machine on a ship, to pull in or let out the sails

winnowing – tossing the grain to make the husks (outer covering) blow away from the solid grains

wolf packs – a large number of Second World War submarines chasing ships like a pack of wolves

workhouse – an institution which housed and fed people who could not support themselves

wrought iron – cast iron that has been hammered or worked on to make it more flexible

XYZ

yeomanry – a cavalry force (soldiers on horseback), made up of local volunteers

Index

Key to crowns

The different crowns represent the different Royal Houses.

 **House of Normandy**

 **House of Plantagenet**

 **House of Lancaster**

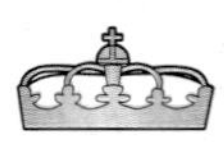 **House of York**

 **House of Tudor**

 **House of Stuart**

 **House of Hanover**

 **House of Saxe-Coburg-Gotha**

 **House of Windsor**